Drama and Intelligence

Drama and Intelligence

A Cognitive Theory

RICHARD COURTNEY

McGill-Queen's University Press
Montreal & Kingston • London • Buffalo

ISBN 0-7735-0766-3

Legal deposit 4th quarter 1990
Bibliothèque nationale du Québec

Printed in Canada on acid-free paper

This book has been published with the help of a grant from the Social Science Federation of Canada, using funds provided by the Social Sciences and Humanities Research Council of Canada.

Canadian Cataloguing in Publication Data

Courtney, Richard
Drama and intelligence
Includes bibliographical references
ISBN 0-7735-0766-3
1. Theater – Psychological aspects. 2. Theater – Philosophy. 3. Intellect. 4. Drama in education. I. Title.
PN2039.C68 1990 792'.02 C90-090178-0

This book was set in Sabon 10/12 by Caractéra inc., Montreal.

For Zina Barnieh
Gisèle Barret
David W. Booth
Judith Koltai
Fabien Lemieux
John McLeod
Brenda Parres
Walter Pitman
John Ripley
H. Howard Russell
Graham Scott
Otto Weininger
Aurelieu Weiss
Joyce Wilkinson

Contents

Preface

Drama is Being "as if." It is a total process, internal and external, that occurs when we transform our creative imagination into acts, when we create mental fictions and express them in spontaneous play, creative drama, improvisation, role play, and theatre. Like life itself, it is an experience we live through. In life we deal with actual thoughts and acts; in drama we deal with imagined thoughts and dramatic acts. The difference is that drama involves "as if" thinking and "as if" action. But life and drama are so alike that contemporary scholars can talk of the drama of life, or life as drama.

This book starts with Being "as if." It looks at dramatic action as an intellectual and cognitive activity, and in a way that uses a variety of analytic tools that cross disciplines to focus on dramatic activity per se. It is therefore a work in Developmental Drama, which I first defined in 1968 as the academic study (as opposed to the direct experience) of dramatic activity, that is, the study of the transformations created by dramatic action. The transformations Developmental Drama studies are personal, social, educational, therapeutic, aesthetic, artistic, and cultural.

This book's focus on the intellectual and cognitive significance of drama does not mean that its social and affective dimensions are ignored. The dramatic perspective is whole: The intellectual, cognitive, social, and affective elements are seen as a unity, as they are when we live through dramatic experience. For our purposes here, however, and for the ease of the general reader, a specific lens has been chosen.

Most of the book is new; small sections are based on material written for journals and specific occasions. Though these have been entirely rewritten, I am grateful to the editors for permission to republish them here. I am also very grateful to Walter Pitman, the director, and the faculty and staff of the Ontario Institute for Studies in Education, for their continuous support; those to whom I have dedicated this book, for conversations and correspondence about the elusive nature of dramatic activity; my graduate students, particularly those who are pursuing or have obtained their doctorates in drama, drama/theatre, and dramatic dance, for perspicacious questions and discussions that have honed my ideas, including Sharon Bailin, Judith Barnard, Bradley Bernstein, Shehla Burney, Robert Campbell, Jay Cheng, Sarina Condello, Don Cordell, Mary Coros, Elizabeth Dickens, Susan P. Eden, Christopher Fitkowsky, Robert Gardner, Poranee Gurutayana, Valerie Kates, Sandra L. Katz, Bathsheva Koren, Brenda Lamothe, Colla Jean MacDonald, Alistair Martin-Smith, Geoffrey Milburn, Peter L. McLaren, Dennis Mulcahy, Alan Riley, Helen E.H. Smith, Elizabeth Straus, Larry Swartz, Audley Timothy, Christine Turkewych, Arie and Frances Vander-Reyden, Bronwen Weaver, Nikki and Michael Wilson, and Belarie Hyman-Zatzman; and my wife, Rosemary Courtney, for both her editing and indexing skills.

R.C.
Toronto and Jackson's Point,
Ontario
1989

Figures

Drama and Intelligence

In everyday life, "if" is a fiction,
in the theatre "if" is an experiment
Peter Brook

INTRODUCTION

Drama and Intelligence

"Drama and Intelligence? Are you joking? Everyone knows that the arts are frills!" A colleague said this when I told him I was writing this book. I was not surprised. In the Western world, drama and the arts do not seem to be very intellectual, at least on the surface. Our societies encourage the image of the romantic artist who acts through inspiration and starves. But most other people spend their time earning money to buy objects that will make their lives easier. From this view, at least, my colleague was not wrong: Drama does not, at first sight, look intellectual.

But was he, in fact, right?

The "live" theatre has survived centuries of neglect and repression but it always reappears, lively and irreverent, when a society is in trouble. No wonder politicians have always feared it. Despite persecution by the Church, the irreverent medieval clowns mocked their betters; later, touring troupes of the *commedia dell'arte* made fun of local townsfolk. Shakespeare's theatre was the conscience of the Elizabethans, Molière's of the French court, Shaw and Galsworthy's of the Edwardians. In the 1970s and 80s troupes of improvisers traveled around the kraals of southern Africa in jeeps resuscitating the life of tribes devastated by apartheid. In the right-wing states of South America today similar troupes travel through small communities keeping the idea of freedom alive. Contemporary dramatists such as Wole Soyinka in Nigeria and Vaclav Havel in Czechoslovakia have stimulated freedom from their prison cells.

The theatre is hardly a frill. At first sight, however, not everyone realizes how significant it is. Perhaps the best-kept secret of the twentieth century has been the slow infiltration of spontaneous drama into the schools of the Western world. Before World War I isolated pioneers realized its potential, but it was not until the 1950s and 60s that real inroads were made into educational systems in Britain, the Commonwealth, and the

United States. By the 1970s it had spread to Europe and, by the 1980s, to Africa and Asia. The growth of educational drama and spontaneous improvisation has been phenomenal, whether as a method of learning ("drama across the curriculum") or as a subject in its own right. In Ontario, for example, few students were using spontaneous drama in schools in the 1960s, but by 1988 there were about 50 thousand in grades 8 to 12 alone. How did this change come about? Quite simply, it *worked:* Good teachers discovered that learners responded quickly and in depth through free dramatization.

Nor was the expansion limited to education. In the early twentieth century, spontaneous drama was used in therapy only by Jacob Moreno's "psychodrama." Later, this method was used with many other dramatic styles in "drama therapy" – a major mode of creative arts treatment for those with mental and physical dysfunctions.

Today, all kinds of improvisations and simulations are used in training programs for business, marketing, social work, jobs, and retraining, for nurses and medical practitioners, and for those engaged in space programs. Recent research has shown that in our post-industrial society many generic skills (those required for work and leisure that can be taught in schools) derive from the ability to read others and see things from their point of view – a specifically dramatic skill. Activities making use of drama are increasing at such an exponential rate that, perhaps, they may be a commonplace in the twenty-first century.

THE SCOPE OF DRAMA

Neither drama nor theatre, then, is a frill. From the way it has been enthusiastically embraced in recent years, and in so many different practical fields, drama appears to be an innate human activity that leads to deep-felt learning at all ages and makes of the players a cohesive social unit. Although dramatic acts are more similar than different, they can be viewed as consisting of two kinds: processes (spontaneous dramatic activities) or forms (theatrical products.)

Through such a loose typology, we can see that dramatic action is a processual activity in concrete form – a direct experience that players live through. It is characterized by acting "as if," either in role, or as themselves in a fictionalized situation. As a process, Being "as if" is the ground on which theatre as an art form rests.

Thus drama pervades life. When we catch ourselves talking to the mirror, rehearsing an upcoming interview, or asking ourselves why we acted "like that" in a particular situation, we have a glimpse of the process in everyday life. We do not take our parent role into the office; if we treated our employer like a child we would soon be out of a job.

We use roles flexibly, adapting them to many social interactions. For most of us, our role playing is unconscious as we go through the day.

For young children dramatic play is a very serious business. It is the way they learn to grow up, and the way they learn to learn. Adults at play (in social gatherings and other festivities) regard it as recreation, which is really re-creation, or the way we re-generate our lives. Theatre, too, can be seen as recreation, but it re-generates our lives in a different way: Tragedy allows us to re-hearse the moments when we face death, while comedy permits us to re-play those little deaths we suffer in our social life. There is more to our dramatic acts than appears on the surface.

It is no wonder, therefore, that drama as a process has increasingly occupied scholars in the twentieth century. Philosophers such as Heidegger, Gadamer, and Fink focus on the play world or the aesthetic world where our fictions are mutually created as forms of dramatization. Thomas G. Pavel interprets our fictional world as the way in which we think. Martin Buber's "dialogism" originated in his student days at the Viennese theatre; his existential "I and Thou," the mutuality we have with others as a model for social interaction, was based on the interaction of two players on a stage. Bakhtin's "dialogism," which has structural similarities to that of Buber, shows how the author and the reader interact: Like stage actors, they mutually contribute to the novel's meaning. Theoretical tools like the model and concepts like the significant Other have been the result.

In criticism, Kenneth Burke's "dramatism" sees both life and literature as drama. His work has considerably affected the sociological theory of Hugh Dalziel Duncan, Ernest Becker, Erving Goffman, Peter Berger, and many others. We can trace a similar dramaturgical perspective in the psychology of, amongst others, Fritz Perls, Eric Berne, Melanie Klein, D.W. Winnicott, Erik Erikson, and Otto Weininger. In social anthropology Victor W. Turner has examined his data in terms of ritual and social dramas. He also experimented in the contemporary theatre, with the stage director Richard Schechner, to explore the theatricality of cultural rituals. Since the 1900s, at least, the avant garde theatre has experimented with improvisation, ritual, and fully spontaneous action using both players and audience, and its innovations have influenced formal theatre.

Dramatic terminology, as result, has slipped into common parlance with our hardly noticing, particularly as a metaphor in newspapers and on radio and television. It has even affected sports writers. Take ice hockey, for example. When the popular captain of the Toronto Maple Leafs, Darryl Sittler, went through months of indecision as the team's owner, Harold Ballard, tried to trade him, the press had a field day: Sittler was "being crucified" and was "in agony," while Ballard was "a traitor" looking for his "thirty pieces of silver." And when Sittler was eventually traded to the Philadelphia Flyers, he was dramatized as having been "resurrected."

INTELLIGENCE

Does dramatic activity affect the way we think? When we act "as if" we are in the "here and now," what kinds of thinking are involved? And does drama improve our thinking abilities? These are questions about the nature of human intelligence and cognition. In order to address them and prevent confusion, we need to be clear about the terms we are using.

Intelligence is not an object. It does not exist like a table or a giraffe. It is an abstraction – a kind of useful fiction that allows us to discuss mental activity and how well it operates in a particular case. People use the word *intelligence* in different ways. In commonsense terms, it is the individual's mental ability, the capacity to function well or badly in the world – with people and information, and in a particular environments. Cultures and groups value different kinds of thinking. Thus we should regard intelligence as those cognitive skills valued in a specific culture. In Western societies they relate to the ability to grasp both relations and symbolic thought, but this is not necessarily so elsewhere.[1] The issue becomes important for drama when we compare one culture with another, or when we analyse it in multicultural societies.

In this book, we accept that the capacity for intelligent thought and action is a mixture of nature and nurture – what we are born with, and what and how we learn. Some scholars emphasize one, some another. We will not venture onto this minefield. It is sufficient for our purposes simply to acknowledge that intelligence is a mixture of both.

We assume that innate capacities are inherited genetically, and that this affects our capability for mental growth. But this is a hypothesis only; any supposed inherited ability depends on an individual's prenatal, natal, and postnatal experiences. There are also other social effects: A child's level of intelligence can rise or fall with environmental changes, and it develops differently in various physical environments.

Intelligence is not one faculty but a variety of mental abilities. Yet what these are is the subject of some disagreement. Howard Gardner has said, in his theory of multiple intelligences,[2] that they include linguistic, logical-mathematical, bodily-kinesthetic, musical, and personal intelligences. Others believe that intelligence is general. Thus we can legitimately ask, is there a dramatic intelligence?

Educational drama teachers constantly tell stories of the student who was exceptional in dramatic expression. In most cases, he or she displayed not merely a great talent but also a dramatic way of thinking. Yet many of these students were unexceptional in other ways; indeed, they could be slow learners in the ordinary classroom. But it is also fair to say that each set of intellectual skills varies with cleverness, or mental efficiency. Some people are quicker in the uptake than others, being good at comprehending, reasoning, and making decisions in a specific skill. Does the fact that some students are good in dramatic activity indicate that there is a dramatic intelligence? Or is it merely a specific case of a phenomenon that occurs with many skills?

This is a chicken and egg question. I may believe that we all possess a dramatic intelligence, but there is no way I can prove it to a sceptic. It is, however, true that on average the performance of students in educational drama seems to parallel their performance in other areas. Thus in most societies children of lower classes and ethnic groups achieve less well than those of upper classes and the major cultural group. This cannot be attributed to inborn intelligence. We know that environment affects how someone is raised and educated. Teachers of educational drama have considerable evidence of such factors – but no one answer to the problem.

People who ought to know better are apt to refer to tests of mental age, or IQ, as tests of "intelligence." They are simply samples of the kinds of skills that someone, somewhere, regards as intelligence. Not everyone will agree what such skills are. Although the tests may be highly objective, they usually omit many human qualities and result in only rough approximations. The IQ test is certainly not a good guide to achievement in higher education and vocations, cleverness, persistence, well-informed thinking, wisdom, understanding daily affairs, creativity, or the ability to dramatize. Good or poor test performance depends on other factors besides the obvious content of the test, such as whether those tested have come across similar questions before and whether they can fully understand the instructions. And the older the person tested, the more unreliable the results.

THE POTENTIAL FOR KNOWING

In this book, the term intelligence will be used to mean the potential for specific types of mental activity. It is useful to think of this potential in relation to three kinds of knowing: personal, explicit, and practical. Personal knowledge is tacit and intuitive knowing. It is largely unconscious and we cannot directly express it in language, although we may do so indirectly in poetry and other media. "We know more than we can tell," says Michael Polanyi.[3] Others say we have a "deep structure" of knowing. Characteristically, personal knowing occurs in the living experience, in the "here and now" of life and the dramatic experience.

When we meet with new information, it must fit our existing personal knowledge in some way in order to be assimilated.

Explicit knowledge is that which we know we know. We can demonstrate this knowing in language. Characteristically we do so when we talk about it, or otherwise express what we know. Yet it is based on personal knowing that is wider and more diffuse in its meaning. Explicit knowledge, on the other hand, is more accurate in its meaning. For drama, when we know IN the dramatic "here and now" we achieve personal knowledge; but when we talk of if afterwards, we obtain knowledge ABOUT it – explicit knowledge.

Practical knowledge, however, is different in kind. It is "know how." It uses forms of personal and explicit knowing but it consists of how to do things. It is knowing how to execute a procedure. There are different kinds of practical knowledge. Thus a teacher has the skills to teach, a sailor to sail, and an actor to act.

In simple terms, it is best to think of intelligence as different sets of potential practical knowledge. In drama, the player knows how to do things through appropriate procedures. This is to distinguish "know how" from "know what" – knowing what those procedures are.

COGNITION

Cognition can mean different things to different people. The word is often used to describe the activities of mind that process information – our perception of information and how we deal with it. But this usage indicates a particular way of looking at intelligence, one that stresses its operational mode. Cognition can also refer to mental structures (concepts or schemas) that are the basis for ideas, and the dynamics between them. The steps by which a child processes information involve a movement from simpler to more complex concepts. A key question for drama is, are these steps best learned through social maturation or through instruction?

The main issues that concern us here are information-processing and concept formation, together with their developmental steps. In contemporary research there are three major ways to address such issues: cognitive science, symbol systems, and semiotics.

Cognitive science studies what happens in the process of problem-solving: how we identify that a problem exists; of what the problem consists; how a solution can be made; and the smallest possible steps in problem-solving as they are learned by a child. For dramatic activity cognitive science is not always satisfactory because it can be too mechanistic, relying as it does on the experimental method and a computer-driven model; or it can be unconcerned with the processes of creativity and dramatization that are important at all ages, particularly at the higher levels of intelligence; or it can be entirely focussed, as is the case with Piaget, on logical-mathematical intelligence.

The "symbol systems" approach addresses the symbolic structures of thought and (in contrast to Piaget's unilinear scheme) how they are linked in a variety of systems. Each symbolic structure creates specific meanings (for example, language, the arts, and mathematics) and its characteristics can vary from culture to culture. One advantage of this approach for drama is that it acknowledges the importance of metaphoric thinking and action. But a disadvantage is that one researcher may talk of one set of symbol systems while another may disagree and propose a different set. The issue comes down to two questions: What are the criteria for the existence of a specific symbol system? and, Is dramatic action such a symbol system?

Semiotics is commonly known as the science of signs. It focuses on the relationship of the signifier (the sign) and the signified (its meaning). It is a research tool that can be used in many ways, one of which is to show the relations between our cognitive processes (the signifieds, or *how* and *what* we think) and our expressions (the signifiers, or the meanings we convey), together with any gap between them. In simple terms, dramatic action is the signifier and dramatic thought is the signified. The difficulty of using semiotics to examine cognition is also its advantage: the science crosses normal disciplines; it unifies what and how we *think* with what and how we *act* (as in drama); and it involves semantics (as in drama, everything hinges on the meanings conveyed and received).

Here we assume that these three methods are relatively valid. Each provides a significant perspective on cognition, and used together they provide a total picture. We will draw less on cognitive science because it is often too mechanical to capture the subtleties of dramatic thought and action. The result is a methodology that is perspectival on the one hand, and consistent and unified on the other – characteristics that make it appropriate for an analysis of drama in its relation to intelligence and cognition.

OUTLINE OF THE THEORY

The theory presented here, in sum, is as follows: Our creative imagination and dramatic actions are experienced as a whole, and together they create meaning. They bring about the "as if" world of possibility (the fictional), which works in parallel with the actual world and is a cognitive tool for understanding it (chapter one). Imagining and dramatic acts work by transformation; they change what we know. This change is learning, or a "knowing how to do." Through "re-play," and with trust in others, we use specific mental structures, dynamics, and skills to reinforce our Being and improve our cognition (chapter two).

The dramatic world we create is a significant element in a universe of cognitive meaning. Although we ground questions of human existence in actuality, we compare the actual with the dramatic world in order to understand it. The "truth" lies in the player and the playing, while ideas are structured through similarity/difference, whole/part, and continua (chapter three). The unity of our imagining and acting transforms the actual world into our dramatic world through media, by substitution and in accordance with specific laws. The result is surface and deep meanings, the latter being both metaphoric and logical (chapter four). Drama is thus seen as the expression of metaphoric activity. Metaphor, or thinking in the dramatic mode, is a whole that is double. But it is not dual; the two parts of metaphor are not separate. Rather, metaphor is nonlinear and continuous and works by similarity. Thus it defines our reality as Prospero does: "We are such stuff/As dreams are made on." For players, dramatic acts are signifiers that stand for imaginings; however, non-players must infer these imaginings (chapter five). But in terms of logic dramatic acts are practical hypotheses; as players in the "here and now," we use experiential logic. Somewhat differently, as observers we use "criteria in contexts" – a rational logic that provides objectivity (chapter six).

From this perspective intuition is a tacit way of knowing learned through dramatic action that provides metaphoric meaning (chapter seven). This meaning becomes cognitively more significant when we externalize it in acts. Then we symbolically understand reality (chapter eight).

The dramatic and theatrical modes are comparable (chapter nine). Human learning viewed in this way can be examined through the Theory of Logical Types, which shows that the dramatic is an advanced style of cognitive operation (chapter ten). The foundation of this activity is the mutuality of dialogue; it underlies all interpretation and understanding of the dramatic event (chapter eleven).

CHAPTER ONE

Drama and Fiction

Imagining and acting are things people do. They are highly complex activities that are not separate as we "live through" them, as we feel them to be. In our experience, they are a unity.

When we think and act dramatically we create a fiction. But this fiction is not false; it is not a lie. It has a cognitive purpose. It is a way of looking at the environment that complements the actual world and, in so doing, it provides us with a new perspective on it. If we put the two together, the actual and the fictional, our understanding of the world changes. We have learned and thereby we have improved our cognitive abilities in highly significant ways.

On the surface, the view I am putting forward is similar to other contemporary ideas about cognition, for example, Dewey's emphasis on activity and consummatory experience, Buber's dialogue, and Burke's dramaturgical perspective. But the idea that all dramatic acts, from children at play to adults using roles, and to actors on the stage, are inherently cognitive is different in a number of ways.

MAJOR ISSUES

The cognitive significance of dramatic action brings to the foreground a number of theoretical issues. We can address them as questions.

When we wish to understand the world we can dramatize it. In what ways? Are there differences between mental dramatizing (imagining, or covert acts) and dramatic (overt) acts? Are there cognitive differences between the creator (player) role and the percipient (audience) role?

We live through *actual* experience in the "here and now." On the surface this appears to be only one state. But simultaneously we live through *dramatic* experience in the same way. Sometimes we can distinguish the two, but sometimes we cannot. When is experience dramatic and when is it not? Do all dramatic arts occur in the present tense, and in a locality that is "here" for everyone who is playing?

Drama creates meaning in a double process: when we compare the actual and the fictional. How, in this double process, do we create meaning from the actual world? Is this meaning a uniquely human perspective on events and on our experience of them? When we dramatize, we create fiction. Do we always understand that this is different from what is actual? When we are very young, the medium we use to create meaning is the self: We act "as if" we are someone else; and the medium of drama gives us a new perspective on an event. With maturation, how do we extend our use of media to create further meaning? When we dance or sing, speak or paint, do we bring more or less meaning to our experience?

For adults, how does meaning vary with the use of media? When we dramatize in thought or in action, we activate the aesthetic mode. How is this related to feeling? What mental structures and dynamics are involved? Do we have one kind of feeling-response to experiences, people, and objects, but another to mental activity? How are feeling-responses similar to and/or different from direct emotion? Do feelings have specific cognitive qualities?

Is our adult attitude to a work of art modeled on how, when we were young, we created meaning when we acted "as if"?[1] There is a close link between spontaneity and dramatization, both in living and in art forms like theatre.[2] Does spontaneity link thinking and action? How free is our spontaneity within dramatization? When we analyse dramatic action, how do we do so? Are some methods better than others? How do we make judgments about dramatic acts? What criteria do we use? Are these the same or different from the kinds of judgments we make about theatre art?

Such questions arise when we begin to discuss the cognitive significance of dramatic action. They are not listed in order of priority. Rather they appear to cluster in particular ways. We begin, therefore, with the double operation of drama. In our cognitive processes, we operate with both the "is" and "as if," with the actual and the fictional.

METHOD

Modern research into dramatic action has been diverse. The research methods of those in the social sciences, who mostly use an experimental design, are different from the historical or critical methods of many theatre scholars. Likewise drama therapists, who often use a medical model, may ignore studies in educational drama that often describe specific events and then analyse them critically.

The methodological stance taken here is that of Developmental Drama. This is empirical in that it originates in direct observation and data, or evidence. But it is not empirical in the sense that it is quantitative; normally the incidents within the evidence cannot be counted. The method is specifically nonmechanical. But it is objective in being rational: It analyses empirical data through logic. That is, it begins from individual practical instances of dramatic action, then proceeds logically to emergents that may be compared by using specific criteria.[3] We will examine this issue in detail in chapter six.

On the surface, the method resembles two others. First, like natural, or anthropological, approaches, it avoids mechanical measurement. But its use of logic for objectivity distinguishes it from these. Second, it uses empirical particulars, as do logical analysts. These scholars for most of the twentieth century were not noted for their interest in dramatic activity; indeed, many regarded it as mere pretence. They adhered strictly to classical deduction and induction. But contemporary logical analysts have different theoretical concerns and their work can help us to understand the process of dramatization.

BEING "AS IF"

Being "as if" is the self's fictional mode of operation. Functionally it is an imaginative or imaginative-"enactive" activity, but modally it is supposition. When we imagine, we think of possibilities. When we take one of these possibilities and externalize it in action, we try to make creative ideas (hypotheses and models) work in the world. The exemplar of this active operation occurs when we "put ourselves in someone else's shoes" – when we try to think and act as they do.

We do this in many spheres of life, not all of which are as obviously dramatic as role-taking or theatre. The world of law, for example, is built on previous stories ("legal cases") which have become so dramatized that the law appears to have a life of its own. Our imaginings and actions can create similar fictions by using a wide variety of media. Thus the suppositions of the arts and sciences are cognitive in that each re-plays our experience and brings about a change in our understanding of it. Or we can create an externalized fiction in words and language; the results can be couched in all kinds of literary forms. The fictions created in myths, fables, stories, novels, and other literary arts parallel those in the many forms of enactment. Where a novel is the re-creation of an imagined sequence of events in language, dramatic action proper is a contiguous process. It is the practical realization in the external world of what is imagined; and what is performed is the projection of particular kinds of imaginings (suppositions, or mental dramatizations) into actions.

In any world of "as if," there are two types of transformation. First, people think "as if" (or think and act "as if") they are different from their everyday selves. They transform themselves into another. Thus ancient shamans became animals and birds, ancient Egyptian priests were manifestations of the gods, Olivier became Hamlet. We play roles. Dramatic action itself has a variety of forms: spontaneous play, educational drama, drama therapy, social role play, theatre, and related activities. Second, "as if" acts transform what we know. Transformation of the persona gives us a new perspective on an event: We learn more about it and this changes our knowledge of it.

How is this cognitive? Primarily because dramatic acts provide us with an explanation of the external world that we can then check against reality.

Forms of fiction, then, are imaginative representations in parallel worlds, and one of these worlds centers on dramatic action. The variety of fictional forms challenges most of the analytic models used earlier in this century, and it defies easy categorization. It may be more easily understood as a cognitive operation – "a laboratory for life,"[4] "a severe testing ground for semantics,"[5] or as hermeneutics through practical trial and error.

COGNITION AND MEANING

What kind of meaning is created by such forms of fiction? Contemporary critical theory has reacted against the search for certainty by earlier linguistic analysts and structuralists. What is sought today are multiple meanings. In modern logic, new logical analysis, and poststructuralism there is no such thing as one universal meaning or structure in a fiction, whether it be literature or drama or any other type. Thus we can ask, What kinds of meaning are created, transmitted, and (if there is an audience) received through the forms of dramatic action?

Can they be described as story meaning? For most of this century, critical theory emphasized that the meanings created in fiction were those of story structures. Carl Jung assumed that story patterns have the same meaning, which derive from psychological archetypes and the collective unconscious.[6] This strongly influenced the theory of visual art. Structuralism and analysis were similarly limited.

Early structuralists said there was both a surface meaning and one of "deep structures" (linguistic and unconscious); they searched for the second within the first. Believing that myths behave like language, Claude

Lévi-Strauss said that story meaning was arbitrary, like linguistic signs.[7] The structuralist search for linguistic models, mediated by narrative analysis, spread to poetics. But methodology was not a major concern of literary structuralism, which theorized more about the general properties of fiction (although phonologism gave a methodological solution to Roland Barthes' early work on narrative structures). Narrative form was central but dramatic action, style, rhetoric, reference, and social relevance became marginal; they were said to be dependent on plot. Representation became unimportant and dramatic action was negated. Indeed, Barthes explicitly stated that mimesis was entirely subordinate to plot: "The function of narrative is not to 'represent': it is to constitute a spectacle still very enigmatic for us, but in any case not of a mimetic order. The 'reality' of a sequence lies not in the 'natural' succession of the actions composing it, but in the logic there exposed, risked and satisfied."[8] By distinguishing between story and discourse, and in identifying the story with narrative structures, a structural examination of discourse and cognition became one of technique. Then, when Vladimir Propp's study of fairy tales showed thirty-one narrative functions (which became known in the 1960s),[9] emphasis was laid on syntax and not on the specific meaning of each story. Similarly, in Lévi-Strauss' analysis of the Oedipus myth as the exemplar of all stories, meaning was said to lie in a pair of binary semantic oppositions. Drama and sequence were of little importance to him.

By giving the text the central place in critical theory, the reader-audience became more important. Barthes even claimed that the idea of the author had to give way to that of "the scriptor." This led to a strongly anti-expressive view of literature, discouraging reflection on style, reference, representation, meaning, and expression while virtually ignoring the significance of drama as fiction.

Early logical analysts had a similar attitude. Many saw the content of fictions as mere fantasy. Novels, myths, fables, plays, and drama were without truth value; they were false or spurious. Bertrand Russell and Gilbert Ryle stressed an economy in ontology and a normative attitude in logic; thus there was, for them, no universe of discourse outside the actual world. Russell, for example, denied any ontological status to nonexistent individuals, and said that statements about fictional persons were false on logical grounds.

Those linguistic analysts who were interested in the semantics of fiction came to rely on noncognitive terms. Thus Ogden and Richards depended on emotion.[10] P.F. Strawson's criticism of Russell[11] allowed for "spurious" statements but, in fact, it resulted in an even greater gap between actual and fictional statements; fictional statements, for Strawson, were always spurious. Gilbert Ryle, who had previously condemned all forms of fiction, agreed.[12] Fictions were not true in the ordinary nonmetaphorical sense because they denoted nothing and lacked truth value: "Nothing is left as a metaphysical residue to be housed in an ontological no-man's land."[13] Others were mainly concerned with the meaning of particular sentences rather than with the totality of the text.

But the significant meaning of dramatic fiction could only remain in an ontological no-man's land for older analysts who assumed that a detailed examination of the parts reconstituted the whole. In fact, as some contemporary logical analysts have shown, the cognitive meaning of dramatic actions lies in the whole, not in the individual parts: "Their micro-truth may well have no impact on the macro-truth value of large segments of the text or on the text as a totality."[14]

ACTUAL AND FICTIONAL

In contrast, today's logic, possible-world semantics, speech-act theory, and world-version epistemology have begun to address fiction from perspectives that show the intellectual qualities of dramatic action. What knowledge does drama provide? What is the relation of fact to fiction in spontaneous dramatic action? How far do play and improvisation resemble actuality? Such questions renew interest in higher-order interpretation, in multiple meanings, and in hermeneutics in general. This allows thinkers to consider that "the world-creating powers of imagination account for the properties of fictional existence and worlds, their complexity, incompleteness, remoteness, and integration within the general economy of culture."[15] What impact has this change of view had?

Like novelists, players create a fictional being within themselves, another persona. The events of the persona's existence make up the story line. Whereas the Western storyteller externalizes this fictional being in words and language, the player does so with the total self – mind, body, and voice in one representation. There are still storytellers in Africa, Asia, and elsewhere who mix dramatic actions with their verbal telling. Thus we can ask, Is there a difference between the Being of a personage and that of a storyteller? Are there differences between the fictional and nonfictional cognitions of the actual world?

Recently popular speech-act theorists tackle such issues poorly, by distinguishing between genres, or the ontological weight of fictional discourse; claiming that all texts and enactments are equally governed by arbitrary conventions; or maintaining that fiction is a discourse "whose illocutory force is mimetic"[16] and which *is* represented speech acts.[17] But John Searle makes a clear distinction between fiction and nonfiction: Fiction results from a particular attitude of a speaker, actor, or improviser who can make virtually any utterance a fiction. Pretence and drama are play, and the playful component of fiction shows that it is a genuine human activity. For Searle, the author of a novel only pretends to make assertions, yet serious (nonpretence) statements can be communicated by fictional speech acts, somewhat in the same way that indirect speech acts imply genuine ones.[18]

Modern thinkers often see the difference between fiction and actuality as a question of belief. The common distinction between opinion, conviction, and absolute conviction[19] places belief on a continuum from the pole of mere acceptance ("the unreasoned absence of dissent") to that of belief proper (assent upon evidence). Indeed, belief in fiction varies widely. It can be assumed to be actual by some schizophrenics who may reject all forms of role playing. Some tribal thinkers regard ritual fiction as more "real" than actuality. Still other people assume, like Ryle, that improvisation is mere fiction and contrast it with truth.

Belief differs, too, according to maturation. In Western cultures the criteria for cognitive activity in the dramatic play of young children are sincerity and absorption; Peter Slade even refuses to acknowledge the term *pretence* in these events.[20] With adolescence, however, students begin to develop two other models: the illustrative, where the fiction is communicated to others in a social interaction; and the expressive, where by later adolescence what is communicated in the fiction becomes important to both players and audience.[21] In terms of theatre, this is to move from Stanislavsky to Brecht.

But belief in dramatic fiction is more of a social imperative than a logical statement. As Pavel puts it, "Speakers who are sincere by participation should not be expected to defend the truth of their utterances other than by reference to the community or to accept readily the consequences of what they say. We do not individually possess qualities such as sincerity, ability to argue about assertions, and readiness to accept their consequences, except for a very limited range of sentences. Most often we behave as if our personal linguistic duties had somehow been waived; we do not always need to perform these duties scrupulously, since at every failure to do so the community is there to back us up."[22] When we say, "It is said that ..." we imply that there is consensus.

As dramatic worlds are created, we come to believe they are important parts of our culture. Thus appear those workaholics who make the fictions of law, business, education, medicine, and politics into social worlds that they believe in as independent entities. They are not required to defend their belief as "the really real."

Contemporary critics, particularly deconstructionists, have seriously undermined earlier assumptions that the structure of language, or the utterance of speech-act theory, constitutes models for cognition and dramatic events. These models do not match with our experience of dramatic fiction as we live through it. The earlier distinction between pretence and genuine acts has today become blurred for all kinds of fiction. Even John Searle distinguishes between fictional and genuine statements inserted by writers in stories: "To take a famous example, Tolstoy begins *Anna Karenina* with the sentence 'Happy families are all happy in the same way, unhappy families are unhappy in their separate, various ways.' That, I take it, is not a fictional, but a serious utterance. It is a genuine assertion."[23] Characters sometimes express their own wisdom, sometimes that of their creator. All fictions mix pretence and genuine statements; in Quine's words, "reference is nonsense except relative to a coordinate system."[24] Fictions refer to systems (such as the worlds of politics, law, and drama), and "in fiction one does not always need to keep track of pretended and genuine statements, since global reference is apparent in spite of such distinctions."[25]

For Jacques Derrida and other deconstructionists, social actions and dramatic events are not simply conventional. They exist on a continuum between two poles; the first, normal and serious acts grounded by a finite set of constitutive rules; the second, unusual or nonserious behaviour (play) that suspends finite conventions and replaces them with creative behaviour. The logical criteria for the one are not necessarily replicas of the other.

While our social behaviours share a considerable number of traits, the operating rules of one society are not the only possible choice. Nor do members of a community master these rules entirely.[26] Thus the conventions used in *this* improvisation are not necessarily the same as those used in *that*. To Searle this is strange: "It is after all an odd, peculiar and amazing fact about human language that it allows the possibility of fiction at all."[27] But it is only strange to those who see culture as grounded in linguistic or speech-act conventions.

Nor is it the case that every actual object has two sets of properties – properties that describe fictional objects within fiction, and those that describe them in the actual world.[28] This view is difficult to maintain in everyday experience, where we work from two perspectives: first, from dramatic action, where objects are always known to be real even if they are assumed; and second, from modern logical analysis, where the actual world cannot be kept out of fiction (fiction often includes "mixed sentences" that combine actual and fictional elements).

The actual and the fictional are not separate cognitive categories. They complement each other. It is better not to speak of the fictional as nonactual. Rather, the fictional world is an alternative to the actual world. The two operate together as a cognitive gestalt, so to speak: they share common properties, such as the concrete reality of the actual, and many of their operations are remarkably similar. The difference lies in our attitude towards them: We see the one as real and the other as "not really real."

In order to know more about the causal or historical chains of reference for fictional personages, as compared with actual persons, we must relax our criteria and accept those relevant to the total fictional context. This is to approach the causal theory of reference somewhat as Thomas G. Pavel does. He says that actual names like Shakespeare, while they are indexical and historical are, in fact independent of the properties of their owners. The names of fictional persons, such as Hamlet, primarily depend upon the referential aspects of the fictional context.

Seemingly, we come to know fictional beings as different from actual persons by unconsciously comparing the fictional and the actual. We innately grasp that their referential systems differ in the criteria they use. But we may not know this consciously. In Polanyi's famous phrase, "We know more than we can tell." This attitude approaches fiction from the inside, rather than making judgments from without – that is, it relies on how the user of fiction, the player, experiences fiction.

POSSIBILITY

To grasp dramatic fiction from the player's viewpoint is not to over-psychologize the issue. Rather, it is to concentrate on the cognitive workings of fiction per se. Just as, when we examine the novel, we must remember the perspectives of the writer and reader together with the meaning they share, so we must use a conceptual framework for dramatic action that emphasizes particular kinds of meaning: those of the players and their interaction, of any audience, and of the possible meaning created between them.

When we conceive possibility we work in the imaginative mode. We activate possibility in our perception of the world; it is this that makes what we hear and see meaningful to us, as David Hume indicated. Indeed, for Kantians there can be no perception at all without imagining. Imagining is also the skill inherent in image making, combining ideas and creating new ones; the inherent freedom of this act derives from to use Sartre's term) "the affective-cognitive synthesis." And our imaginative capacity is an inherent precondition for negotiation, the dramatic skill of seeing others in their own terms.

What kinds of possibilities are inherent in dramatic fictions? There appear to be two: those that are *realizable,* for example, "Hamlet is uncertain"; and those that are *unrealizable*: "Hamlet would have made a good king." These possibilities are available to both players and critics. In dramatic play, creative drama, and improvisation, where spontaneous dramatic action is the focus, the players have a choice between the two possibilities in the "here and now." They decide, as Ortega says, what happens next. Critics, from their choices, can infer a variety of things, such as This player consistently makes choices that are realizable, or He is inconsistent in his choices, choosing realizable alternatives for fantasy themes, and unrealizable ones for scenes of everyday life. Moreover, one possibility can be transformed into another, as in the play *Rosencrantz and Guildenstern Are Dead.*

But when Saul Kripke says that "Sherlock Holmes doesn't exist, but in other states of affairs he would have existed," he assumes that people and things in dramatic and fictional worlds are compatible with life.[29] Kripke has some agreement with Aristotle, who said it is the poet's business to tell us what would happen, or might have happened – "what is possible according to possibility and necessity."[30] Then there are two kinds of dramatic fiction: first, that which is true according to the real world – possible according to necessity; and second, that which is true according to possibility – possible as an alternative to the actual world. In theatre, this issue becomes Stanislavsky versus Brecht. Yet in both kinds of fiction, the fictional world is inhabited by persons who might have existed: both fictions are presented to the spectator in "hypothetically actual" worlds, but in different degrees.

Kripke's view is tangled. Fiction cannot be literally identified with metaphysically possible worlds, which would imply that it is independent of the novelist or the player – that Shakespeare did not create Hamlet but simply identified him as existing in a possible world.[31] Nor can Kripke's approach account for contradictory fictions: Should Sherlock Holmes draw a square circle (as Pavel says), the fictional world he inhabits would no longer be a possible world. But to say that all possible worlds are as real as the actual world does not make sense; we do, in fact, cognitively distinguish the real from the "not really real." Although we may value a fictional world as highly as the actual world, we recognize that each has a different level of reality.[32]

The paradoxes and contradictions that result from dramatization are not necessarily experienced as errors, so we cannot reduce fiction to a Kripkean theory. In a dramatic world mistakes can be made. Take *The Merry Wives of Windsor* as a simplistic example. Shakespeare wrote the play in haste and, as a result, the Justice Shallow and horse-stealing scenes are incomplete and not fully integrated into the plot. But in a great performance, how much do Shakespeare's mistakes matter? Mistakes and paradoxes do not negate the idea of a fictional world, though we might say that this world appears more unsymmetrical than the actual world. Pavel calls the Kripkean form a "distant" model of a theory of fiction; what is required, he says, is rather "a typology of worlds to represent the variety of fictional practice."[33] A number of contemporary philosophers have made attempts to this end. Some have used an ontological metaphor for fiction; others have created a whole aesthetic theory from fictional worlds, or used fictional terminology in phenomenology, or provided a categorization of fictional worlds.[34] In so doing, they have begun to use the cognitive power of dramatic fiction in ways similar to those of scholars in criticism, social role playing, sociology, anthropology, religion, ritual, critical pedagogy, and so forth.[35]

CONCLUSION

In what ways, then, can dramatic action as a cognitive operation be called a fictional world?

When we put ourselves in someone else's shoes, we try to think and act as they do. This act of identification and impersonation is the bedrock of all dramatic action: Infantile identifications lead to it, and theatrical acts result from it. But when we act in such a way we also cognitively engage the other person. We try to understand them and, by doing so, understand more about ourselves. This is why, for example, spontaneous dramatic action is so effective in overcoming bigotry and stereotypes. We learn not to stereotype when we put ourselves in someone else's shoes. The fiction of drama allows us to live through an alternative to rigid attitudes, giving us a world of dramatic possibility. The more we do so, the more intelligence becomes a factor in our lives.

This is probably best stated philosophically by Alvin Plantinga, who says that a possible world defines "a way things could have been ... a possible state of affairs of some kind."[36] He provides three parameters. First, he links the idea with Being "as if" – a notion that psychologists and educationalists believe is fundamental to play and enactment in children, and which they and others consider establishes play worlds and aesthetic worlds. Second, this "possible state of affairs," viewed as a world, does not violate the laws of either logic or the laws of dramatic action, but is whole and complete. Third, the possible state of affairs identifies such a world as cognitive and intelligent. This leads us to consider, in the next chapter, the intellectual qualities of fictional worlds.

CHAPTER TWO

Drama and Cognitive Processes

Does dramatic activity improve our thinking? What do we know from it? Is this different from other ways in which we know? This is to raise two issues: that of cognition (how we think), and that of learning (how we can improve our intelligence).

KNOWING AND BELIEVING

Knowing is a confusing word. Much is clarified if we ask: What does my knowing mean to me? What is it that I then have? When I know I am certain. But some people say they know things that, to you or me, are patently false. Then we might say, "They think they *know* something but actually they only *believe* it."

In popular usage, we say we know what is true but we believe what may or may not be so; we are sure we know something when we are certain of the facts, but we only believe it if we are not so certain. Despite popular usage, there is not a diametric opposition between knowing and believing.[1] From the utterance, "He drinks from a cup," we know some facts about a person and his actions with a cup. But when we watch an improviser drinking from an imagined cup, we know some mundane facts about the player and his actions with an imagined cup; we believe that a character is engaged in some actions with a cup in a fictional context; and we know and believe these things at the same time. They coexist. One level alternates with the other. From this, a logician might say that drama conveys two meanings: one we know, and one we believe. But this is not likely to be so at our *feeling* level as we live through the "here and now." Then knowing and believing can be remarkably alike to us.

That is, in life or in drama we function as if there is no difference between knowing and believing. We attend to both the player and the personage alternately. It is only after the experience (that is, as we look back on it) that we distinguish them. When I say, "I think such and such is the case," I usually mean I believe it to be the case, rather than I know that it is so. But what I *really* mean is, It is the consensus that it is so. Usually I cannot substantiate my view with rigorous proof. It is no wonder that in common parlance believing and knowing mean roughly the same thing.

What about the audience? Is there a difference between its knowing and believing? The people in the audience are observers. In most forms of inquiry, we gain knowledge from observation. If this is done properly (it is said), good data is exposed to rigorous treatment so as to reveal objective knowledge. This may be the case in highly abstract research, but it does not coincide with our experience in an audience, when we live through a performance much as we do events in life, even though we are not actively participing. We both believe in the dramatic action and, paradoxically, we know that it is merely fiction; we unconsciously compare it with life. We can also alternate our experience with thinking about the performance, that is, by distancing ourselves we may distinguish between actor and character, actual and fictional, and so on. Then the kind of meaning we obtain from the performance can be more significant than the meaning obtained from a mundane event. Once we see a stage character drinking from a full cup (imagined), and we know that it is poisoned but he does not, our believing is pregnant with meaning.

MUTUALITY

We create our knowing reciprocally with others. This mutuality may be direct: We may meet face-to-face with the person communicating with us, as in all forms of improvisation. Or it may be indirect: The author of a book may be assumed to be communicating with us.

Mutuality is functional. Its purpose is to communicate, and the fundamental agents of communication are human performers. Computers are able to pass information between performers, but only people can genuinely communicate. No two computers can communicate with one another with the nuances and subtleties of two improvisers. It is usual to say of communication that the sender and the receiver use transmission channels and codes determined by the culture of the users, their attitudes towards signs, and the nature of the medium when "the medium is the message."[2] In addition, however, the human actor as sender/receiver is dynamically engaged in creating unique meanings with another person (or persons).

When two people act in reciprocity, they are not neutral. Both are active in the exchange (or dialogue). They create change of two main kinds: of transformation and of Being. First, players act to change, or transform, something; this is a "knowing how to *do*." Second, they change Being. One person presupposes the virtual existence of the other, which reinforces the other's Being; this, in turn, reinforces the first person's own Being. In some way, what each of the two knows is changed. This is a "knowing how to *Be*."

In one sense, players in communication persuade one another. A teacher in a class, an actor performing on a stage, the author of a book – each persuades another person (or does not) that such and such is the case. The receiver comes to believe. In fact, players demonstrate several degrees of "coming to believe": from partial belief to that believing which is synonymous with knowing. Thus we can say that knowing and believing are poles of a continuum. Created in dramatic mutuality, they are unified by a player's actions and they operate within the mode of persuasion.

What are the dramatic processes we go through when we operate in such cognitive ways? Observation of children at play and adults using roles shows that a player functions on at least four cognitive levels, where he or she:

1 Has a store of existing knowledge and belief (a state of Being).
2 Presupposes the virtual existence of the other ("knowing how to *Be*").
3 Communicates what s/he knows or believes to another (communication).
4 Transforms what is received from the other ("knowing how to *do*").

For example, a class of French teenagers is improvising about life in China, although none of them have been there. In their preparations ("We'll do it like this") and their group improvisations, cognitive work is mainly tacit (observers must infer it from what the players do and say). In model form, the teenagers operate with their existing knowledge (based on learning and consensus); with other persons (based on the assumption, They are Beings like myself); with communicative and interactive skills in the "here and now" ("If I do Y like this, what will you do?"); with what they receive (aware of the meaning both for the other player and for the self); and with transformation ("If you do X like that, I will do Y like this"). Each of these operations includes a variety of cognitive skills.

This is an exemplary model for the mutuality in all dramatic action. Most obvious when the actions are overt, it is implicit in covert operations; and it operates in those cases where the presence of an other is assumed (like the author of a novel).

TRANSFORMATION

Drama *is* transformation – hunters possessed by animal spirits, children playing mother and father. But it is also a basic principle of human cognition: To understand something new, we must transform it into a pattern we already know. A classic instance of transformation took place when Captain Cook landed at Nootka Sound on Vancouver Island in 1778. The first night he and his men witnessed a winter ceremonial with masked Indian dancers transformed into frightening spirits. The second night, the men saw Indians dancing in masks and costumes made to resemble English sailors!

Whether one is an Amerindian dancing as a bear, a child playing bears, or an actor performing the bear in *The Winter's Tale,* the transformation brings about a change in the player's knowing. This occurs in two practical modes: the virtual and the actual. "Virtualization" is dramatization in the head, or imagining; actualization is "knowing how to *do,*" or making the virtual actual. Although there are many variations, the normal sequence for a player's transformation is (1) imagining the possibilities for action – if we doubt its possibility we do not move it into action, but if we think it is likely we do; and (2) trying out the dramatic action – if it works it becomes part of our knowing, but if it does not we reject it.

Transformation is a dynamic that brings about learning. Children at play or in creative drama are "coming to know." For example, by acting "as if" they are mothers and fathers, they act out old ideas and try out new ones in a reciprocal performance. They "come to know" more about mothers, about fathers, and about their relationship. What is transformed in dramatic action is learned.

Transformation also occurs in theatre art. Actors on a stage interpreting Ibsen's *A Doll's House* effect various changes in us when we are members of the audience. We attend to them as actors and also "as if" they are personages (a double reality), both actors and personages being "human beings like ourselves" (at another level of reality). They present us with acts which, if powerful enough, can change our knowing. In a great performance we feel that we have been changed, that we have learned in some way – although, as this change or learning is largely tacit, it is difficult to put into words.

Both play and theatre parallel the genuine educative act where teacher and student meet in an act of mutuality. The two engage in an exchange: The teacher tries to see the issue from the student's point of view and the student tries to do the same with the teacher. When this occurs, the student's knowing changes and learning happens.

We have described this (in play, theatre, or education) as a movement towards knowing or believing – from what is not known, to what is believed to be the case; from doubt to acceptance. The transformation is given power by its human context: It is acted by ourselves (in the case of children playing mother and father or of teacher and student interacting) or by the actor/character (in theatre). Thus the issues become deeply embedded in us.

This is illustrated by the telling of the parable of the good Samaritan. Jesus was clearly a powerful storyteller. Before he told the parable his listeners believed that Samaritans were bad and that Pharisees were good. When he had finished telling it, they were confronted with two views: their old belief and the new perspective. The result would have been felt when they next met a Samaritan or a Pharisee; one view or the other would have been confirmed. But, even if they returned to their old view, the experience of hearing the parable would have changed that view somewhat.[3]

The remarkable power of this type of cognitive change derives from its human context. It is ontological; it is a form of knowing how to Be. Identification with the other clearly takes place (much as Buber said) with either the actor/character or a person who is highly significant to us (like the teacher or Jesus).

But the change is as likely to be one of thought structure as of content – as much part of *how* we think as of *what* we think. Dramatic activity mostly produces a change in how we understand the deep rather than the surface level of meaning (although this is not always the case). The purpose of the parable, for example, is not only to change our attitude to this particular Samaritan but to change all forms of stereotypical thinking.

This issue is important for both instruction and interpretation. It affects instruction because in educational drama the content of the action is not necessarily progressive. "The mirror game," for example, can be played with all persons, from the youngest to the oldest. This is different from math, where addition normally comes before differential calculus and the learning of content is explicit and cumulative. In dramatic activity, where change occurs at a deep structural level, what we learn cumulatively is often tacit. As far as interpretation is concerned, we use inference to interpret dramatic action, whether this be children's play or a performance of *A Doll's House*. Any interpretation must proceed from a surface to a deep level.

For communication to take place effectively, activity must occur on the same hierarchical level of meaning. Ways of understanding the conversion of structures (such as the semiotic square)[4] can be applied as we move from one level to another. If activity does not take place on the same level, players or members of an audience are likely not to understand the dramatic message, and communication will break down; as a result they may understand dramatic activity (transformation) as a state and not as a dynamic. Thus they may view the inherent belief/doubt as being of the past and not of the present.

Although transformation is dramatic, a great variety of persuasive procedures are involved in it. These always exist in the "here and now" and can be viewed as dramatic variants. They include storytelling and narration in the present tense, direct demonstration, illustration, argumentation, debate, and so on, all of which share with drama the invitation to reciprocity. For example, someone playing a policeman, like the proposer in a debate, persuades the other to respond to his or her role. These procedures cover such a wide range of activity that a taxonomy of them would not be productive.

RE-PLAY AND INTRINSIC COGNITION

Yet all these variants can be reduced to forms of re-play.[5] As we have seen, dramatic activity and transformation involve re-playing what is already known. Even when we face something new, it must be incorporated into what is known in order for it to be learned and understood. This involves re-cognition – "to know again" or "to really know." It is not always realized that all cognitive processes involve some form of re-cognition; and that the various forms of spontaneous drama (play, creative drama, improvisation) operate in a parallel way. This is particularly the case with intrinsic cognition and learning.

Spontaneous drama encourages players to perceive in increasing depth and width. The dramatic action assists them to fully experience the environment through the senses and to organize and interpret their sensations. From this base, the players' consciousness and cognizance of their surroundings, and of others, increases. The process is circular, for it expands the players' awareness of what is perceived. It also focuses their attention on the task at hand, to concentrate. The task is specifically practical; it moves the action forward. In order to be successful, players must concentrate on the immediacy of the dramatic experience – a cognitive ability closely related to self-confidence. Educational drama has variously demonstrated that dramatic action improves players' belief that they can accomplish particular or general dramatic tasks. This applies whether tasks are generated internally by the self, or externally by others and the environment. Continued dramatic success promotes players' sense of their own worth as persons. The importance of this cannot be exaggerated. That a sense of confidence and self-worth promotes all kinds of cognitive and intellectual skills has been recognized in education for many years. Spontaneous drama is an exemplar of how this sense can be achieved.

A player is continuously responsible for his or her choices. At every single dramatic moment the improviser faces a number of choices and, to be successful, must discover one that will drive the action on. The player has a wider range of choice in freer forms (in play, creative drama, improvisation, and life) and less in those that are more formal (ritual and theatre). But even in the latter, players continuously choose. They exercise judgment in deciding which items to keep and which to jettison, according to the dictates of dramatic truth. This is very much a pragmatic truth; they keep what works in the "here and now," their criterion for judgment being the adequacy of the act in the dramatic world. The actions they use are those that propel the dramatic event – that project the dramatic action into what happens next.

The spontaneity necessary to move dramatic action forward encourages players to develop a wide range of styles of thought and action. The players take on all kinds of personage, each requiring its own thought-style and also the expressive ability of the player to convey this in representational forms. The thought styles can be divergent/convergent, creative/noncreative, and so forth. Dramatic activity enables each player to choose a unique thought style and also to work through to a solution by making a series of discriminating choices.

Two instances will serve us here. The first example is a grade 7 class in Toronto which demonstrated the ability to proceed through a series of discriminating choices to a solution while improvising an ancient Egyptian ritual. The students began by creating ancient Egyptian "music" with all kinds of found objects. Starting with this concrete and practical action, they began to focus on smaller and smaller elements. They improvised a religious procession where some of them carried and played the instruments. They discovered that Egyptian priests conducted a ritual in which they acted the roles of the gods of the Osiris myth, and cast some of their members as Re, Geb, Osiris, Isis, Nepthys, Seth, and Horus. This group worked out a ritual drama among themselves in considerable detail. The other group concentrated on the procession, getting the music and the movement "right." Then the whole was put together: An Egyptian religious procession entered the temple using music and stylized gestures, performed the ritual-myth, and departed.

The second example is taken from Shakespeare's *King Henry IV, Part 1,* act III, scene iii. When Falstaff, after teasing Bardolph about his great red nose, says, "How now, Dame Partlett, the hen!" the stage directions indicate that the Hostess enters. This presents a performance problem: Why does Falstaff refer to her as Dame Partlett, the hen, when her name is Mistress Quickly and there is nothing in the play to link her to chickens? A group of adults trying to solve the problem may after much agonizing find no solution. But dramatic action can be effective in problem-solving; the same question could be directed to groups in a grade 11 class who are experienced in improvisation, and within a few moments they discover that Mistress Quickly comes into the room cackling with laughter.

The impact of dramatic activity on the cognitive processes involved in problem solving is strong because drama is always directed to a specific practice: the need to keep the action moving forward. Players become more and more ingenious in problem-solving with increased dramatic experience. Play, creative drama and improvisation, in particular, encourage spontaneity and inventiveness in the identification and solving of problems.

Motivation is similarly affected. Motivation, whether initiated by the self (intrinsic) or by others and the environment (extrinsic), has been recognized as a vital factor in cognition for centuries. Even Rabelais made it the basis for the education of Gargantua. Play is, by definition, something people wish to do. It is always characterized by intrinsic motivation; and the dramatic quality of play extends this form of motivation into all kinds of different activities. This results in two other cognitive skills that become increasingly important with maturation: concentration and the ability to complete a joint task with others.

STRUCTURES AND DYNAMICS

The nature of the mental structures and dynamics involved in intelligent acts can provide us with insights into a person's patterns of thought and action. We must note, however, that all such insights are based on inference from the evidence of human action.

Mental structures and dynamics are highly complex and space precludes more than a cursory glance at them. Mental structures are the stable elements of thought. Mental dynamics are the energies that move between elements, or between thoughts. There is least energy when the mind is at rest, more when it is highly active. For instance, when we use computational skills specific structures/dynamics are highly active while those related to, say, eating are not. At all times, even in sleep, all structures/dynamics are active to some degree. We may be less conscious of some than others at a particular moment, but all of them operate at a low level of energy. In dramatic events, many mental structures and dynamics are highly active.

Second, mental dynamics oscillate. They move back and forth at great speed between the parts of any one structure, and between different structures. When we use computational skills, this oscillating energy is directed to specific aspects of the mind; it is directed intentionally, say, to the structures that will solve the particular computational problem. While we are engaged in dramatic action, the same kind of oscillation occurs, but in contrast to, say, mathematical skills, it is liable to affect a great many different mental structures that are activated as the players require them. Dramatic action activates a wide range of structures, while computation activates a narrower range.

Third, structures and dynamics can "flip." That is to say, what is a structure in one operation may become a dynamic in a different operation and vice versa. At first sight, this may seem paradoxical, but one of the major characteristics of dramatic action is its ability to generate ambiguous and paradoxical meanings based on its capacity to make structures and dynamics reversible. Normally structures are thought of as spatial, dynamics as temporal. But under certain circumstances they can reverse themselves. This most commonly occurs in spontaneous creative thought, with hypnopompic and hypnagogic images, in liminal conditions, and through festivity, clowning, and humour. The most obvious example in theatre is the reversible world of a particular "topsy-turvey" style in English comic plays from Ben Jonson and Henry Fielding to W.S. Gilbert and modern radio and television drama (Spike Milligan, John Cleese, etc.)

Fourth, dynamics are not merely linear but can function in all dimensions, including loops. Thus, while many thoughts flow along well-worn paths, others appear to be linked by association. The former are usually linked to the tragic, the latter to the comic.

Fifth and most important for our purposes, like all aspects of mind, structures and dynamics are double: Those that function in the "as" mode are homologous to those that work in the "as if" mode. (Indeed, the "as" and the "as if" may be the same; perhaps it is only our attitude to them that varies.) The homologous relation ensures that learning in one promotes learning in the other. When we talk of dramatic structures and dynamics, in most cases we imply both.

What structures and dynamics do we use in dramatic action? There are two fundamental mental structures inherent in all human activity: similarity and doubling. They work simultaneously.

Similarity

The first is similarity. When we are born we lack the ability to differentiate. After a few days we turn our head if a light is turned on in a darkened room. Slightly later we do the same if someone drops a book – the beginning of the structure of similarity/difference. Then the structure becomes more complex: part/whole (what is different is the part and what is similar is the whole) and continua (many different degrees of the whole).

This fundamental structure is formed around our experiences of juncture/disjuncture, which affects our use of transformation. Our knowing is constantly transformed by dramatic actions, which with maturation becomes increasingly complex. However, in each case we assess the results on two continua: from affirming the action to doubting it, and from believing the action to denying its truth. We discover whether what we do creates juncture (then we affirm or believe it) or disjuncture (then we doubt or deny it). With disjuncture, dramatic action fails: In life, communciation ceases; in improvisation, "overload" can be used for resuscitation;[6] and in theatre, more rehearsal is required. There are many different positions between juncture and disjuncture.

Doubling

The second fundamental structure begins with doubling. No sooner is a structure created in the "as" mode than it is doubled by one that is "as if"; the actual is paralleled by the fictional, or dramatic. The two effectively become homologous.

Thus, for example, once the part/whole structure is firmly established we complicate it with a parallel metaphoric structure. If I say, "My mind is a little rusty today," I create a fictional relationship between my mind (main subject – whole) and a machine (second subject – part) for the purpose of creating meaning through language. But I can also create metaphors in any medium – paint, photography, dance, theatre, etc. I can further complicate this structure through the use of symbols and/ or comparison.

There are three additional dynamics inherent in all human activity:

1 An "inner-outer movement." Based on the baby's identification and affective relation with the mother, this begins with empathy for her (projection) and a sense of being like her (introjection). Upon this are built the many complex dynamics focused on inner-outer, for example, inside-outside, here-there, me-you, and near-far.
2 A movement of change, or transformation. We transform, or change, people, events, and objects into mental forms with which we can deal. Linked to the inner-outer dynamic, when we transform an external object this also changes the relevant internal structure (which is a learning activity).
3 Substitution. This is another movement of change, from a lack of differentiation to precision. When we meet a concept with such a lack

of differentiation that it is difficult for us to deal with, we substitute for it one that is more refined or precise. By doing so, we lose much of its particularity and gross meaning but retain a more abstract if accurate meaning.

We develop aspects of these structures and dynamics for particular worlds. Thus when we turn to the mental structure that most commonly gives rise to dramatic activity, the metaphoric, we discover that it functions as a pole on two different but united continua. First is *similarity* (which is analogic, nonlinear, and continuous – metaphor) versus *differentiation* (which is analogic, continuous, and linear). Second is *opposition* (which is digital, nonlinear, and discontinuous) versus contiguity (which is discontinuous, linear, and digital – metonymy). This structure is energized by three dynamics: the contrary, contradictory, and complementary (see figure 3).

A further cognitive skill is the ability to understand the relation of drama to metadrama (for example, the play within the play). Understanding this relation in practice is the experiential ground for the abstract understanding of the function of metalanguages (see pp. 141–5).

TRUST

Fundamental to the dramatic process, as we have seen, is reciprocity. Players attempt to put themselves in someone else's shoes and see things from their point of view. This action is the model dramatic act; this is what characterizes an act as dramatic. It further establishes the cognitive context as a dramatic one.

In order for an act to function in a genuinely dramatic way, however, it has to engage the trust of two or more players. Thus it can also be called the fiduciary contract: Two persons implicitly agree to operate reciprocally, and to do so on the same "as if" level.[7] The fiduciary contract is the operational foundation for all those actions inherently dramatic in nature: storytelling, debate, dialogue, negotiation, and the like.

The contract of trust is entered into when both protagonists commit themselves to two positions: "the vaunt," and "the proposition." The vaunt announces that the fiduciary contract is in place, and the proposition begins the action.

Implicitly or explicitly, all players announce who they are in role. In early ritual drama they are likely to do so explicitly. In the English Mummers' Plays an actor in role typically enters saying, "I am St George," and there are similar examples in the medieval Mystery Cycles, the Noh, the Kathakali, and other traditional plays. In contemporary Western theatre the vaunt is usually more subtle. While children at play may explicitly state the vaunt ("I am Julia in my pretty dress..."), in most social dramatic forms it is likely to be unconscious. But when one player gives a vaunt and a second player responds with another, the dramatic context is established. This announces their mutual trust: in terms of opposition, as in ancient Greek tragedy; or of cooperation, as in many examples of children's play. The vaunt establishes the reciprocal contract between two players and allows dramatic action to begin.

The dramatic proposition sets the action in motion. Whereas the vaunt refers to Being, the proposition refers to knowing or believing. The protagonist's initial proposition (dramatic action) states or implies that he or she knows something ("I think that..."), which begins the dramatic action. It is a de facto invitation for the antagonist to respond – a persuasive statement to which both players can address themselves. Then they can engage in mutual action and dialogue. The proposition also involves the identity of the sender and invites the same level of personal commitment by the receiver. It initiates cognitive activity which, in the "here and now," operates on the surface; it is essentially practical and deeply personalized (ontological). It is specifically not abstract. Only after the mutual exchange has begun can the dramatic meaning move to a deep level.

This occurs with the skills of reciprocity. It requires interpersonal skills which, once the dramatic action has begun, enable the protagonist to move it forward with the help of the antagonist. The major skills of reciprocity are three:

1 *Wanting*. The player who wants the dramatic action to proceed in a specific way uses implied temptation and/or seduction. Things are said and done to persuade the other to a desired way of working. These can vary from the more obvious to the most subtle. Examples from theatre include Lady Macbeth's exhortation to her husband to keep to their murder plan; and Macbeth's eliciting of Banquo's opinion of the witches.
2 *Being able to*. An actor in role can use implied threats or provocations. This can be an obvious physical threat or a subtle provocation (for example, Macbeth's persuasion of the First Murderer to kill Banquo).

   These first two skills bring about a fundamental relationship between the two protagonists. They cause the antagonist to believe.
3 *Negotiation*. This primary skill of reciprocity pervades all dramatic actions. Human interaction and communication rest on the ability of one person to read the other by seeing things from the other's point of view and then putting things in a way that relates to the other's viewpoint. Success here lies in persuading the antagonist to move the

action forward on his or her own terms, but also in a way satisfactory to the protagonist. Negotiation is particularly dramatic in that it acknowledges the attitudes of both protagonist and antagonist.

These skills develop the mutuality of dramatic action. The better they are manipulated, the more effective the action. They work in three ways,

1 as double structures, which are skills of both the player and the character. Here they are usually intended by the player to be executed by the personage;
2 in the "here and now";
3 as persuasions, intended by the player to move the action forward.

Although these skills and their operations are largely tacit for the player who works with them, for the observer they can represent a cognitive test as to whether the action is dramatic or not.

CONCLUSION

Dramatic activity affects human intelligence by improving important cognitive processes. First, drama improves our knowing. We come to know what we play and act through varieties of believing. In order for a dramatic action to be accepted and used, players affirm its truth value through a "knowing how to *Be*" and a "knowing how to *do*." Second, dramatic activity improves learning. Learning is synonymous with the change in knowing achieved by re-play, an element of dramatic transformation that brings about re-cognition. This is particularly the case with intrisic learning and the improvement of judgment, problem-solving, and motivation to learn. Third, dramatic activity improves intelligence by activating the fundamental structures and dynamics of mind.

But, additionally, drama works with doubling and metaphor. Thus it improves specific cognitions and general intelligence by providing a necessary fictional frame of reference against which we check our direct perception of reality.

These improvements are possible because dramatic activity rests on reciprocity: the mutual trust between players, who commit their Being to action, and express their Being and their knowledge in action and dialogue. This level of existential commitment to the dramatic world gives the knowing of the players a degree of certainty that allows us to accept it as a valid form of cognition. The kinds of worlds to which players become committed are examined in the next chapter.

CHAPTER THREE

Cognitive Worlds

Cognition separates truth from falsehood, develops and changes concepts, assimilates information, and uses mental frameworks so that we can make sense of our experiences. When we talk of brain cells being connected at synapses, we describe aspects of human physiology. Alternatively we can discuss "mind", where we can picture cognition as groups of activities. The latter are worlds, one of which is our dramatic world.

WORLDS AND MEANING

My actual world is the way I think about and act with the total environment as I know it to be – as I eat my lunch or contemplate a sunset. This is the actual. It concerns sticks and stones, how I stub my toe, what happens when I wash my face, and the people I meet. In the abstract, we can distinguish my actual world from various fictional worlds we create. The latter are of two kinds: the dramatic world of each individual and the social worlds people in a culture share.

Each individual works with an actual world and a dramatic world. My dramatic world is a fiction. I have created it with my imaginings and my acts; and I have done so over a long period of time – it has its own history. It consists of my perspective on the actual world, which comes from my personal experience. That is, the actual world provides the materials with which my dramatic world works. The cognitive purpose of my dramatic world lies in comparisons between that world and the actual world; from these, I can make judgments of validity and of truth.

But what happens when two players (you and I) improvise together? You also have a dramatic world that you have created and that has its own history. Our two dramatic worlds, yours and mine, may well involve similar dramatic skills – those of role playing, improvisation, and other forms of dramatic expression[1] – as well as criteria for judgment. This enables us to improvise together with reasonable success. But my dramatic world is as unique as yours; it is based on my personal experience of the actual world, some parts of which we may share, together with other parts we do not share. There are, therefore, moments in our joint improvisation when I do not quite grasp all that you imply, and vice versa. Indeed, there are some gaps between us when we improvise. The skills of improvisation include the ability to overcome such gaps.

The dramatic world differs from social worlds, although both are fictional. The world of law or the world of politics, like those of education, therapy, and so forth, are primarily built on human ideas of a social kind. So are those worlds of a particular culture that many share, including myth, story, history, arts, sciences, etc. (This has particular importance at the end of the twentieth century as the major cities of the world grow increasingly multicultural.) Such worlds are socially fictional; they are created by many people's imaginings and actions, often over a long period of time. But they enter the actual world as acts that are socially significant, and thereby they construct social reality. They too have a cognitive effect: They develop their own particular concepts, and these can change what we perceive, know, and believe. But my dramatic world is clearly different from, say, the world of law, in that while we share most of the latter, the former is primarily mine. It has cognitive elements in common with other worlds, but most of its elements are felt to be unique.

A group of worlds make up a cognitive universe: the actual world[2] and both kinds of fictional worlds, the dramatic worlds of the players, and the social worlds within which they play. Together they provide a universe of meaning available to me. One perspective (or world) has only limited meaning. But when perspectives are available from a variety of worlds that constitute a cognitive universe, meaning becomes multidimensional.

However, universes and worlds may require different languages to describe them. Phenomena in one fictional world, or universe, may coincide only approximately with that in another. All fictional worlds are linked to the same actual world; but they vary in their meanings. What you and I come to know, through our different dramatic worlds as we improvise together, coexists; those worlds are variant descriptions of the same actuality. A dramatic world, yours or mine, carries explicit and tacit meanings; but not all dramatic worlds are explicable in a specific language. It is not the case that any content can be appropriately expressed by some linguistic means or other.[3] A natural language is a medium with a finite numbers of referents and constructions; it cannot adequately describe a cognitive universe that has (at least in theory) an infinite number of possibilities.[4]

The difference between actual and fictional worlds lies in their attitude to actuality. However, the difference between fictional worlds is of another kind: "Like various theories each positing its own level of actuality, fiction employs a multiplicity of bases, of worlds 'actual'-in-the-system. Don Quixote's universe develops around a basic level that is different both from our actuality and from the world described, say, in *Persiles and Sigismunda* or *The Pickwick Papers*."[5] Each fictional world carries a different kind of meaning. Yet each has cognitive reference to the actual world in which it is framed, its own historical and cultural context, and its own internal models. That is, each indicates "the ontological status of fictional entities... embodied in the experience of being caught up in the story."[6] This happens "because works of fiction are not mere sequences of sentences but props in a game of make-believe, like children playing with dolls or pretending to be cowboys... [Such] propositions are true in the world of that game. And just as children pretending to feed dolls that in the game are (fictionally) babies become themselves fictional moms and dads fictionally feeding their offspring, readers of *Anna Karenina* who cry at the character's tragic end fictionally attend Anna's suicide, that is, participate (as spectators) in a game of make-believe."[7]

TRUTH

Truth lies in the player and in the playing. A fictional proposition is true in the world of the fiction itself – of the game that is played. A fiction, that is to say, provides a frame of reference for itself.

We live in fiction. Those who read a novel or witness a performance do not contemplate a fictional world from outside that world. Rather, as Kendall Walton says, they are within the fictional world; and while the game is played, they take the fictional world to be actual.[8] The reader or audience applies this intuitive judgment to all fictions that exist in time: story, drama, theatre, dance, music, opera, ballet, film, puppetry, and so on.

It has also been said that there is a cognitive distance when we read a novel or go to the theatre – that we do not live within the fiction at all but, in Coleridge's phrase, we willingly suspend our disbelief. In fact, as all theatregoers know in their bones, we do both. As members of an audience, there are times when we assume that the fiction is true and that we are in it. At other times, particularly when we think ABOUT it, we can say that it is "only" fiction. These audience frames of reference are cognitive. The first frame is significant to our feelings, intuitions, and judgments (the aesthetic-cognitive), and it is also cognitive by providing deep inner meanings (personal knowing). The second frame provides a kind of discursive cognition – a Knowing ABOUT. We achieve our sense of reality through a comparison between the two frames.

When we are caught up in a story, says Kendall Walton, we become part of the fiction by projecting a fictional ego; this ego attends to the imaginary happenings (but does not participate in them) and it is moved by these events (which we are not). Here Walton seems to describe two kinds of fiction. He begins with those fictions most distanced from us. But he says that we can feel, in addition, "a psychological bond to fictions, an intimacy with them, of a kind which normally we feel only toward things we take to be actual." Here he seems to describe the fictions closest to us, as when a reader cries at Anna Karenina's death or feels pity for Olivier in a tragedy.

This enables us to say that our feelings participate in fiction by degrees: distanced/involved, or indirect/direct experience. In the modern theatre, for instance, there are two theoretic exemplars of this polarity when we are members of the audience: Stanislavsky would have us deeply involved with the situation, identifying with the characters and participating (as voyeurs) in the event; but, in contrast, Brecht would have us distanced from the event and the story, recognizing the actors as actors and the theatre as a theatre, and not involved in any way. In practice, however, as members of the audience we may alternate between states of belief and nonbelief in the dramatic action – more deeply with a great performance, less so with other performances. We experience fictional worlds through relative similarities and differences.

What is truth in a dramatic world? In play, it is what is played. It is the playing in this specific case – the *what* and *how* of a particular dramatic action. When we dramatize, truth emerges in several ways: when players express truths of the human condition as personages through their Being, words, and action (ontological truths); when their seeming spontaneity is in the present tense (temporal truths); and when their acting area provides the truths of contexts as the significant "here" (spatial truths). Other truths can be added by incorporation (any truth not ruled out by the rules of the game) and by constructions derived from the rules and incorporated truths.[9]

There are continua of such truths. An example is given by a comparison between enactments in play, where truths are created entirely by and for the players; and enactments in formal theatre, where truths are created mainly for meanings to be conveyed to the audience. These are specifically not digital oppositions but two actions linked through correspondence – through the relations created "as if." This relation is a double one.

In a playhouse, the primary world is the actual one; the performances include only those cognitive elements that correspond to the actual in a homologous relation.[10] The secondary world of the theatre is a mirror of the first. But performances are existentially creative: Pretending to be chased by a dragon has some cognitive meanings that have no correspondence to the actual world.

FICTIONAL WORLDS

Fictional worlds include cognitive, aesthetic, ontological, and other elements that are overlapping parts of the whole. Such worlds are cognitive because in our use of them we come to know more of both the fictional and actual, so that our concepts change and develop. Fictional worlds are also aesthetic: Our intuitive cognition is grounded in feeling. Such worlds are formed from our choices. Thus when we make good judgments they are likely to be mainly tacit; they feel right, in an intuitive way. These worlds are also ontological. As they are created by us, they are an expression of our Being – who we *are*, who we imagine ourself to be (Being "as if"), and who we will *become*. Such inclusiveness raises many difficulties for more conservative scholars: Worlds are not categoric; they cannot be thoroughly described as this or that. When we speak of them as being cognitive, therefore, we are selecting only one attribute of a fictional world that is, in essence, whole.

Other confusions arise because some aspects of one fictional world may also be aspects of another. For example, the *hic et nunc* of the dramatic, theatrical, and religious worlds share certain beliefs and practices. The combined ritual-myth is played by priests and believers; the living ritual (the enactment) re-plays the origin myth (the story) in the "here and now" of Inanna and Damuzzi, Osiris and Horus, Dionysos, Jesus Christ, the cannibal spirit of Pacific Northwest Coast Indians, or the dreamtime of Australian aboriginals. These rituals are performed in "sacred time," where past and present are collapsed into the "now," and in "sacred space," where the acting area is elevated beyond the mundane. These similarities between the dramatic, theatrical, and religious worlds show that, in the fundamental ontological model, the actual and nonactual of fictional worlds are parallel. In the religious world the contrast is profane/sacred, but in the dramatic and theatrical worlds it is mundane/significant.[11]

In one sense, therefore, we can distinguish between the various ways in which worlds *use* enactment for cognitive purposes. The actual world uses it for externalizing imaginings in many media. Our dramatic world uses enactment to test our knowing of actuality. And social fictional worlds enable us to work within our society and culture in a variety of ways. Yet fictional worlds are not entirely discrete entities. Enactment is used by the play world in children's activities and adult festivities; by artistic worlds in creating art; by aesthetic worlds in feeling constructions; by religious worlds in ritual and myth; and so forth.

So what characterizes the dramatic world in cognitive terms? Some key factors are externalizing the inner (covert) dramatizations of the creators in "as if" actions (overt); making valid the created world as an alternative context; and projecting hypothetical possibilities and what-happens-next into the *hic et nunc* by the player and/or the audience. Thus Arthur Danto shows that when we say, "This actor is Lear," we engage in artistic identification: "It is an *is*... which has near-relatives in marginal and mythical pronouncements. (Thus, one is Quetzalcoatl; those are the Pillars of Hercules.)... [T]he artworld stands to the real world in something like the relationship in which the City of God stands to the Earthly City."[12] In the dramatic world, the "as if" is treated as an "is" – it is believed in. Yet the "is" and the "as if" are known to be different forms of reality. Dramatic worlds, in other words, are inherently paradoxical.

The prime cognitive relation to actuality of both the dramatic and the ritual worlds is ontological. Personages in both worlds are alternatives to actual persons. But F.E. Sparshott notes some differences: "Either the place and the participants are conceived on the model of familiar types, in which case the element of fantasy becomes scarcely more than decoration, or the story becomes thin and schematic, because we cannot tell what sort of background to provide for what we are explicitly told."[13] However, worlds can be distinguished from one another through the styles of playing for which they call:

1 The actual world, where the human actor is "a mundane costumed player."
2 The dramatic world, where our spontaneous and improvised gestures, words, presence, clothing, and Being, based on the actual world, are the foundation for other fictional worlds.
3 The socio-fictional world, which works within the actual world when the human actor takes roles as "a social costumed player." In addition, groups improvise and create fictional subworlds within culture (for example, business, education, law) which can appear to function independently.
4 The social-aesthetic world is characterized by enactments that mix personal and social meanings. In spontaneous play, educational

drama, drama therapy, and social and related enacted worlds, the human actor is "an exploratory costumed player" – beyond the mundane but not always significant – who creates meaning through absorbed, illustrative, and expressive models.

5 The (aesthetic) artistic world of theatre where, in improvised or formal styles, the actor is "a significant costumed player" who jointly communicates and creates with the audience a significant space, time and meaning.

6 The religious world, characterized by varieties of improvised and formal performances in which the ritualist is "a sacred costumed player" who jointly creates and communicates with others a sacred space, time, and meaning.

These five categories are far from rigidly discrete. There are many examples of enactments that fall between their cracks; for example, some educational drama with senior students, and some activities in drama therapy, are close to theatre while others are close to social ritual. Rather, dramatic worlds are located on a continuum between the informal and the formal.

ONTOLOGY

All the different types and styles of fictional worlds derive from the dramatic world, and this leads us to ontology. Ontological issues concern human existence. They play a significant part in all fictional worlds, particularly the dramatic world, through the fundamental use of Being "as if" – human supposition. Ontological issues are those of Being and Becoming. We might ask, "Who am I? Who am I for you? Who are you? Who are you for me?" These questions are answered in dramatic action when we put ourselves in someone else's shoes. All fictional personages do this, whatever the dramatic form in which they operate. Jocasta and Portia do it, each improviser does, and each child at play.

But ontology is best illustrated by theatre. Ontology is directly addressed not only by Hamlet in his "To be or not to be" speech but also by Laudisi in Pirandello's *Right You Are (If You Think So!)*, when he asks, "Who am I for other people?" and replies, "An image in a glass." Ontological issues lie at the centre of tragedy *(Oedipus Rex, Phèdre, The Wild Duck)* and are also the focus of comedy *(Twelfth Night, Tartuffe, Waiting for Godot)*. They pervade modern plays from Archie Rice who, in John Osborne's *The Entertainer*, says, "I'm dead behind these eyes," to Arthur Miller's *Death of a Salesman* where, for Willy Loman, "attention must be paid."

But ontological issues are not addressed so directly and obviously all the time. Thus it is not always possible to rigidly distinguish the ontology of the sacred from, on the one hand, that of theatre and, on the other, that of spontaneous play. Take, for example, the sacred among the three Amerindian tribes on Vancouver Island. In rituals, the Coast Salish fully believe they become spirits and are possessed; but the Nootka (West Coast) and Southern Kwakiutl ritualists, while they are supposed to be possessed, recognize that they are being highly theatrical[14] – like Western players who can alternate between distance and absorption in their roles. Simultaneously, each of the three tribes regards their ritual performance as playing – relaxation and spontaneous enjoyment.

From this example we can see that the ontology of dramatic fiction ranges across a number of continua whose poles are distance/absorption, mundane/metaphysical, and so on. This may, perhaps, account for a major characteristic of our dramatic worlds, our ontological commitment to them. If we do not believe in them in quite the same way as we believe in our religious worlds, we do however regard them as coherent and cognitive wholes to which we are devoted. Calling children in for lunch while they are playing can be as difficult as persuading the workaholic businessman that he might be wise to change his life style. While working within our fictional worlds, we can ignore the fact that they are only possible and not actual worlds. The language we use about them also ignores their nonactuality. We work "as if" they are actual worlds.

A dramatic world is a double but not a copy (or, as Aristotle would have it, an imitation) of the actual world. We operate within the one as a double of the other. Life is like drama, and drama is like life – a metaphor at least as old as Pythagoras. Or we can say with Prospero that life *is* drama, "such stuff as dreams are made on." This might account for many of the doublings that have previously posed intellectual difficulties for positivists: actuality dramatized as a double of the world of the spirits (in tribal cultures) or the world of the gods (in early agricultural societies); in fiction, the appeal of twins, the figure of the doppelgänger, and pairs who complement each other (male/male, female/female, male/female, or human/animal in myths, legends, and allegories); and the universal use of the mirror, from the transformation of ancient shamans to the symbolism of Pirandello. To perform in or watch an improvisation, to write or read a book, to paint or contemplate a painting, is to already inhabit its world. As with Heisenberg's uncertainty principle, we can alternate between the two perspectives (actual and fictional) by switching from one to the other at will, although they may seem to exist simultaneously.

Dramatization centres on persons: who they *are,* and who they are likely to *become.* This ontological factor is the cognitive focus not only of our dramatic world but also indirectly of all our fictional worlds. Each world is created by dramatization, but some are more distant from Being than others. Those of direct dramatic action (dramatic play, improvisation, theatre, and speech) come close to who we *are;* our self-in-role creates them. They are on a different ontological level from those indirect worlds that substitute for direct dramatic action the creative behaviours used in other media (music, visual arts, writing, etc.).

Ontological complexities in fiction are common in late Renaissance and baroque literature, particularly in the play within a play of *Hamlet* and the fiction within a fiction of *Don Quixote.* These complexities, at their best, are specific. They are based on the actual world and are essentially playful – like *Tristram Shandy,* they are usually self-conscious, drawing attention to themselves as fictions. Such works create a feeling of spontaneity and provide another perspective; they make us re-play and so reassess our experience. They draw readers/audience into a world and make them work cognitively – either by stimulating them to put flesh on the bones of a fiction; or more narrowly by stimulating reactions through specific techniques (allusions, puns, quotations, etc., in novels) or strategies (deixis in theatre). Obviously, playfulness is more prevalent in some creators than in others, for example, in Shakespeare more than in Corneille, James Joyce more than in George Eliot.

The most primitive actors, wandering players, had the skill to imitate the speech, facial expressions, gestures, and character of a slave (or servant), a peasant, a procurer, a scholastic pedant, and a foreigner. This was the case in classical times. Such personages still appear today at the annual fairs in southern Italy. A *commedia dell'arte* improvisation in the Renaissance, as with all theatre forms, took actual persons of the day and made them into stock types. But it had its own Renaissance conventions, its own degree of playfulness, its own forms of deixis. The stock characters (Arlecchino, Pantalone, etc.) altered as ideas of personality changed. By the early eighteenth century this tradition had become codified in a particular way: There was a mixture of *commedia dell'arte* masked figures and *inamorati* in improvisations framed around *lazzi.*

Goldoni and Gozzi transformed this view of personality into scripted plays and so changed the inherent ontology. By "the Great Season" of 1750, Goldoni had added realistic characters so that, in *The Liar,* all three styles – caricatures, elegant lovers, and the realistic – peopled the stage, and Goldoni could draw a central character made up of elements of each with a pathological multipersonality. That same year Goldoni also created *The Comic Theatre,* a play-cum-dramatic theory that fictionally examined such a chaotic view of Being; this he "corrected" in later, more naturalistic plays. It was not merely that his personages became more bourgeois – he also changed the level of ontological treatment.

In the 1920s, Pirandello brilliantly adapted *The Comic Theatre* to his masterpiece, *Six Characters in Search of an Author*, where he dramatized an Einsteinian view of Being. In the world of this play, a person's personality is known differently by others and, quite consciously, the central questions for each character become, Who am I? And who am I for other people? On the surface, human personality may appear to be even more chaotic than Goldoni conceived it, but Pirandello turns Goldoni's comic world on its head. Now it has a relativist logic: Cognition is a matter of perspective. Within any one dramatic world there are various subworlds that fit together like a set of Chinese boxes. Thus in *Six Characters* various alternative views of Being appear to be the-actual-in-the-drama:

1 The (actual actors performing as) fictional backstage personnel preparing the stage for a rehearsal.
2 The (actual actors performing as) fictional actors being themselves.
3 The (actual actors performing as) fictional personages in a play they are rehearsing (a different play by Pirandello).
4 The (other actual actors performing as the) fictional six characters (at a different fictional level from the personages above).
5 The (original actual actors, as those at 1, 2, 3 above, performing as fictional actors re-performing (rehearsing) as the fictional characters (as in 4 above).
6 The (actual) audience.

But, as audience, we are also confronted with subsets of each of the subworlds, a kind of infinite regression, in fact. For example, Madame Pace is one of the characters, but unlike the other five she can only live with the real objects of her trade around her, and her sudden appearance among the props of her establishment is a theatrical tour de force of startling proportions.

The ontology in the world of *Six Characters* is highly cognitive. Pirandello himself saw his plays as a mixture of emotion and intellect. As this one proceeds, we learn of the human condition in the modern world: Being is fragmented, but multiplicity is unified when the fragments are seen as aspects of all humanity. Commonly called Pirandello's levels of illusion, the fragments are also inherent ontological frames of reference within the play; they enable us cognitively to examine the nature of both his dramatic world and humanity itself from a variety of perspectives.

These examples from theatre illuminate what has been happening in philosophy and criticism in recent years. Instead of studying fiction from a model of language or speech acts, critics increasingly use dramatization. When Marie-Laure Ryan suggests that literature originates in the activity of impersonating,[15] she implies that the author of the novel pretends to be the narrator – for example, Tolstoy impersonating the narrator of *War and Peace*. This is to distinguish between narrative discourse performed by the impersonated speaker, and metanarrative comments performed by the author him or herself. In effect, Ryan complements Walton's theory of reading fiction with a theory of creating fiction.

But drama has no narrator. Or at least a narrator is not necessary to dramatic form, which is concerned with showing, not telling. Dramatic action is created on the spot by the player. The ontology of dramatic action is specified from within itself, through references made to it by the players. Here lies the crux of the matter. Fictional worlds are the result of mutual creation (reader/writer, audience/dramatist, witness/improviser), as the young Martin Buber understood when he went to the Viennese theatre: There is a "mutual dialogue" in all human relationships. That is, cognitive meaning lies in the dynamic *between* – between dynamics, between forces, between processes – which is a tenet of poststructuralism.

DRAMA AND DECONSTRUCTION

Barthes in *S/Z* was the first to indicate that, as the reader adopts different viewpoints, the text's meaning separates into a multitude of fragments that appear to have no unity. Those who look for a cognitive and hermeneutic code discover, instead, an enigma. But deconstruction goes further. It is fundamental to Jacques Derrida, Jacques Lacan, Julia Kristeva, Paul de Man, and others that fiction is mutually created:[16] The writer allows for what the reader will "fill in." Their case is made stronger with the instance of theatre: The dramatist and player allow for the audience's creation of meaning. This has considerable cognitive significance.

All human communication is mutual for Jacques Lacan, but it is only possible through reversing ourselves, that is, putting ourselves in someone else's shoes (the exemplary dramatic act). This develops with maturation. In the baby's first months there is no clear distinction between subject and object; no central self exists that can set object apart from subject. Child therapists have identified "the mediate object" (a doll or a piece of cloth, like Linus' security blanket) as the focus that differentiates the inside from the outside.[17] Lacan shows that later, in the prelinguistic "mirror phase," the baby starts to project a unity onto the fragmented self-image in the mirror: S/he creates a fictional ideal, an ego, which continues the maturational development of differentiation. I have shown elsewhere that this codifies at about ten months into "the primal act":[18] The baby begins to act "as if" s/he is the self in another situation. An act of genuine dramatization occurs between the self and the-self-as-other. The baby, now able to distinguish subject from object, becomes a child.

This is the generic basis for the cognitive activity of dramatic action. The two sides of a concept (subject and object) are linked and gradually seen as element of the whole – as whole/part or as continua. The two are specifically not seen as binary oppositions but as similarities that have degrees of difference. But the two parts can also be seen on alternating continua: The mental principle of similarity is doubled so that contrasts, contradictions, and complementaries can then be imagined and acted. This process is developmental: It continues throughout life; it changes with learning and cultural shifts; and it can be explicated through the semiotic square of similars and metaphors.[19*]

Cognitive activity is a process: a continuing, emergent, and changing dynamic, as exemplified in speech. When Jacques Derrida says, "Speaking is life but writing is death," he is giving primacy to the processual. Speaking is nearer to our Being than writing. Derrida also says that every linguistic sign is but "a trace of the absence of all other signs." There is, indeed, more to fiction than meets the eye. Speaking is as near as media can get to the self. In much the same way we can say that spontaneous dramatic action, as a medium, has priority in terms of creating meaning. The costumed player, as the double of an actual human presence, incarnates that person. Playing gives cognitive meaning to human existence.

A particular world has its place on a continuum of near/far in relation to Being. That place depends on the paramount medium. Thus, for example, drama, dance, and speech are near the Being of persons, while writing and drawing are far from it. This is not to classify any medium as better or worse than any other, but merely to characterize media in ontological terms. The near/far continuum can be used to examine each world's structure and to make aesthetic judgments about it. We have to

---

* We should note in passing that the view of subject and object as similarities is considerably different from the view that has driven Western intellectual thought since Aristotle. Opposition and competition were basic to the Greek view of life. The Greeks competed in the Olympic and other games and also in poetry and theatre. Democratic man (not woman or slave) functioned continually in opposition to something – ideas, people, states, the gods. His heroes were combative and the world was engaged in continuous warfare. Once we view the two sides of a concept as similar, however, opposition, competition, digital thought, and warfare are no longer a predominant view. They are replaced by similarity, mutuality, continuity, love, and peace.

ask: What are the fundamental fictional properties of this specific world? What kind of ontology does it express?

This is to reverse the normal hierarchy, much as Blake did in believing that Milton was on Satan's side, and as Shelley in believing that Satan was morally superior to God. Such reversal is essential for Derrida; it is the deconstruction showing him that genuine meaning lies in the gaps between ideas, not necessarily in the ideas themselves. In a similar vein, for Julia Kristeva existence is process and is capable of being other than it is. Not only the novelist but also the dramatist allows for the filling in of the text; his dialogue on the page allows the stage actor to respond to a warm or a cold audience. The improviser fills in even more; s/he relies fundamentally on audience response before taking another step on the dramatic tightrope. Theatre as a form closely resembles the freedom of play.

Derrida treats ideas as process – a dynamic of interchange, like Buber's mutual dialogue. But Derrida reverses the normal hierarchy of the actual/fictional. For him, an actual courtroom oath is simply a special case of the performances people play in films and books. As Oscar Wilde believed, life copies art.

In addition Derrida has much to say about mimesis. From Aristotle on, the term has broadly indicated "the imitation of living actions," as a synonym for "replica," "representation," "reproduction," "resemblance," "simulation," "analogy," and so on. To these Derrida adds "presentation/presencing," "production," "appropriation," "the original," "the model," and "the authentic." Ultimately mimesis transcends all such concepts; it is virtually untranslatable. For our purposes, however, Derrida defines mimesis as the dramatization that leads to enactment. This is different from literature, where dramatization leads to story.

In *Dissemination,* Derrida tells us that Plato, in a particularly abstruse passage, describes how the breath of Thoth, the enigmatic Egyptian god of the moon, created the world. Thoth mainly existed by wearing the masks of the other gods; he was the "masker," the "masquer," the dramatizer, related to the ancient trickster. He was also the ancestor of Hermes, the messenger of the Greek gods, "he who puts play into play." Similar to Thoth is the hero of Plato's dialogues, the fictional representation of his master Socrates, for whom speech was life. As a man and as a teacher, Socrates' essence was dialogic: It consisted of his self-presentation, his dramatization of himself as one who knows nothing. For Socrates, *our ontological reality is that we dramatize who we are in life;* this is the nearest we can come to Being.

Derrida also says that Kant performs "a miracle" through the mediating figure of the genius-poet who is the unconscious mouthpiece of God. Using the genius-poet, Kant permits the dramatic world to be both imitation and a free activity through analogy; this occurs in the operation of "as if," which Kant essentially sees as a way of knowing. Working from this example, Derrida says the transformation of imagining into fictional worlds, through media such as speech and self-presentation, has many cognitive implications. Life and art, when described by Derrida, originate in "speech," "breath," and "self-presentation" – a dramaturgical perspective more cognitively revealing than even that of Kenneth Burke. Mimesis, in this context, is a powerful all-inclusive term.

This case is made somewhat differently by Lacoue-Labarthe,[20] for whom mimesis is in incessant movement "in-between." It precedes, or is anterior to, re-presentation or fiction proper. This would place mimesis after the thought and before the act – a primal proto-act on which all other acts depend. The implication is that the mimetic origins of education are inherent in Plato's *Republic.*

But it is Paul de Man who delivers the coup de grâce to the linguistic analysts of the early twentieth century. He says that tropes and figures of speech in general pervade language, and that they convey more significant meanings than mere syntax. Tropes allow creators of meaning (writers, dramatists, players) to say one thing but mean something else, that is, to substitute one sign for another (metaphor), to displace meaning from one sign in a chain to another (metonymy), and so on. The classic instance of this in the playhouse is the work of Chekhov. In *The Cherry Orchard,* for example, the play's subtext is covered by the plain, homely words in conversations which, nevertheless, carry major messages to the audience. Performance conveys more meaning than is contained in spoken words.

Thus Paul de Man destabilizes classical logic and prevents a simple or straightforward reference to language about the actual or the fictional. Language, used within fiction, is more meaningful because it is inherently figurative. Thus contemporary thinkers work with metaphor as a way of understanding deep cognitive meanings. (see chapter five).

CONCLUSION

The player, even more than the writer, reveals fiction at heart to be a human exchange which, while rooted in actuality, provides an alternative reality, somewhat in the manner of the dialogue of Buber and Bakhtin, or Burke's dramatism. Exchange takes place in the creative imagination – in the imaginary world of a specific medium, the model instance of which is dramatic. A fictional world is cognitive: The "as if" is the way we understand life and existence. Although both player and writer experience the dramatic world as a "switch" from the actual world, the boundaries between the two are not precise.

Creators of fiction use dramatization within fictional worlds but also retain the actual. As Pavel puts it:

> Impersonation moves them across the critical distance not so much by abolishing it as by dulling their awareness of it... Impersonation works only so long as the fictional setting is taken seriously, imagined as real. In order to make fiction function smoothly, the reader and the author must pretend that there was no suspension of disbelief... [Fiction] does not necessarily entail a weakening of the usual methods of inference, commonsense knowledge, and habitual emotions... Fictional distance appears to boil down to difference and, in order to be manageable, difference must be kept to a minimum.[21]

Our fictional worlds, created for the purpose of cognition, must be grounded in actuality.[22] But this is tantamount to saying that cognition is actual and fictional at the same time – that it is metaphorical.[23] According to this view, we dramatize differentiation by primal similarity. We do so within a variety of fictional worlds, but when in the dramatic mode we create the source and exemplar for all forms of fiction.

Finally, we should note that unlike many other styles of fictional discourse, dramatization in its creation of fictional worlds has a profound effect on many facets of practical life: educational drama, drama therapy, simulation, social role playing, and so forth.[24] The practical results of fiction meant little to Gilbert Ryle and those who denied its validity in terms of their particular view of truth. But at the end of the twentieth century, as the notion of possibilities begins to take its proper place as the focus of human cognition, fiction has considerable importance.

CHAPTER FOUR

The Dramatic World

What are the inner workings of our dramatic world? How do we dramatize the actual and make it into a fictional world that operates in the ways we have discussed? In this chapter, we will examine these questions from three perspectives: first, the personal, the internal mental processes that are involved; second, the mediate processes that relate mind to the external world; and third, the external processes that affect how we create such worlds.

A COGNITIVE MODEL

We create a dramatic world that provides a valid perspective on the actual world. The dramatic world expresses what players cognitively know, believe, and understand of the actual world.

What occurs in the mind that allows us to describe the process, or events, as dramatic? When we put physiological evidence together with research from cognitive and dramatic studies, a relatively clear picture emerges. The human mind appears to operate much like any organism. In outline, this model shows that at the personal level a variety of events occur in the cognitive process. We:

1 Perceive the environment with our senses.
2 Transform our perceptions into mental images.
3 Combine images in various ways to create thought patterns.
4 Use these patterns to dream, remember, fantasize, live, and imagine.
5 Select and transform elements of thought patterns into action.
6 Perceive our actions as feedback.

While each of these events is affected by dramatic action, mental dramatization sui generis occurs the moment we combine images to create thought patterns (structures and dynamics), as we will see below.

The organismic model is progressive, developmental, and synergetic, for our actions both affect the environment and become feedback to our perceptions. The model appears linear in descriptive form, but in our lives the events making up this loop take place instantaneously.

THE NATURE OF THE MODEL

How do we perceive? Through sensation, and under the influence of our culture. First, we perceive the environment with our senses. Human perception depends largely on three factors: the appropriate functioning of the sensory organs; the state in which we improve our awareness of self, of others, and of the environment; and the ability to concentrate, to focus on what we perceive. Research indicates that the latter two factors are honed with increased dramatic practice, and that these improvements can be transferred to many other cognitive activities, including persistence. How we perceive is affected, second, by our culture and our environment. Thus Arabs in the Sahara Desert tend to see in horizontals, pygmies in the equatorial forest in verticals, Westerners (who live in "a carpentered world") in rectangles. Most contemporary evidence shows that within a particular culture there are significant individual differences, for example, some people tend to be more sensitive to sound than others. Skin sensitivity, which is high at birth but lessens with maturity, can vary widely among individuals.

Images are mental units that are both transformations and representations of what has been perceived. Images are created in all sensory forms – visual images, oral images, etc. Much research has been devoted to show that, in Western societies at least, the predominant images are visual. These findings are open to question, however, for a number of reasons. First, natural human perception has been distorted in Western cultures by a predominantly visual orientation derived from the alphabet and the printing press; yet many of the tests have been verbal and visual. Second, some perceptual responses are specifically not conducive to such tests, for example, kinaesthetic or bodily perceptions which, mostly unconscious, are difficult to put into words.

Once an image is created it persists over time in an increasingly condensed form while losing some of its vividness and clarity. When images are used in dramatizations, however, this tendency is reversed; this is particularly the case with synaesthesia, for instance when a visual image is dramatized in dance. Further more, over time as images lose their initial character, they tend to take on the character of the context in which they are remembered.

Images grouped together may be called thoughts, ideas, or imaginings, depending on the context. Individuals group images into imaginings differently: Some produce ideas quickly, some slowly; some delay closure, some tend to premature closure; etc. Despite the views of determinists, individual differences in grouping images can be remarkable. Even in the Soviet Union under Stalin differences appeared; note the varied imaginings in the music of Prokofiev, Shostakovich, and Kabalevsky, all written at the same time.

It is with the formation of imaginings that dramatization proper occurs. Humans are purposive: Our intentions double all mental activity so that we can compare ideas – as between inner/outer, I/Thou, self/role, etc. The resulting energy oscillates between the poles so that specific structures and dynamics are created.

There are two common ways of grouping images into imaginings: first by sets, or well-worn paths, where ideas are grouped in ways often used by the organism; and second by associations, or leaps from one frame of reference to a contiguous framework. There are many variations of the latter; "Knight's-move thinking," for example, is a leap from one frame of reference to another that appears (at least as far as one can observe) to be unconnected to the first, although there are often remote links.

Spontaneous dramatic activity improves a player's ability to produce creative imaginings, to adjust to the thinking needed in practical and concrete situations, and to recall images, etc. Some players (the gifted, talented, highly creative, and intelligent) use association more than others, but personality factors and thinking styles can produce considerable variation. Introverted highly creative people think in terms of association less than extroverted people; and players who imagine mainly in sets but who have high persistence levels increase their use of association over long periods. Evidence from different kinds of spontaneous drama (play, creative drama, improvisation, etc.) leads us to infer that the imagining process involves continual doubling.

We should note, also, that gathering evidence about imaginings from players engaged in spontaneous drama is complex in certain instances. One case is an inquiry into the nature of imagery and imagistic life as related to the developmental stages of children aged 6 to 11 years old. Improvisation with European children aged 7 to 9 being often an experimentation with picaresque form,* observers tried to "bracket off" such experimentation to ensure that the data more clearly represented the imagistic life of the children in this age group. They discovered that

* Different stories linked by the presence of the same characters, for example, Dickens' *The Pickwick Papers* and Cervantes' *Don Quixote*.

this was not possible, that the children's expression of imagining was interlocked with the picaresque form. The data that resulted was complex and cumbersome. Often it is easier to collect such evidence from younger rather than older children. Another difficulty is that human intention appears to ensure that when images are strung together in imaginings, the idea created is quickly complicated by an alternative perspective on the same issue. This complication usually stems from similarity; that is, the two perspectives represent part/whole or two poles on a continuum, not opposition. Doubling, as an integral part of mind and imagining, may originate in two ways: physiologically in "bihemisphericity," and developmentally in the infantile sequence of mastering media.[1]

When imagining is transformed from the player's dramatic world into the environment, an overt dramatic act results. This specific transformation resembles the description by Jean Piaget of learning a new schema:[2] The player imitates parts and plays with other parts of an original schema in order for a new one to emerge; in Piaget's own terms, accommodation and assimilation lead to synthesis. Once "the primal act" has been achieved at about ten months of age (see p. 54), it remains overt for some time. Increasingly with age (as gratification is delayed) these acts can become covert.

Dramatic acts can vary over time, too. Primarily, a dramatic act is a performance in a role; this can be unconscious, as in the drama of everyday life; or partially unconscious, as in children's play; or conscious, as in theatre. A role can be performed in a fictional context ("I am a bear in the forest") or in an actual context ("I am a bear sleeping in my bed"), or as the self in a fictional context ("I am me in a spaceship").

The dramatic act provides feedback to our mental processes. It is a channel for introjection; that is, through it we come to understand the environment dramatically. Thus in the dramatic world, the way our mental dynamics and structures form and change is based on the nature of dramatic activity itself. Human beings act in the external world, either in role or as themselves in a fictional environment. When one protagonist interacts with another, both come to affirm the action by working with their believing and knowing.

We should briefly note that emotions tend, under certain conditions, to block or encourage specific elements of the dramatic model. The player who says, "I can't do that" when engaged in a specific dramatic task is usually reacting to some deep-seated fear. The only major pattern emerging from research on this issue is that percepts are blocked less than images, which are blocked less than acts.

THE DRAMATIC ACT AS MEDIATOR

But what happens when we externalize our imaginings through a dramatic act? This is also a highly complex issue, as we can observe from the number of common terms for this act; transformation, representation, expression, symbol (of what we imagine or have imagined). Much is clarified when we see that the dramatic act is a mediator:

1 Human intention initiates the dramatization of imaginings.
2 Imaginings are externalized in a dramatic act.
3 The dramatic act creates effects in the external world.
4 These effects provide feedback to mind in ways it can grasp.

This is to say that dramatic action is a mediator; it is the dynamic between mind and the external world; it is the action that generates meaning within the environment and incorporates that meaning in mind.

To cite McLuhan's adage, "The medium is the message." The acting human being (the costumed player) is the medium that carries meaning from the self to the external world and vice versa. When we perform a dramatic act the medium we use is the total self – our Being.

If we look at this process from the ontological perspective, the dramatic medium is *what* and *how* we are; it is the medium closest to the self. But when we are very young two other media are also close: the medium of Sounding, for speech, music, and all forms of language; and the medium of Moving, for dance and forms that use three and two dimensions (as we shall see below). From this perspective, our intelligence both initiates and depends on dramatic action as a medium.

MEDIA AND SUBSTITUTION

The processes whereby we start to master media can help us understand this complex issue. The baby progressively learns to control media through identification, the mediate object, the mirror stage, and at about ten months old, "the primal act," as we have seen.[3] In the case of my son at this age, we observed "the primal act" when he acted "as if" he was himself going to sleep at night, in the middle of the day, by putting his head on his teddy bear, closing his eyes, saying, "Night, night!" and then roaring with laughter. We can say he was pretending or acting "as if," or playing. We can also say that this "primal act" was his first fully controlled use of a medium (his self in the external world) in order to convey meaning.[4]

No sooner has the ten-month-old acted "as if" than s/he complicates (doubles) the action. Immediately after my son pretended to go to sleep, he did the same thing with his duck, his bus, and any other toy that was on hand. This represents a fundamental human trait: One meaning is insufficient; it must be tested through the use of further media. We have already seen an instance of this in Captain Cook's arrival on Vancouver Island (see p. 25).

In the next year or so the child progressively learns to use media in a functional way by the process of substitution.[5] It was Sir Ernst Gombrich, the distinguished art historian, who first commented on this phenomenon. Subsequent research has shown that substitution is a major mental dynamic: The human mind has the functional inclination and capacity to substitute for a whole an element of that whole. The element retains the total meaning of the whole, albeit in a tacit and condensed manner. The way this occurs varies with each child.

We can distinguish numerous developments of media. "The primal act" is the ground for these developments (level 1). As the first full ontological act, it is the essence of Being – the initial moment of great success when the baby has turned the inner outer, and vice versa. It is Being in the expressive mode, Being "as if," Being expressed in a dramatic act – "I am an airplane."

The media in level 2 are the first substitutes for Being "as if." These occurs in two dimensions. The first dimension evolves in degrees of near/far to Being "as if": The media nearest to Being "as if" are Sounding ("I make the sound of an airplane") and Moving ("I make the movements of an airplane"). At the same time, the second dimension evolves in degrees of inner/outer to Being as if: The child discovers that for direct dramatic play ("personal play") there is an alternative, "projected play," where imaginings are projected onto an object, as when a stick becomes an airplane.[6] In other words, styles of substitution occur in more than one dimension.

Meanwhile the first dimension continues to develop into subsequent levels. This happens in three main ways. First, from Sounding emerges the medium of music – love of sound for its own sake. This grows into the use of specific sounds (words) for particular things, people, and actions – "naming" is a medium when we are about one year old. Eventually words and music develop into the medium of language. Second, from generalized Movement emerges dance – the love of creative movement for its own sake. Shortly dance grows into an understanding of three dimensions (felt by the child to be "frozen dance"). This leads to the medium of two dimensions (it is often forgotten that two dimensions cannot be understood in early childhood without an understanding of three dimensions). Third, Being "as if" develops in a variety of ways: as growth from personal and projected play, and as dramatic play that is more/less sincere, more/less absorbed, and so forth. Thus, before the end of the second year the child has used functional substitution to experience all major media by externalizing imaginings.

The pattern of how media emerge in early life touches on our earlier discussion of media in terms of absorption/distance.[7] In adult life, the medium nearest to Being is self-presentation, similar to what Socrates does in Plato's dialogues. But Socrates was also Being "as if" by dramatizing himself as ignorant. Being and Being "as if" are close, if not exactly the same. "I am that I am," say the Hindu scriptures, and the earliest player introduces himself with the vaunt ("I am…"). This cluster of ideas has significance for our theme. It shows that dramatic action is intertwined with cognition in the growth of the individual personality. Drama allows the individual to express the self externally by using media. The use of media begins with the self as a costumed player and is then extended to all other mediate forms. These representations, acts within our social and cultural worlds, tend through feedback to improve our intelligence.

LAWS OF THE MEDIA

The genetic emergence of media demonstrates four laws of growth, or maturational learning, that improve our potential for intelligence.

L1. *As expressive forms emerge, they increase in discrimination.* When we "put on" a new medium, it is more discriminating and accurate than older media. "The primal act" is gross and relatively undifferentiated. The medium used when we act "as if" is the total self – body, gesture, voice, Being, all existing in time and space. What the actor is tacitly saying is, "I am a costumed player. "Cognitive learning is involved: The dramatic act ("I am my mother") is more gross than the refinement of pure sound ("mumumumum"), which in itself is less accurate than the evolving word *Mommy*.

L2. *Later expressive forms are less rich than earlier ones.* Increasing discrimination of evolving media automatically produces meanings less rich than those of earlier forms. More sophisticated masks and media are less meaningful than undifferentiated expressions and extensions. Newer forms of signification may be more precise and accurate in their meaning than earlier ones, but they allow for a less whole expression and extension. What is conveyed, the signified, may be more sophisticated but its connotations are less.

Thought is whole. It is intuitive and rational, affective and cognitive, unconscious and conscious. The form of expression in a medium signifies total thought, but its signifier does not. A mask that uses a medium cannot represent total thought, although it can signify it. Thus no expression is as holistic as thought itself. Moreover, expressions differ in degrees of signification. Initial masks (such as those of "the primal act") are richer in meaning than later ones (such as drawing in two dimensions), although they are less discriminating. That is to say, a dramatic act is richer and less discriminating than speech, which is richer and less discriminating than writing.

L3. *The more discriminating expressions contain, implicitly, the context of earlier expressions.* Later media contain (tacitly as signifieds) the implications of earlier media. Advanced expressions may be more sophisticated, precise, and refined, and they are less holistic; yet at the same time when we use them we assume a greater context than they appear to have on the surface (as signifiers). Advanced expressions, masks, and media are flexible; they are open to many implied meanings. Earlier forms can he incorporated in them by choice. For example, "hullo" can be said with a variety of emotional overtones (the signified), each more subtle than the word itself (the signifier). In contrast, the possible implicit meanings of the sentence, "My computer has 64Ks," are far less. In the same way, the symbolism of art and religion is richer (if less discriminate) than the signs of mathematics. Yet as Einstein said, even the abstraction of mathematics can reveal "the mystery of life"; behind its empty figures and signs there lies something greater to be revealed.

L4. *All forms of expression and all masks provide feedback to the mental activity that gave rise to them.* Expression produces an act, a signification within a medium, that alters the environment; and this act, through perception, affects subsequent mental activity. Further, expression in one medium provides feedback that will, through subsequent imaginings, affect expression in any medium. For example, initial expression in visual form affects later expression in verbal form, and both visual and oral expression affect later meaning expressed in a written medium.

In semiotic terms, thought expressed in language is liable to be more rational than thought signified in dance, yet the signification of dance has a rational context and the signification of language has an affective context. The meaning inherent in a dramatic signifier is more gross and less refined than the meaning implied in a linguistic signifier. The former, in terms of semiosis, is more holistic than the latter. A dramatic sign or symbol has a unity of meaning that includes the rational and the affective; it tends to work from equivalent hemispheres. By comparison, a linguistic signifier is more rational and has a dominance of the left hemisphere.

These four laws apply to all media throughout the life span. They also affect all aspects of the model discussed on pp. 50–3, including language, which I have examined elsewhere.[8]

SOCIAL AND CULTURAL WORLDS

Dramatic events are essentially social. In genuine communication, the dramatic worlds of two protagonists mesh. The dramatic world of the sender must closely relate to that of the receiver – so closely, indeed, that each attempts to identify with the other and see things from that person's perspective. One examines his or her own dramatic world with the eyes of the other. Identification and empathy are used by both, and impersonation adds incorporation to projection.

We have seen that dramatic action hinges on mutuality, trust, and the fiduciary contract. Dramatization teaches us to act on behalf of the other and, indeed, is a major tool for instilling the values of cooperation. When meaning is created by the activity of two players working *for* each other, they are actively encouraged to work on behalf of other people. This is most simply illustrated by pointing out the great social and personal unity that can be felt by those who mutually engage in dramatic activity. This is the case not only in theatre companies, as with the Group Theatre of New York earlier in the twentieth century, but also in classes of drama students who become devoted both to their teacher and to their work.

While such acts are linked closely to emotion and feeling, they are also specifically cognitive: The unknown is integrated with the known on the one hand, and on the other, the known authenticates the unknown. The protagonist and the antagonist exist on the knife edge of spontaneity – more spontaneously in play and improvisation, less so in ritual and theatre.[9] What the antagonist receives from the protagonist is not exactly the total meaning of the protagonist. The antagonist interprets the received meaning and responds accordingly. What he too communicates is not exactly his total meaning. But provided that, in this curious isomorphism, both focus on the action between them, their spontaneous reciprocity proceeds onwards. The dramatic nature of the action encourages them to respond creatively to the gap between them.

The fact that human beings interact in such a highly complex way, taking all the personal and social risks that they do, and in activities ranging from simple social communication to the art form of theatre, indicates a high degree of intelligence. People demonstrate this intelligence in their actions but not necessarily in the way they talk about them. Note the stream of books by famous actors that have been published since the late nineteenth century. Few of them tell us anything valuable about the process of acting (the notable exceptions are John Hare, Jean-Louis Barrault, Michael Redgrave, Lupino Lane, Morris Carnovsky, and Tony Curtis).

The double relationship underlies communication in all media: author/

reader, painter/viewer, and so on. But with, say, a novel, the relationship is assumed and indirect; the reader's response and interpretation does not take place in the presence of the author. Moreover the reader can turn back the pages of a novel. Reflection erodes spontaneity and is a luxury unknown to players and audiences.

The sharing of our mutual dramatic worlds is intelligent, both cognitive and social. It is not cognitive in an abstract sense. Rather, it is cognition invested with the practicality of human meaning. When players improvise, they mutually create and intuitively recognize the relations between the molecular units of dramatic action. The players validate these relations pragmatically – if improvisation works, it exists, or as Picasso said, "Art *is*." Mutually created meaning grows as actors continue to work together. In terms of the model, one dramatic world linked with another builds a storehouse of constantly changing knowledge and beliefs through shared dramatic action.

The shared dramatic worlds of players are also part of a universe of meaning. If these worlds were abstract, we might call this a collective universe. But the specific nature of shared dramatic worlds enables us to describe a universe as a community of worlds. Collectivity rests on abstract needs, but community hinges on human needs. In a genuine community, each player contributes elements of his or her dramatic world to a new whole – the drama enacted by a community of persons. This reflects beliefs and systems of thought that in most cases are shared but in some cases are not. The dramatic world of the individual player is changed in some way, not only by the impact of a shared dramatic world, but also through shared social worlds and a shared dramatic universe. In other words, while a player's dramatic world is continually transformed through mutual action, this same player's world is also changed by a universe that is a community of worlds.

It is clear that we are talking about human culture, or what Martin Buber, Victor W. Turner, and others call communitas. This raises different questions in terms of drama: Do children at different ages have particular maturational worlds, as Piaget implies? How is it that European civilization created tragedy, while all other cultures created mixed forms (to use Aristotle's phrase)? If Western worlds differ radically from Asian ones, what kinds of mutuality can exist between them?

Without detailing the changes in cultural history,[10] we can say that a dichotomy exists in the Western world that is not present in most other cultures. The schism rests on the difference between objective (or "scientifically proven") knowing on the one hand, and subjective (or "scientifically unproven") knowing on the other. This is the issue of knowing and believing raised in chapter one, where it was noted that in common parlance, or in life and in drama, there is little difference between them.

The mental revolution brought about by Einstein has shown this dichotomy to be false, and yet it is still a popular (if false) idea in Western societies that life is a duality – objective versus subjective, sacred versus profane, reason versus faith, and so on. Still, recent multiculturalism in the Western world has shaken this schism to its foundations even at the popular level. It is slowly coming to be accepted that there is a variety of cognitive universes related to different cultures. But it is not the substance (content) that mainly affects the relation a person will have to such universes. On the contrary, it is the form that is central. That is, the way content is structured in a cognitive universe tells us the place knowing and believing hold in it.

The nature of dramatic performance in a culture reflects the cognitive universe of those who participate it. Two examples show that there can be a vast difference between cultures, even today. Among Amerindians on the Northwest Coast of Canada,[11] it is assumed that there is a direct relationship between the world of the spirits and the world of the everyday – actions in one affect actions in the other. These combined worlds are structured as a "quaternity" (the four winds, the four directions, etc.) focused on the "quincunx", the spiritual and physical centre of life, the place of power. Past coexists with present and all dynamics are circular or spiral. This cognitive structure is reflected in the Mystery Cycle of the Southern Kwakiutl ("the winter ceremonial"): The protagonist is possessed by a spirit in the mundane life of the longhouse; this is to repeat what happened in "the old times" (the origin myth) as a ritual-drama where time is collapsed into a permanent present. All dramatic performances have a fourfold pattern within the place of "power", and the total cycle regenerates life and the cosmos on a seasonal and cyclical basis.

This is in strict contrast with the bifurcation of the cognitive universe in Western cultures. Here the sacred is contrasted with the secular; while God can affect human life, the reverse is not the case. Knowledge has a binary structure (either/or) that leads to the oppositions of classical logic and mechanism. Thus the rules of deduction and the machine lead to the objective knowledge that contrasts with faith and belief. From the time of Newton, this dual cognitive model has dominated Western thought. Coincidentally, the profane world of comedy has dominated the playhouse. Tragedy and the spiritual have become minor traditions (as we can see from contemporary television). Just as science concentrated on what was perceived and was less concerned with the metaphysical, so the theatre concentrated on perceived social life and was less concerned with the great issues of existence.

But post-Einsteinian Western theatre reflects the coexistence of quantitative and qualitative judgments. Pirandello's *Six Characters in Search of an Author,* which Bernard Shaw said was the greatest tragedy of the twentieth century, is called a comedy. It reflects the covalidity of opposites: A comic illusion (the human mask) hides the tragic reality of existence (the face), and both are different from judgments of emotions and feelings (of the characters of the title). In the worlds of Einstein and Pirandello, the paradox exists.

From these brief illustrations we can see that the structures and dynamics of a culturally cognitive universe can be encapsulated in the theatre of that culture. But what applies to theatre can also be found in all forms of dramatic activity. For example, in 1970 a drama teacher in Sydney, Australia, was having great problems with a class engaged in improvisation. The students refused to divide into mixed groups because 80 percent of them were newly immigrated Moslem Turks whose social mores prevented adolescent girls from mingling with boys – another form of bifurcation. In other words, our dramatic world is an exemplar of the cognitive universe of our culture.

SURFACE AND DEEP MEANINGS

At the surface level of dramatic action, we use imaginary masks ("seeming") to cover our face (Being), the deep level of meaning. This act is essentially social. It leads us to ask, How far can this social act be generalized – that is, from the dramatic world through the social world to the cognitive universe? Are the surface and deep-level meanings in the dramatic world similar to those in other cognitive worlds and universes? Can the tacit and implicit meanings in the dramatic world be the same kind of phenomena as those on the surface level when they have different styles of representation? Indeed, can we ask if drama, which by its nature reveals "Being" through "seeming," is "a science" that sees through manifestation to immanence?

A major factor in our deliberations must be that the masks of social life, formed upon "as if" thinking, generate functional actions of a figurative kind. These actions are mostly metaphorical and metonymical. For example, a person can be "as strong as a horse" and we can use "a crown for a king." At the level of "seeming," masks bring about intra- and extradramatic referents; they exist to dramatize something other than themselves, the latter, considered as media, being "put-ons," in McLuhan's phrase. That is, we use them as extensions of the self: Clothes and costumes are masks in this sense, while the pen is an extension of the hand, the wheel is an extension of the foot, and radio and television are extensions of the circuitry of the brain. Masks also create the possibility of other significations: analogic, anagogic, and parabolic. This brings about a further referent – the thematic, or deep level.

Yet the relation of surface and deep levels is not causal. United by the fiduciary contract, players project a double string of reasoning. There is a meaning within a meaning, just as there is a a face within a mask and a play within a play. If not causal, the link is more than haphazard. It is rational, but in a unique way. In Pirandello's world, as we have seen, the rationality is based on Being/seeming and reality/illusion. The surface drama of the "here and now" creates a further drama that moves two ways: (1) deeper (it is more abstract, more thematic than simple narrative), and (2) laterally (it creates a new parallel figurative structure).

We can take two related examples: Shakespeare's *Macbeth* in the theatrical interpretations of Edward Gordon Craig[12] and G. Wilson Knight.[13] Craig finds a theme parallel to the narrative of the play at a deep level – from chaos to order in the state. This theme is not causal. Craig expresses it laterally (figuratively) in his stage design: A mountain is initially covered by fog that slowly dissipates until, at the end, the air is clear. Wilson Knight on the other hand, discovers a deep structure, that contrasts profane/sacred power, which he expressed figuratively in theatrical terms by a throne on one side and a statue of the Virgin Mary on the other. These different views are interpretations which, because they are expressed figuratively and reflect both the play's surface and deep meanings, are valid as alternative perspectives. Whereas the rationality of surface drama is found in narrative expressed in the "here and now," the rationality of deep drama is found in themes which, expressed figuratively, are of equivalent importance. While this is the case in theatre, it also manifest less formally in improvisation, play, and life.

But what is the epistemological status of these parallel kinds of knowing? In the case of *Macbeth*, Shakespeare has superimposed on the themes of chaos/order and profane/sacred a series of surface figures, for example, the great storm, the horses that eat one another, Macbeth wearing clothes that do not fit him, and so on. But superimposition is more apparent than real because the figures create specific sequences in the dramatic narrative. Even more, the play changes the underlying themes, which start with profane greed for power and conclude with the use of power for order and the sacredness of the true king's dynasty. This is a case of dramatic progress, a form of metaphoric and metonymic reasoning where there is not a one-to-one relationship between surface and deep figures. Rather, the parallel figures and meanings do not exactly correspond to or even, on occasion, resemble one another. This kind of intellectual reasoning is more like a set of gestalt structures that nest within each other to provide a holistic meaning.

We can apply such reasoning to all dramatic forms. Whether children are at play, students are improvising, adults act social roles, or actors perform on a stage, they engage in a particular kind of reasoning that links surface, figurative, and deep meanings in a unique way.

We have seen that in our dramatic world figurative reasoning is directly involved. It is primarily metaphoric and metonymic but with close ties to the parable and the analogy. It is not exactly parabolic, yet some parables use similar figures, and it is more parabolic than analogy, which requires a direct likeness between figures. It is not causal, although there are clearly links between surface and deep figures. Rather, it has a number of specific characteristics that make it unique:

1 In terms of knowledge (epistemology), the fiction of the dramatic world is a way of knowing so that the protagonists come to believe in the explanatory power of the dramatic world and extend it to the cognitive universe (see chapter one).
2 In human terms (ontology), it is obviously fiduciary, with trust existing between the two protagonists (see chapter two).
3 In terms of mediation, it focuses on the whole person as a meaning-giving medium linking imagining and dramatic actualization in the "here and now" with deep covert meanings (see chapter three).
4 In figurative terms, deep meanings are based on a structure of living metaphor and metonymy (see chapter five).
5 In logical terms, the link between surface and deep meanings is not causal. It is essentially suggestive and allusive and able to generate multiform meanings; it has some similarities with analogic reasoning but more with parabolic reasoning; and it uses practical thinking based on plausibility (see chapter six).

CONCLUSION

We have examined the workings of our dramatic world from three perspectives: the personal, the mediate, and the cultural. The picture that emerges is a dynamic one. The dramatic act is an energizing movement that creates a fiction that provides meaning to the self and the external world. What the meanings are cannot be predetermined; they are created in the process we live through in this time and place.

Thus far the theory has been shown to disagree with early positivists but to resemble theories of contemporary analysts of fiction, philosophers of process (pragmatists) and existence (Buber), modern critics of various persuasions (Burke, Derrida), and major scholars in the social sciences (Turner, Winnicott). It follows that conceptual idealists (like

Plato and Samuel Alexander) and determinists (like Darwin, Marx, and Freud) would have some difficulties with this theory. To adapt it to their views, they would probably have to focus upon intention, showing that it is a version of either the absolute (for conceptual idealists) or the energy that fuels the machine (for determinists). This would be unsatisfactory for our purposes, however.

A major feature of our dramatic world is that it accepts, accounts for, and uses ambiguity and paradox. This places the theory very much in the contemporary world and therefore it is probably unfair to compare it with intellectual positions prior to Einstein. Dramatic worlds can operate only in the contexts available to them. Ambiguity and paradox are very much part of our modern world, as is metaphorical thinking, the subject of the next chapter.

CHAPTER FIVE

The Dramatic Metaphor

Metaphor is the imaginative root of dramatic action. In the mind, groups of imaginings constitute fictional worlds that have a metaphoric character; these worlds project metaphors through dramatic acts. That is to say, a metaphoric thought is expressed through the medium of dramatic action. But, as we shall see in chapter 8, once a thought is put into action it may or may not remain metaphoric.

THE IMAGINATIVE BASIS FOR METAPHOR

In simple terms, a metaphor combines two thoughts in order to create a new meaning. Often mistakenly thought of as only existing in language, the metaphor is inherent in human thought and can be expressed in all media. Imaginings are expressed in metaphoric form. How?

Groups of images and imaginings cluster in the mind so that, when an idea begins to form, specific clusters are activated. They coalesce around the idea as a series of choices and alternatives. This occurs, for example, when an architect has the initial idea of building a bridge; he chooses between a number of possibilities, each focused on the half-formed idea of the bridge. His choices (say, the use of concrete and not steel) activate some possibilities and do not activate others; thus the possibilities take a particular pattern or order based on alternatives and comparisons. When the idea has fully formed, there is a complex of meanings within one overarching idea. (The structure and dynamics of such ideas are discussed on pp. 29–32.)

Imaginings explore possibilities. An architect designs a bridge with the contents of many imaginings: conditions in wind, rain, snow, ice; the nature of the terrain and the span necessary; the weight it must carry; the materials necessary and available, etc. He may mentally try out one of the elements (the use of concrete) against all the others; then he may compare it with another (the use of steel). He will have to conduct many similar imaginary tests with each element. What will the effect of expected temperatures be on, say, concrete, steel, or other materials? Using his previous experience, together with both logic and intuition, his idea will become clearer.

At a particular moment he will try it out in action. He begins drawing his plans according to the specific criteria he has chosen. At this point, he is still examining his ideas, projecting (expressing) his thought in action. He thinks "as if" the bridge is such and such and acts "as if" it is such and such by drawing it. The act of drawing the bridge is not overtly dramatic. The architect is not putting himself in someone else's place like a player on a stage. But his action is covertly dramatic. The "as if" process is involved when he tries out his idea through a representation.

Significantly, his representation in action is not all he thinks about. Although the architect may be trying out a concrete bridge in the drawing as he proceeds, he also retains thoughts about steel and other materials. They have not vanished merely because he is focusing on something else. Nor have they gone into the unconscious. Rather, they remain just below the surface of consciousness and can be re-played at a moment's notice. As a result, the architect can swiftly alter his idea, for example, by changing concrete to steel. Then he will activate a whole series of mental imaginings that were tacit and, vice versa, make tacit a number of imaginings that were explicit. He can flip from one to another, a particular variant of doubling.

At this stage, both idea and action are fictional. The bridge does not exist in the actual world. It exists in the architect's fictional world. He is attempting to make what is fictional to him into a bridge that is actual. One step on the way is through the medium of drawing. He has created a double relation in this mind between the fictional bridge and the possibility of the actual bridge. Through the act of drawing, his metaphorical thought starts to become actual.

At a later stage, once the drawings and specifications are complete, he moves his fictional world into the actual world. With the assistance of many others who closely follow his representations, the bridge is built. Only then can the architect discover if his imaginings, which worked well in his mind and in his fictional representation, are effective in actuality.

THE NATURE AND FUNCTIONS OF METAPHOR

An example of metaphor in language is "The roses in her cheeks." A primary idea (cheeks) is related to a secondary one (roses). The assumption is that her cheeks are "as if" they are roses. Roses and cheeks are viewed as a new whole, and the meaning of the whole is greater than the ideas it contains. While metaphors are popularly known as linguistic expressions, or figures, they can be expressed in all media.

Aristotle's comments in the *Poetics* show that metaphors are forms of dramatization.[1] They operate so that one thing is "as if" another thing – by comparison. Like all dramatic acts, they transform ideas "from *genus* to species, or from species to *genus,* or from species to species, or on grounds of analogy."[2] In order to be expressed, imaginings are made metaphoric in action.[3] The function of metaphor is to present people as acting and all things "as in act." Metaphor has an ontological function whereby every latent capacity for action is actualized. For Aristotle, metaphorization is a cognitive activity.[4] As the best metaphors "show things in a state of activity," they provide knowledge of the actual; they bring together two ideas of the actual world so that there is resemblance "even in things that are far apart."[5]

In common usage, however, metaphor can be described in two ways: either as a figure of speech or as a mental operation. As a figure of speech, metaphor is part of rhetoric and language. It is a form of the mental structure of similarity that is here expressed in speech. But when metaphor is used of mental acts (imaginings), it implies that a person's expression of an idea in a medium such as a work of art is considered metaphorical. We might say, for example, that when Leonardo was painting the background of the *Mona Lisa* he was thinking metaphorically, just as he was thinking metaphorically (but with a different metaphor) when painting the woman herself. These two acts are different but related. The first act is based on likeness, where one thing is seen in terms of another – "as if" it is another, a concept basic to dramatic action. The second act works "as if" it is the first. Ironically, the two acts relate to one another as whole/part. In a more generic sense, both involve doubling. Mind, through intention, is constantly seeking to know; it complicates any initial idea by similarity, and one important way it does so is with metaphor.

Once we move beyond common parlance, as Umberto Eco and many others have shown, metaphor defies all definitions and even encyclopedic description. In order to understand the relation of metaphor to dramatic acts, therefore, it is better to examine the functions of this relation. The first function, as we have seen and Ricouer indicates,[6] is to work through *a structure of similarity*. This suggests that imagining cannot be seen as a function of the image. Perceptions provide us with images, but once formed, images do not operate as quasi-sensations. This is the case despite Merleau-Ponty's point that in our experience perceiving happens at the same time as thinking and action. Although true in our experience, the elements of our experience have diverse functions. Images, once they are created and they cluster in imaginings, become functions of mind. True, when they are recalled they can sometimes activate the recall of the initial sensation, and when the original sensation is reexperienced a similar image can be formed again. But images as part of an imagining have become condensed and they do not function in a sensate way. As Wittgenstein put it, imagining is "seeing as"; that is, imagining has the power of seeing the similar in the dissimilar. We can say that the resulting metaphor creates a family resemblance between two ideas which, previously, may not have been related in any way. An initial idea is given complex meaning when it is related to a similar idea that is seemingly dissimilar (but the result is not necessarily an opposition). "The roses in her cheeks" carries more meaning than the two ideas that constitute it. This meaning results from tension – between the first two ideas, and between the parts and the whole, both of which function in terms of similarity/difference.

The second function of metaphor is to provide us with a different form of perception, an *alternative to perceiving through the senses.* It gives us a unique frame or perspective, a way of looking at things. When we move from perceiving through the senses to perceiving through a metaphoric frame, we change how we think about things or how we make sense of reality; we can even establish the problems that we will later attempt to solve. This is an instance of Wittgenstein's "seeing as."

The third function of metaphor is to *define our reality.* We understand the external world in which we live (our social reality) by the use of our fictional world, a metaphoric and processual construction of mind that, when activated, separates the inner self and the actual world and yet mediates between them. Something new is created when a metaphor is understood, and some metaphors lead us to understand elements of reality that they help to create. Lakoff and Johnson show that metaphors as part of everyday speech affect how we think and act.[7] This has support from laboratory studies of metaphor.[8] Human interactions are performances: People metaphorize themselves which, projected by dramatic action, become persona, masks, or roles in interrelation. But as metaphors vary from culture to culture, so do the realities they define. There are few realities in tribal cultures, many in contemporary pluralistic societies.

The fourth function of metaphor, as we have seen, is cognitive. It preserves and develops the heuristic power of fiction[9] and provides "a split reference"[10] that in usage indicates an advanced form of intelligence. This occurs in various circumstances, one of which is the "negotiation" of social order. One human being enters a problematic situation with a certain self-concept and a metaphorized imagining (the fictional world) that when dramatized in action meets similar constructions by another person (two dramatic worlds). By communicating, they construct their own social worlds. We might like Camus see this as absurd. "The actor taught us this: there is no difference between appearing and Being." Cognitive it may be, but as Northrop Frye once said, in modern educational systems there are no classes in "remedial metaphor."

The fifth function of metaphor is to *think in a dramatic mode.* From an abstract perspective, metaphor's dramatic quality appears when images are transformed into imaginings; doubling occurs and tension exists between the parts of a metaphor; but as we live through experience the metaphor becomes instantaneous and unconscious. Metaphor is grounded in infantile empathy and identification, characterized by a tacit "as if," and inclusive of Wittgenstein's "seeing as." The "as if" also implies "as if not," which means we can speak of metaphorical truth.[11] This was certainly the case in the Middle Ages when Honorius said that the priest's dramatization in the mass represented Christ's drama and thus truth.[12]

The sixth function of metaphor is to *allow us to interpret what people do and say, and thus infer what they are thinking.* This is a question of interpretation, a hermeneutic problem. From the metaphors people use, and the metaphorical framework of any "text," we make inferences. We have two perspectives on inferences: the evidence they present and the criteria by which they can be tested. This affects dramatic action by indicating:

1 *the kinds of inferences underlying interpretations.* Inference is made from a metaphorical framework. When inferences are made from diverse metaphors, reciprocal frameworks are reconstructed so that alternative inferences are generated.
2 *the sorts of evidence inferences require.* Inference arises not from givens but from the view of the metaphorical framework. Each metaphor provides a particular frame and turns our attention to different facts.
3 *the criteria by which inferences can be tested.* Metaphors and the inferences they produce can be constructed from the story line of the dramatic action: either from the story itself, or at a deeper level from the themes implied by the dramatization, or at the deepest level from the structures and dynamics of thought.
4 *the level of intelligence of the player.* The use of metaphor shows the degree to which players have developed their intellectual potential. When players cannot use metaphor, if indicates that they do not "see the forest for the trees." These persons require Frye's classes in remedial metaphor. Those who can use metaphors effectively, however, have moved from literal thinking towards a multiperspective.

Thus, for example, we can make inferences from the metaphors that scientists use and from the metaphorical framework of their scientific performances. The foundations of physics are metaphors of human consciousness.[13] For Newton, space was connective, organic, and alive, time was spatial, matter was "stuff," and number was quantitative. But today space is extension, distance, separation, and isolation; time is uneven, cumulative, and cyclic; matter is not stuff but is understood through indeterminacy and probability; and number is qualitative and symbolic. Clearly the inferences made from these two frameworks are very different.

The seventh function of metaphor is *creative*. Metaphor is ubiquitous. It is an everyday phenomenon for people, particularly children. This applies to the imagined metaphor, the metaphor in the process of being expressed, and the metaphor in action, but in each case there are different styles of meaning. Each style, however, if taken literally, asserts something that it plainly is not. Cheeks are not roses. This is not to work with a lie, as Plato and Ryle would have it, but to create out of the actual an alternative yet fictional meaning. Thus it is that both Coleridge and Max Black claim that metaphor can be creative. By changing the relationship between its two constituent parts, the metaphor can often function creatively. It can change our knowing and insight; it can enable us to re-play aspects of reality incorporated by its parts and the new whole; and it can give us a new perspective on events and experience.

Finally we should note that, despite these functions, the initial meanings of the elements of a metaphor do not change when they are returned to their normal usage. Separated from each other, cheeks remain cheeks and roses remain roses. That is, the metaphoric application of any element does not alter its previous meaning. That we can "flip" between the literal and metaphoric elements of, say, roses contributes greatly to the multiplex semantics of imaginings expressed through media. This is particularly the case when the medium is dramatic action.

THE *THEATRUM MUNDI*

When Shakespeare said, "All the world's a stage," he was giving his version of the theatre metaphor, the *Theatrum Mundi:* Life is like a theatre/theatre is like life. The idea was ancient even then. It may have been used by Pythagoras and it was the last thing said by Augustus Caesar. Cervantes used it, but Shakespeare made it uniquely his own, altering and expanding its meaning from play to play. At the end of his life, he transformed it significantly: "We are such stuff / As dreams are made on; and our little life / Is rounded with a sleep." So said Prospero in *The Tempest.*[14] With one rhetorical sweep, Shakespeare's last great poetic vision changed the theatre metaphor into "the dramatic metaphor." For Prospero, life is not simply like a theatre; it *is* a play we all perform. Human existence is a dramatic illusion that, like a dream, melts and dissolves.

The dramatic metaphor has many implications, one of which we have addressed a number of times: Thinking in the metaphoric mode is the core of imagining, which when expressed in action is dramatic. The child at play and the salesman who tries to "get into the skin" of the customer, the student improvising social studies, the socialite who takes the role of the hostess at a banquet, the politician who says what he thinks the voters want to hear – all of these individuals are experimenting with the dramatic metaphor. Each is engaged, as Plato and Northrop Frye have said, in the "great lie." The world we know is not actual but dramatic. It is created out of possibilities we imagine and then act. According to this view, we are, indeed, such stuff as dreams are made on. It is not, of course, a lie but a fiction.

THE EFFECT OF THE DRAMATIC METAPHOR

Today the dramatic metaphor often appears in the newspapers and on radio and television. Considered historically, this is a new phenomenon. It would have been unthinkable in their day for, say, George Washington, Wordsworth, or Goethe to have been conceived as role players in quite the same way as Ronald Reagan, Mikhail Gorbachev or Ezra Pound are today.

There has been a similar change in our view of theatre. A century ago it was an increasingly popular view that theatre was a reflection, or copy, or "a slice of life." The audience had became voyeurs looking through "the window" of the proscenium arch into the lives of others. The influence of the naturalistic plays of Ibsen, the "cup and saucer" school of Tom Robertson and the Wiltons, Antoine and the Théâtre Libre, the Saxe-Meiningen company, and Stanislavsky's early Moscow Art Theatre – all led theatre towards naturalism. This increased until early in the century. Then David Belasco dismantled an actual house and placed it on the New York stage to make the production "more natural." (Unfortunately the critics were not impressed; they thought it artificial!) Few listened when Oscar Wilde said that life imitates art. Stage melodrama, the music hall, and vaudeville all wilted before the naturalism of the stage and, then of films and television. But a reaction against theatrical naturalism, initiated early this century by Artaud, Craig, Meyerhold, Brecht, and others, has brought the late twentieth century to a theatrical perspective of theatre. After Pirandello, dramatists like Sartre, Anouilh, Miller, and Osborne raised issues of illusion and reality while directors like Joan Littlewood and Peter Brook firmly acknowledged that the audience was in a playhouse. As the twentieth century draws to a close, naturalism is dying.

Another effect of the dramatic metaphor has been to revolutionize the idea of education to the point where it is seen as a dramatic event. In recent years, researchers have refocused their views of teaching and learning with metaphors derived from drama and the arts. This research has been of three sorts:

1 *Curriculum metaphors.* The dramatic metaphor has been very effective in curriculum research where issues are analyzed with metaphors from aesthetics and art criticism, literary criticism, journalism, music, theatre, and drama.[15] Geoffrey Milburn has called this discipline stripping – the use of one discipline's concepts and methods to provide a new perspective on the educational process. Researchers in drama, however, have taken this one step further. Dramatic action, by definition, is conceived through the dramatic metaphor and is said to infuse all of life; similarly, teaching and learning are thought of as dramatic processes.
2 *Praxis research.* Educational research has taken place at the level of praxis, a combination of theory and practice, although the point of departure may be one or the other. Those who start from theory always relate it to practice. Kenneth A. Leithwood and his colleagues[16] have developed "procedural knowledge," the kind that permits curriculum planners "to gain control over an otherwise muddy sea of complexities" but that can be applied to most, if not all, types of human performance. From experience of complex phenomena, players generate a model of performance containing a series of steps, or sequences. The player successfully negotiates these steps by understanding the model and by performing the role(s) necessary in the model – a direct use of the dramatic metaphor.

   Somewhat differently, studies of personal-practical knowledge by F. Michael Connelly and others[17] are based on Polanyi's work. They attempt "to understand and conceptualize the nature, origin and expression of a practitioner's metaphors, images, rules, and principles," which constitute "personal-practical knowledge." To do so they examine the rhythms, rituals, procedures, and habitual actions of school teachers; the results are teachers' narratives of what they do. Although this approach is less overtly concerned with dramatic action, it is still remarkably revealing of the gap between what teachers think they do and what they really do.

More directly dramatic is Peter L. McLaren's *Schooling as a Ritual Performance.*[18] McLaren uses a case study approach to discern the various unconscious and conscious rituals of school life. He then uses the emergent rituals to examine life in other contexts.

Though this author's own research studies of arts education[19] are diverse, each analyzes the date according to metaphors (as cognitive processes) and actual practice (as dramatic action).

3 *Practical research.* At the same time, others in educational drama have engaged in class-based research. This type of inquiry focuses on dramatic activity in classrooms – the immediate experience of students and teachers – with results seen as emerging from the data.

These different approaches to educational research have not only improved the quality of drama teaching and learning in the past half-century but also given rise to a remarkably informative body of recent literature in educational drama.[20] Research styles that use the dramatic metaphor have also resulted in an acceptance of the dramatic perspective for both players and observers in a variety of situations: social life, education, therapy, theatre, etc.* In sum, we can say that it is commonly held that the fiction of dramatic action occurs at two fundamental levels: actual and fictional frames, and fictional content.

1 *Actual and fictional frames.* At the moment drama begins, the present is transformed from the actual to the fictional. The actual world and its events are transformed into what is "real for me." In the playhouse, the audience and the players gather in an actual time and place, but when the drama begins both acknowledge that the players' fictional actions take place in (a) the actual time and place, and (b) the fictional time and place. That is, (a) is the contextual frame, (b) is the inner frame. Similarly, in spontaneous and educational drama the inner fictional frame is surrounded by an actual frame, "a special place" that is actual for improvisers, like a classroom for teachers and students.

But what the players act is a fiction; the story being performed is not actual but fictional. Dramatic metaphor and action express the "real" meaning; they transform an obdurate environment into a fiction with which we can deal. Those engaged in theatre, play, and spontaneous drama bracket off mundane life and live through a fictional "here and now," but within an actual context. The fiction of

* The researcher, however, must not confuse the use of dramatic metaphor as a research *method* with the use of this metaphor by the players (the dramatic metaphor as *content*). It is essential that they remain conceptually distinct.

drama requires an actual context in order for us to recognize it as fiction. Those who have difficulty doing this are marginalized in Western societies.

2 *Fictional content*. The audience in the playhouse experiences at least four levels of meaning as the fiction progresses on the stage. First, they are immediately aware of the story in the sequence in which it is shown (not "told") by the players. Second, as the story continues they mentally reconstitute it as plot, adding to the story all events referred to by the characters (action offstage, things that have happened prior to the opening of the drama, etc.). Third, to the story and plot the audience consciously adds surface meanings (for example, "At *this* specific moment, Hamlet represents good, Claudius represents evil"), and all three together make up the manifest content of the fiction. Fourth, these factors lodge in the unconscious to become the latent content of the fiction – the deep level of meaning that each member of the audience may intuit.

To put this another way, the dramatic metaphors inherent in the fictional present have both manifest and latent content. Manifest content is the subject matter of the fiction: the story, the plot, and the meaning-giving experience of living through the performance. Latent content is of two kinds. The first consists of the themes that underlie the story. For example, a group of 13-year-olds was so keen about improvising a scene about coal mining in the nineteenth century (manifest content) that they worked on it in their spare time. Not until later did the teacher discover that the latent content was the students' interest in the miners kissing their wives goodbye as they left for work.[21] The second consists of themes at a deeper level. Much depends on the perspective of the observer. For example, Freudians infer themes of sexuality, and Lévi-Strauss assumes common latent themes based on a digital structure.

But to observe dramatic action in appropriate dramatic terms and not in terms of another discipline (say, psychoanalysis in the case of Freud), we cannot begin from ideas outside the dramatic framework. Rather, to obtain specifically dramatic meaning we must begin with what players do, that is, with their actions at the manifest level (the signifiers). And we must then infer the metaphors used (the latent level, or signifieds) in dramatic events.

METAPHOR AND METONYMY

Metaphorization is a mental mode of operation that includes the use of metaphor and metonymy, "a condensation of entities which were previously related through contiguity. Hence, similarity (metaphor) and contiguity (metonymy) are not independent; linguistic similarity actually consists of shared associations of contiguity."[22] What, in dramatic terms, is the difference between metaphor and metonymy?

We have seen that "The roses in her cheeks" is an example of metaphor: Her cheeks are viewed (dramatized) "as if" they are roses. The two concepts are parallel. Cheeks is primary and roses is secondary. Metaphors allow an active selection of elements between two subjects; the secondary subject gives a perspective on the primary subject.[23] Creating metaphors is an intellectual method that capitalizes on the poetic nature of human minds.[24]

Metonymy works differently. It refers to something that already exists. The two subjects relate as part/whole; they come from the same context. In the playhouse, "a crown for a king" is an example of metonymy because a crown is seen as part of the concept of kingship – the part stands for the whole. The secondary subject is contiguous with the primary. As we have seen (p. 62), for a production of *Macbeth* G. Wilson Knight sets a throne on one side of the stage and a statue of the Madonna on the other. He uses two forms of metonymy (one a part of kingship, the other of Christian belief) to metaphorize the play. However, in the live production his metonymies join with other metaphors and metonymies to become symbolic of the whole play. (We shall deal with symbols in chapter 8.)

In metaphor two concepts are parallel. But the structure of metonymy is that of part/whole, contained/container, and cause/effect. Metonymy is generated through spatio-temporal-causal contiguity; its meaning hinges on the cultural context in which it is used. Yet it can also be used syntactically in a linear fashion through grammatical contiguity. Metonymy thus has a dual function: linguistic and extralinguistic. While metaphor's association is by similarity, that of metonymy is by contiguity.

The mental imagery of metaphor is analogic and parabolic; it works by parallelism. Metaphor contrasts with metonymy, which like opposition is a digital form. However, metaphor and metonymy both refer to concepts beyond the relations between linguistic signifiers. They are not arbitrary and autonomous. Both are context dependent. They communicate relationships and messages of all types between one player and another.[25] Thus, in cognitive terms, metaphor and metonymy in dramatic action provide meaning, metaphor through similarity and metonymy through part/whole. But both metaphor and metonymy are dramatic in that they transform experience. They provide frameworks in which different entities are structurally related.[26]

In fact, however, and specifically in dramatic events, not many situations are totally metaphoric or metonymic,[27] nor is there an absolute distinction between the two. This is the case in Knight's *Macbeth* where, as we have seen, the total "living" play is symbolic to the audience and we can only distinguish the types of metaphor and metonymy in abstract, not as we live through the play.

This lack of precision can lead to two important types of confusion about dramatic action. First, Anthony Wilden shows that metaphor and metonymy can slide into each other.[28] Consider the relationship of two dogs: "Nip" and "bite" are metonymical when two dogs begin to communicate – nip is part of play and bite is part of war. But they can become metaphorical; nip and bite are then metaphors for bite and war. A second confusion is that powerful metaphors, because of their aptness, often appear to be understood and treated metonymically,[29] for example, when ritual is treated "as if" it was theatre and vice versa. In this example, one activity is reduced to the properties of another activity.[30]

METAPHOR AND SEMIOSIS

The complexities in the dramatic metaphor and action are considerable. How then can we grasp the cognitive processes that occur when the various forms of metaphorization are externalized in action?

One solution is to use semiotics, a research tool that can tease out issues from highly complex problems. Each of the many semiotic styles starts from a basic distinction: the meaning of the dramatic metaphor is signified by a dramatic action that is the signifier. But the version of semiotics developed by A.J. Greimas[31] has the advantage of including semantics, as does the activity of drama. Greimas is famous for developing the semiotic square, a way of analyzing and describing transformation, the movement from one "state of belief" to another. We might also call this use of the semiotic square the change in thinking that constitutes learning, or cognitive algorithms, or the dramatic dynamic whereby we develop our potential for intelligence. (see figure 1).

The semiotic square charts transformations, the various dynamics of changes in believing and doing (or in imagining and action in metaphor and the dramatic act, etc.) We begin by identifying two poles on the continuum of doing/not doing (say, A and Z). Both poles generate their differences (say, A7 and Z9) and the result is four positions of a square in continuous change (A, A7, Z, Z9).

That is to say, when we externalize a metaphor in dramatic action (A), we have made a choice not to use another metaphor/dramatic action (Z). But in the very act of choosing *A*, we have generated the differences of A and Z, which are A7 and Z9. The four positions refer to poles on the similarity/difference continuum. Fundamental to understanding the semiotic square is that it is processual: The four positions are not distinct opposites but gradations (one dramatic action is not the direct opposite

Figure 1
The Cognitive Square (after A-J. Greimas)

of another, but a gradation on a continuum)); and in any moment of time the square changes as we and events change (the dramatic event of *this* moment becomes the dramatic moment of *that*).

In the case of cognition, or "coming to believe" (figure 1), the transformation is from certainty to doubt or vice versa. One pole on the first continuum (A) is "to affirm" (certitude); its difference, "to doubt," is the second pole (A7). The opposite of "to affirm" is "to refuse," or exclusion (Z). This becomes the first pole on the second continuum, with "to believe" (or "to admit") as the second pole (Z9).

Returning to the parable of the Good Samaritan, we see that Christ's listeners went through various stages of "coming to believe" with each appearance of a character. These stages can be plotted on a square whose poles are of certitude/doubt and refusal/belief. As the listener's beliefs change, this semiotic square would be transformed into another.

With the dramatic metaphor (see figure 3), transformation hinges on the poles on the first continuum, *similarity* and *differentiation*. Contradictory to differentiation is *opposition*, and contradictory to similarity is *contiguity*. Opposition and contiguity thus become poles on the second continuum. Similarity and opposition are gestalt wholes of which contiguity and differentiation are parts. For example, there are two continua in the metaphor "Macbeth is a beast," that are expressed in the play (see figure 2).

Needless to say, the player is not conscious of all this intellectual

Continuum 1

Macbeth = beast ↔ Macbeth = different from a beast

Continuum 2

Macbeth = not a beast ↔ Macbeth = not not a beast

(e.g., Macbeth and beast are contiguous)

Figure 2
The Continua of "Macbeth Is a Beast." The metaphor in continuum 1 is transformed into dramatic action at a specific moment in the play's process, only to be changed by continuum 2 as the action progresses.

activity. In the dramatic act the actor's knowing is whole; he or she focuses on the gestalt of living through the experience of the "here and now," while the action itself deals with relations between wholes. Opposition is not directly required in the protagonist's own metaphor; the single actor is more concerned consciously with similarity than with differentiation. But once two actors perform together, opposition is a necessary precondition of the action. If the vaunt of one is answered by that of another, dramatic action exists. Thus the child at play obviates contiguity because he or she emphasizes wholes, not parts. Yet the child complements differentiation when he or she distinguishes the parts that make up the whole.

From the ground of the dramatic metaphor, the dramatic act re-plays wholes and creates similarities, the axiological bases for knowing, meaning, and learning. This process underlies what others have called models, scientific paradigms, root metaphors or world hypotheses, world views, and forms of life[32] – the way our dramatic world deals with what happens next. Of the figurative forces that work against our dramatic world, opposition bifurcates the universe. As a result, systems arise in hierarchies that attempt to organize cosmic chaos; differentiation assumes that knowing the parts is to know the whole; by extension, contiguity and metonymy relate concepts abstractly and cognitively. Metonymy is pure imagery. Contiguous images (for example, a crown for a king, a sail for a ship) are incomplete wholes revealed by the dramatic metaphor and action; yet at the same time they allow us to live with ambiguity and paradox.

How do these considerations affect learning? John McLeod suggests that current educational systems and methods are insufficient, that the nature of metaphor within drama and arts curricula must be addressed. Examples should be grounded (he says) in an explicit and apparent context, and the dialogue between structure and transformation, together

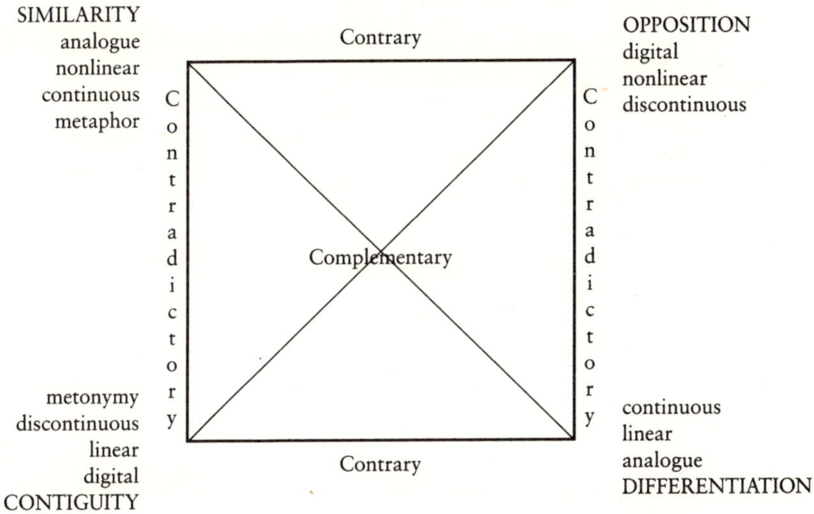

Figure 3
The Dramatic Metaphor: Semiotic Square (after A-J. Greimas and Floyd Merrel)

with their metaphoric relationship, needs to be exposed. Specifically, more emphasis needs to be placed on the tacit domain.[33] Primarily, the strategies for learning must be firmly grounded in the dramatic world. How can the teacher become the agent of such strategies?

Figure 4 illustrates how the teacher can conceive the learning sequence of four major cognitive qualities in developmental stages. This typology, initially developed by Robert W. Witkin[34] from a research study with thousands of British students, concerns aesthetic development, which is different from but similar to the cognitive development described by Piaget. Witkin says that preadolescent aesthetic knowledge has four qualities: harmonies (corresponding to multiplication), semblances (addition), discords (division) and contrasts (subtraction). The higher-level and more complex mental operations of adolescence order these into syntheses, identities, dialogues (dialectics), and polarities. As the four qualities of knowing correspond exactly to the metaphoric typology of Greimas, we have here an example where research and theory come together for the use of practitioners.

CONCLUSION

When others use the dramatic metaphor in its expressive or active form we can assess if learning occurs. How do they use metaphors – in action?

	SIMILARITY	CONTIGUITY	OPPOSITION	DIFFERENTIATION
Pre-adolescent operations	HARMONIES wholes	SEMBLANCES tension of parts	DISCORDS conflict of parts	CONTRASTS separation of parts
Piaget's terms	multiplication	addition	division	subtraction
Adolescent	SYNTHESES totality of individual wholes is absorbed into a synthesis	IDENTITIES various semblances are ordered as identities within wholes	DIALOGUES discords in various wholes are seen as dialogues	POLARITIES contrasts in various wholes are seen as polarities

Figure 4
Cognitive Qualities in Developmental Stages
(after Robert W. Witkin)

language? other media? Do they use metaphors uniquely and, if so, how? When a metaphor is adequately activated, it is a whole that is double: It relates one thought to another so that a new meaning is created in the mode of similarity/difference, and thus it defines our reality. How does person P define reality by expressing metaphor? If a metaphor is truly cognitive, we come to know through the fiction it creates. Compared with person P, how does person Q define reality by expressing metaphor?

We all have our own metaphor. We use it to express our Being, our ontological reality. Most of us are not aware what it is or even that it exists. If we do not know what it is, we can begin to discover its identity by playing a Victorian parlour game. "If I was a chair, what kind of chair would I be?" "If I was an animal, what kind of animal would I be?" And so on. The process of identifying our personal metaphor can be a long one. After all, as Northrop Frye has said, our educational systems do not offer courses in remedial metaphor.

As we live through experience, the metaphor and the dramatic act are one entity; we come to know by using both at the same time. As observers and researchers we may use intellectual tools like the semiotic square to discover how others use metaphors in action. But this is an abstract activity; it is different from the player negotiating with another player by expressing his or her own metaphor. This is cognitive. When drama is life, life drama, the metaphoric/dramatic mode is the way cognition and intelligence function; it is how we deal with the environment we perceive, how we form and develop concepts, how we cope with experience as a whole, and how we do so through the stages of transformation.

CHAPTER SIX

Drama and Logic

If we make cognitive sense out of our experience by comparing what is actual and fictional, how do we ensure that we gain the "right" meaning? This is a question of logic. Whereas the Victorians thought classical logic was the only kind, and that it provided absolute truth, contemporary logicians work with several kinds of logic. Each kind provides what is right for a particular framework. From this perspective we must ask, in imaginative thought and dramatic action, what form or forms of logic can we use? Do these differ when we talk ABOUT it?

These questions are complicated by two key issues: the nature of meaning, and the logic inherent in the comparison of the actual and the fictional. We should acknowledge at the outset that the issues are so intertwined, misunderstood, and clouded by uncertainty as to whether we are discussing the view of the players or that of the audience members, that our inquiry can only be a beginning.

MEANING

What does a dramatic action "mean"? In semiotics this question becomes, What does this sign mean? when "this sign" is a particular signifier, namely, a dramatic act.

The cultural relativism of the Sapir-Whorf hypothesis[1] tells us that people living in a particular culture and language think differently from others. This may be true at the surface level of attitudes and language, but it is not the total picture at the deep level of intersubjective communication. Among players, the fiduciary contract is the focus of meaning and provides a framework for logic. Critics may use critical criteria and audiences may distinguish between liking and not liking, but only the most conservative philosophers, seemingly, work through classical logic to find abstract truth. From day to day, most people function on a more mundane level. They look for "what works in this context." Their cognitive activity searches for pragmatic meaning. They wish to improve their practical knowledge and thus their intelligence.

Mutual trust is the bedrock of meaning for players. Each focuses on moving the action forward. In the dramatic "here and now" their mental functions are not predominantly inductive or deductive. Meaning for both lies primarily in their interaction and what is happening. The workings of the fiduciary mode do not lend themselves to the neat and categorical opposition of either/or, like those of classical logic, which can lead to abstract truth. Rather, opposition is seen as an aspect of similarity/difference. That is, ideas are not in diametric conflict but exist on continua. This is particularly the case in dramatic action; it is also the case in various aspects of life, for example, languages, which contain indefinitives (a little/a lot, early/late, near/far, etc.) alongside categorical terms.

Previous semiotic analyses of language provide no direct answers to our question, but they are some help. Semioticians have found the dictionary insufficient for interpreting linguistic signs; it lacks the subtlety and richness necessary for adequate interpretation. The dictionary is simply a pragmatic device, a tool, whereas the encyclopedia is a semantic concept. Umberto Eco considers that even the encyclopedia is adequate only when governed by the metaphor of the labyrinth. This provides three possibilities for interpretation: the classical labyrinth, an ancient symbol for solving the riddle of life and death; the maze, which offers choices through alternative paths but with only one way out; and "the net," of which the best model is that of the rhizome, a tangle where every point is connected to another point and not one element can supply a global description of the whole.[2] With "the net" we grope our way toward cognitive meaning. It has been variously called a probe[3] and a myopic algorhythm.[4] Eco develops the metaphor of the labyrinth-net-rhizome into Model Q, a polydimensional network that can reconstruct itself through the continuum of similarity/difference. From this perspective we can say that:

Dramatic Signs
are signifiers and
are the human actions
that we create and perceive
to stand for something else (the signified)
(yet which can include codes)
that must be interpreted by others through inference
&

Dramatic Meaning
is the signified of dramatic action
structured by a network of interpretants
that is virtually infinite while it
registers both truth and
commentary on what is true/false
(probably to be communicated)
yet is always incomplete
while structured within its context

PERFORMANCE LOGIC

We are concerned with the specific logic we use while we are within the dramatic experience and the logic involved when we observe it.

As we live through dramatic action we use various interlocking experiential logics: of trust, action, life, and "inner logic." The logic of trust hinges on the fiduciary contract. This is linked to two forms of knowing: personal knowledge, where the functional structure between two players must intuitively feel right if it is to work; and practical knowledge, where the players have the "know how" to interact productively.

The logic of action functions in terms of human skill. Some players act well, some act less well. Some are good conversationalists or salesmen, some are not. Skills can be improved: Improvisers learn them in spontaneous drama with specific techniques. The logic of action derives from practical knowledge, the "know how" to present oneself (as self or in role) to others, and to move the dramatic action forward together. As improvisers work, the logic consists of a series of action clichés, such as "Keep your eye on the ball" (the focus on the progress of the event itself), "Show don't tell" (do it, do not talk ABOUT it), etc. The accumulation of such skills in practice demonstrates this type of logic.

Closely related to the logic of action is the logic of life skills. Players use virtually the same logic that works in everyday experience: simple and commonplace forms of cause and effect, deduction, induction, comparisons, and so forth. Much is trial and error, and we are liable to make mistakes as we are not using abstract logic, particularly the kinds of mistakes Popper calls the foundation of knowledge.[5]

Our inner logic while playing consists of six closely linked elements. First are our intentions, aims, and goals. Immediate, midterm, and long-term purposes arise from who we are (personality, beliefs, etc.) together with our perspective on existence and the action at hand. Second is content, or the *what* of our actions, for example, washing up or killing a king. This is affected by our purpose in doing it and the way in which we do it. Third is method, or *how* we do it: fast/slow, comically/tragically, overtly/covertly, spontaneously/rehearsed, etc. Fourth is assessment. As we act we assess what we are doing: Do I feel right in doing this? Our answers will change how we proceed. Fifth and last is the context in which the action takes place. If I wash up and then kill the king there will be some difference in the two sets of actions depending on their purpose, method, content, assessment, and context (for example, a Dickensian slum or the Palace of Versailles just before the French Revolution). These logical elements intersect on the planes of space and time, in the "here and now."

In addition there are two major variables, time and communication. The main difference between the logic of life experience and that of dramatic experience lies in the player's attitude to the "here and now." In everyday life we concentrate on the "here and now" but take into account both past and future. During a dramatic event, the player is constantly aware than an effort must be made to forward the action. Although operating in the "here and now," the player is aware of what happens next in anticipation of the next "now." In other words, in life we work in the perpetual present but with reference to all pasts and all futures; in the dramatic experience, we function in a perpetual present, which is in tension with an immediate future. This difference affects less the kind of logic used than the attitudes of the users to logical processes. Also, the logic of dramatic action may alter according to whether the act is intended for an audience or not. Examples of the two poles are children at play who do not necessarily need the skills of communication and actors on a stage who do. The players in these instances will assess their actions in very different ways.

THE OBSERVER'S LOGIC

When we observe and/or analyse dramatic events, the logic necessary ("exterior logic") is different from the logic used in dramatic experience. Exterior logic must be objective if it is to be recognized as valid. This may create some false difficulties, as dramatic phenomena do not respond well to empirically mechanical methods, particularly the experimental and behavioural. Here the position is taken that the *logic is objective if it is rational* and undertaken with intellectual rigour.

Dramatic ideas are relative and comparative. Thus in *Hamlet* meaning is gained from the values and meanings of the whole, not from those of any one character. To the question Is this Japanese play performance good? we cannot give a quantitative answer or one based on abstract logic. We must ask first, What are the criteria for judgment? and, In what context? The context in this instance is Japanese drama and theatre. Unless the person making the judgment has a good background in these, any assessment is objectively invalid. *The criteria to be used emerge from the context.* It would be patently absurd, for example, to use criteria from Western stage speech and movement as a way of assessing a Noh or Kabuki performance. Similarly, when a teacher says, "Is this creative drama good?" the question must first be addressed in the context of the age, ability, aptitude, and setting of the students. If they are eight years old, one set of criteria the teacher might use is that suggested by Peter Slade:[6] How sincere are they in role? How absorbed are they in the activity?

An observers we describe dramatic action in a metalanguage, that is, when we talk ABOUT it, not when we are IN it. This metalanguage is logical, but it is based on the use of criteria in contexts and not on natural laws. Aristotelian logic resulted in natural laws (rules and absolutes) but, subsequent to Einstein's theory of relativity and Russell's denial of Aristotelian logic, Wittgenstein developed his own form of modern logic.[7] When he said, "Philosophy is not a science," he was stating that philosophy is a way of working, or a method, not a body of doctrine. For Wittgenstein the skill, or inner logic, of any study of temporal events (including the dramatic) must be showing, not telling. Showing is demonstrating by using particular criteria within specific contexts.

Which criteria? That depends on our frame of reference. In physics, Heinsenberg's theory of indeterminacy[8] shows that a particle may be said to have position (that is, it can be examined in terms of space) or velocity (it can be examined in terms of time), but it cannot *in any exact sense* be said to have both. In other words we as observers are always part of the experiment. Our personal frame of reference gives us the parameters for a particular perspective, or map, of the dramatic event. Mine is different from yours. But the map, as Korzybski said, "IS NOT the territory."[9] In this sense all dramatic events are territories. Each can be studied through maps, by using metalanguages from specific perspectives and by using the criteria of those maps. Just as there are geological, archeological, and other maps of the same ground, so each of us has our own criteria within our own perspective. The important thing is to ensure that our criteria emerge from the evidence – that is, from our practical knowledge and intelligence – and can be substantiated.

Possible criteria to be used in a specific situation are many but not limitless. The criteria of one framework may be similar to, or different from, the criteria of other frameworks. Thus it is possible to consider a painting from aesthetic criteria (its aesthetic value) or from economic criteria (its financial value). In a similar way we can observe dramatic events from a cognitive map (as we do here), an aesthetic map, an affective map, and so on.

Criteria are to be contrasted with evidence. David Best (whom we will follow here) has shown that this distinction has considerable logical significance.[10] The appearance of raincoats and umbrellas in the street is *evidence* of rain, but my sensations of wet drops are *criteria* of rain. Evidence and criteria are to be distinguished; they are indirect and direct ways of knowing. Thus the statement "It is raining" does not necessarily imply that people are carrying umbrellas, but it does indicate that wet drops are falling.

Behavioural investigation deals with indirect evidence. Sometimes behaviourists take behaviour as evidence, but strictly speaking this is a form of dualism. They assume that behaviour is evidence and, also, that for which it is evidence. At other times, an unsophisticated form of behaviourism can assume the position of monism, that is, it can assume that behaviour "just is" the emotion or sensation. But clearly I can feel pain or sadness without behavioural manifestation, and vice versa. In contrast, the appropriate criteria provide logical connections between behavioural statements and mental-experience statements. The actions of other people are criteria of their mental experience; but the behaviourist can mistakenly view their behaviour as evidence. Thus Best can say (in terms of aesthetic metalanguages) that "if we take the movement to be evidence for, or to be standing for, the emotion which is being expressed, we thereby create a gap between the ... movement and the emotion ... Expressive movements do not stand for anything, they are not evidence of anything. They are criteria of the emotions which they express. And this is true not only of expression in the art of movement, but also of expression in the arts generally."[11]

There are two familiar methods of substantiation, the empirical and the logical. Empirical substantiation is undertaken by "going and seeing",[12] that is, by gathering information or by investigation. This method answers the question, How many? Logical substantiation is undertaken by means of argument or reasoning. An example is the proof of the Pythagorean theorem by steps of deductive reasoning using the axioms and rules of inference. An empirical investigation of various right-angled triangles is unnecessary to substantiate the theorem; it follows as a matter of logic. To put the matter another way, mechanistic scientific study proposes or considers a hypothesis that is subjected to rigourous empirical tests; in effect, such study tries to refute the hypothesis by reversing induction – seeing if all examples obey it. By logic does not try to do this. Rather, it attempts to refute or confirm an argument by reasoning. Human behaviour is amenable to two quite different modes of explanation: in terms of reason and in terms of cause. Reasons are confirmed in terms of logical criteria. Causes are confirmed in terms of empirical evidence.

Both forms of substantiation are objective. Both the logical (explained by reason) and the empirical (explained by cause) are objective because substantiation is made by what actually occurs or exists. But the logical is not empirical, since no additional investigation or information is required. Because scientific explanation is assumed to be causal, it is tempting (but false) to believe that it is the only genuine sort of explanation, and the only "proper" kind of objective inquiry. But reasons, not causes, are the foundation of logic. In this study, therefore, reasons and not causes are emphasized.

Reasons

Although various logical reasons are useful in metalanguages, the idea is still prevalent that "proper" reasoning must either be inductive or deductive, as in classical logic. But today there is more scope for reasoning than just these two forms. For example, neither inductive nor deductive reason is characteristically (or at least exclusively) employed for an emotional reaction, for a view of life, or for an aesthetic judgment. At the same time all reasoning must be answerable, at least in principle, to what is or could be perceived.

In contemporary logic, as Best has shown,[13] there are at least four types of reasons: *inductive, deductive, moral,* and *interpretative.* The inductive is characteristically used in science. It relies on repetition: It looks for as many particulars as possible that "match" and makes a generalization from them. But Popper shows that the repetition at B of event A does not give an event identical to A. All repetitions are approximations only. Their similarity is no more than approximate because they can similar in different respects.[14] Deduction is characteristically used in mathematics, as we see in the classical syllogism: All men are mortal; Socrates is a man; therefore Socrates is mortal. It is now a commonplace to say that deduction is based on an unproven assumption (as with the first statement of the syllogism) and that it is also, as Russell showed, a single linguistic statement that has nothing to do with whether the statement is true or not.

Moral reason is characteristically used in the moral justification for direct experience. Justifying, commending, and explaining direct experiences by reference to moral attitudes have strength because they draw on the fundamental beliefs of the person who gives them. Two sets of opposing moral reasons may be equally sound and internally consistent; but the less the overlap of fundamental belief, the less the possibility of reaching agreement. Interpretative reasons are characteristically used in attempts to discern or convey the salient features of behaviour as it relates to moral character. For example, two persons might interpret an improvisation or a play in two different moral ways, yet both might be right. Although moral and interpretative reasons do not necessarily yield conclusions as definite and specific as those of inductive or deductive reasons, this does not mean that any conclusion is as good as any other. Each person might be able to give good reasons for a conclusion, but not just any conclusion can be put forward. There must be a logical relationship between the event (or situation, or drama, or work of art) and our interpretation of it. As Best puts it: "It is true of objectivity in any sphere as it is in the arts that it has to allow for the indefinite but not unlimited possibilities of valid or intelligible interpretation."[15]

The criteria of a particular frame of reference must be placed within a specific context in order to be logical. A dance by Pavlova or the performance of a play by Shaw, when examined out of its normal context, is unintelligible. As Wittgenstein says, "The very fact that we should so much like to say: 'This is the important thing' – while we point privately to the sensation – is enough to show how much we are inclined to say something which gives no information."[16] Context is an obvious factor when we attempt to assess a work of art created in a culture or time different from our own – say, a medieval morality play performed today, or a Balinese ritual drama performed in Paris. Every feature of an event or art work is relevant to an analysis of it: Reasoning must function in a total context.

There is a logical relation between meaning and the medium in which meaning is expressed. In the case of linguistics, the meaning of a word is given by the various sentences in which it is expressed; those sentences derive their meaning from the whole activity of language of which they are a part. The same is true of dramatic meaning, which is given by the context of the action, or the complex of actions, of which it is a part. A gesture or a dance movement may have different meanings (that is, it may *be* different actions) in different contexts.[17] Nodding the head, for example, means "yes" in the English-speaking world but "no" in Bulgaria, while shaking the head means "no" to the English but "yes" to Bulgarians. An English-speaking tourist using his or her own cultural head gestures in Bulgaria could cause considerable confusion, particularly with the opposite sex.

The influence of context on logic is particularly related to moral and interpretative reasoning. Not everyone can see the same thing in a work of art. One person interprets Picasso's *Guernica* one way, another person in a quite different way. The facts about an action, as opposed to the physical movement involved in it, depend on how the event is seen, that is, on one's attitude towards it. We must take into account not an isolated physical event but, implicitly, wide factors – the circumstances under which it occurred, our knowledge of the person concerned, and so on. An aesthetic judgment is bound to a whole cultural tradition and the life of a society. Although we all have our individual frames of reference, these only make sense against a background of objective meaning; and objectivity is relative to both logical criteria and cultural differences.

Cause and rational strings

When the dramatic world uses deductive, inductive, moral, and interpretative reasoning, causes can be different from one instance to another. Performing players create new meanings – those in theatre less so, because they use the structures of the dramatist, those in life, play, creative drama, and improvisation, more so. They create a typology of relations for a particular context, so that meanings, reasons, and causes can differ from performance to performance. A pair of young children playing mommy and daddy draw on different relations than another pair. Examples in theatre are less extreme, although a fascinating example occurred in 1946 when Olivier, playing Lear and taken ill, was replaced with William Devlin, who succeeded in making the same production into a different interpretation. Both performances were equally memorable.

Meaning, reason, and cause are linked in the dramatic "here and now." In the re-cognizing that takes place in drama, a story is told through action but in some kind of sequence – a form of action-narrative that exists in the present tense. There has been much recent research about the organizing principles of narrative and temporality where,[18] in some cases, dramatic events have been seen as a causal series. This view might well be true if it were not for the fiduciary contract on which all dramatic relations hinge.

In drama, the causes that link one action to another are less like those used by logicians and more like those of everyday life. They are liable to appear false in the light of abstract logic but true in other circumstances. For example, improvisers, noting the appearance of thunder and dark clouds, might think of the causes of mythological thinking ("The gods are angry, we will suffer for it") or of practical thinking ("The clouds are getting nearer, it is going to rain"). This is similar to the kind of reasoning used in sacred and profane rituals. Observations of children at play show they naturally link ideas causally; and in creative drama classes there is an increase of socialization in children's reasoning. Piaget reads causality in children's natural play usually because he reads their actions from left to right; but sometimes these actions can also be seen as "logical presupposition" if we move from right to left. Yet many strings of action in drama do not have such implicit logic.

In play and all forms of dramatic activity there are various rational strings. First is thinking that results from Being – through the Being of the player, which is more significant in natural forms (in play and life) but is less emphasized in more socialized forms (like theatre); through the Being of the role ("Policemen act like this"); and through the fiduciary contract ("This is the way people negotiate with one another"). Second is thinking that results from doing. Dramatic doing is action. It is a whole, with the elements of the self, the voice and the body, each separately and together, providing an intuitive form of reason in the "here and now." Acting is thinking on the feet; it involves spontaneous, tacit, and largely unconscious reasoning. Thus Keith Johnstone[19] may ask advanced improvisers, while they are acting, to count backwards in their heads from 100; in this way they release their unconscious creativity from unnecessary playwriting (or telling, or talking ABOUT it). Any causes, therefore, are likely to arise from the player's unconscious in a kind of serendipity. Third is thinking that results from predictable events. Such thinking depends on the co-occurrence, in temporal contiguity, of acts in succession. This kind of thinking can be considered by personages in the "here and now" as predictable, or perhaps plausible, or even necessary – for example, among the characters in Chekhov's *The Cherry Orchard*. In the initial steps of play and creative drama, such thinking can be stereotypical; in theatre, in contrast, it can be highly sophisticated. Fourth is interpretative thinking. The player's attitude to the action affects its meaning; how the player feels about it is transmitted to others, and this alters the way they feel about it. How I see and respond to an event may be different from how you see and respond to it; this difference will give variant interpretations. Fifth and last is moral thinking, as in the clash of views between major personages in the theatre: Oedipus *versus* Creon, Portia *versus* Shylock, Pizarro *versus* Atahuallpa. Most moral reasoning does not result from abstract logic. People differ in their moral attitudes to facts, or to the significance of facts, which determine their reasons. Moral cause can be the result.

But the focus of dramatic reasoning and cause is the trust established between two players and, thus, between two personages. Knowing that something is true in a dramatic context is twofold: Does it work? and, do I trust the other player? At the same time it is confidential, in most cases for the players, and in theatre for the audience as well. In tribal societies members of the audience are "witnesses" in the Biblical sense. For example, in the Northwest Coast Amerindian potlatch the audience-guests share "the secret" for its being given; as witnesses, they are trusted to take the secret home to share with their families and thus confirm it. In many dramatic and theatrical cases, it is as though the dramatic truth of contents implied or hidden is confirmed among players. Even explicit reasons and causes functioning at the surface level of drama are bound to exist at tacit and deep levels. Whenever the fiduciary relation is used, meanings are generated at a deep level.

Hypothesis and other logical concepts

We work by hypothesis not merely in abstract and scientific thinking but also in everyday life. Indeed, most of our mundane operations are based on tacit and unconscious hypotheses. This has been the subject of many modern logical studies.[20] According to Eco, there are at least three types of hypothesis. The overcoded presupposes some hypotheses about the circumstances, the speaker, and so forth. Examples in language are "Man is a rational mortal animal," and "Theatre is a temporal form." A law is given automatically or almost automatically. The undercoded hypothesis selects a rule from a variety of possibilities but not necessarily the most correct one. Examples in language are "Man is a brave male," and "Theatre is an actor's form." The creative hypothesis is a new explanation or theory, for example, the theory of Copernicus, all poetry, and all spontaneous drama where the events and how they are played are new at least to the players. We work with these three types of hypothesis in abstraction, estimation, tacit operations, and dramatic actions such as thinking on the feet.

In addition, however, hypothesis is assumed by all dramatic acts in whatever form. In each case there is a hidden assumption: "If I play my role in way *A*, then the resulting actions are *Y*. But if I play my role in way *B*, then the resulting actions are *Z*." Such an assumption can be called tacit, or unconscious, or deep-structured, etc. But in cognitive terms it is creating a hypothesis in the spheres of doing and Being in order to conduct an experiment in an intelligent way. Our research also shows that people with rich experience in creating dramatic hypotheses often gain earlier understanding of logical scientific hypothesis in the mode of Piaget (when compared with people without such experience). That is, those who experiment with dramatic hypothesis improve their ability in abstract hypothesis. They improve their intellectual capability.

In recent years, logical concepts have been introduced from semiotics, of which some of the most important for us are isotopies, the analogical/digital comparison, and homologies. Isotopies are complexes of whole meaning communicated by works. Thus the whole meaning of an improvisation, or the total production in the theatre, is an isotopy, that is, the fundamental and total meaning of it. Similarly, an isotopy is "a complex of manifold semantic categories making possible the uniform reading of a story."[21] An isotopy differs from a topic. A topic is activated by a reader or member of an audience, or it is a question asked of a text or art work; an isotopy is the semantic property of a total text or work of art or of theatre. For Greimas, an isotopy is the "concept of the meaningful whole set forth by a message" and "the principle of the equivalence of unequal units."[22] We can use this idea to justify the study of a total dramatic or theatrical experience and without considering the artist who creates it. This is to reverse the mechanical method of criticism where parts are analysed and assumed to add up to a whole. In contrast, the use of isotopies permits us to take one part of the whole and study it "as if" it is the whole – a dramatic way of working. (This bears some resemblance to the use of the hologram.)

The comparison of analogic and digital systems occupies semioticians in a variety of ways. In logic, analogy is the process of reasoning from parallel cases. Analogues are processed and perceived holistically, while analogic systems are continuous. In number, digital means any unit from 0 to 9, while digital systems are generated from bits of information into messages that can be broken up (analysed) and perceived as isolated parts. Digital systems are therefore discontinuous.[23] Dramatic events are nearer to the analogic and parabolic: Players and personages both reason from parallel cases (analogy) and from heightened reality (parable). In recent years some theoreticians have used analogy and/or parable as criteria for analysis. Much of Sartre's theoretical work, for example, is based on the analogy of life and theatre.

But the comparison between actual and fictional worlds is more than merely analogic or parabolic. It is homologous. Like isotopy, homology is another term that Greimas borrowed from natural sciences for use in his logic. Homology is the structural parallelism of two notions or elements of meaning (or concepts). Using homologies we can say that, as our dramatic and actual worlds parallel each other and we make cognitive sense out of living by comparing them, these two worlds are homologous. This is to make a comparison beyond the analogic and the parabolic, one that obeys our experience of the actual and the fictional.

CONCLUSION

Previously we examined the cognitive qualities inherent in dramatic action (chapters 3 and 4, and the metaphoric nature of its processes in chapter 5). In this chapter we have examined just how far dramatic action is rational and logical. But intelligence is more than all these things put together. For example, although play and drama may be logical and rational they can also be as illogical and irrational as the occasion demands. They must be practical. As players, we must be able to use our intelligence to gain "know how," which is a composite of the manner in which we function, the procedures we use in life, the way we negotiate with others, and our flexibility and adaptability in coping with such ever-changing skills.

Those who have these skills often seem to perform them in an unthinking way – "it just comes naturally to them." In the next chapter we will address intuition.

CHAPTER SEVEN

Drama and Intuition

Perhaps the most neglected area of cognition and intelligence is intuition. The popular view holds that intuition, whether it be guessing or playing a hunch, having an inspiration or just being lucky, has little to do with intelligence. Yet those people who cultivate their intuition usually feel more successful in their tasks than those who do not.

In all societies one group that relies on intuition is artists and creative arts teachers. Both explicitly and implicitly, their talk about art, how they teach, and how they and their students learn focuses on the intuitive. Our research shows that theatre artists and teachers of educational drama use intuition even more than other artists and creative arts teachers. For those whose life-work is dramatic activity, the rational and the intuitive go hand in hand. Perhaps recognizing that dramatic acts can be inherently paradoxical, they commonly express the view that both kinds of cognitive activity are necessary, although the intuitive is more important. Moreover, they say that in any one instance they do not necessarily know how they "come to believe," or how they grasp a new concept or intelligently solve a problem. For them it just happens, and they are willing to trust their intuition.

Our research has shown that the intuitive and dramatic processes are homologous. By interviewing and observing artists, learners, and teachers, we discovered that intuition works through dialogue and a kind of quasidramatization – that the mental activity upon which dramatization hinges, particularly doubling, is also inherent in intuition.

INTUITION, INSIGHT, AND PRACTICAL KNOWLEDGE

Despite this homology, there are many dramatic actions that are not intuitive. In the same way, there are many instances of intuition that, at least on the surface, do not appear dramatic. We must therefore address the intuitive before we consider its dramatic character.

We can talk about intuition from three angles: the psychological, the philosophical, and the mundane. Two groups of psychologists are concerned with intuition. Behaviourists are inclined to talk of "logical intuitions" – inherited or learned dispositions. In a simplistic sense we all have such dispositions, but an appeal to them does not illuminate the nature of intuition. For behaviourists who believe that all can be accounted for by an input/output model, any other kind of intuition is an ambiguous paradox to be ignored. Others have treated intuition contemptuously or denounced it as imprecise thinking. Thus they avoid a process that has produced some of the most important advances in the sciences, arts, and humanities, and they cut children off from one of the most exciting areas of learning.[1] Much of the problem can be attributed to the difficulty in grasping the nature of intuition through the low-level mind-sets of mechanical thinkers.

Some psychologists recognize the value of intuition, but most do not deal with it in detail. Eric Berne found intuition to be integrated perceptive processes working on both sides of consciousness, shifting their emphases according to prevailing conditions.[2] Piaget implies that intuition is knowing the world in terms of "our actions upon it rather than relations among objects."[3] Jerome S. Bruner, in reference to "informed guessing" (hypothesis) and the ability to solve a problem without formal proof in mathematics,[4] says that "intuition implies the act of grasping the meaning or significance or structure of a problem without explicit reliance on the analytic apparatus of one's craft."[5]

The most famous philosophical discussion of the issue is that of Plato. He described grasping the forms of ideas as a kind of vision: Our "mental eye" (*nous*, reason) operates through intellectual intuition, which enables us to "see" an idea, an essence, or an object that belongs to the intelligible world. Plato claimed that this intellectual intuition is infallible, but others have doubted this; some have maintained that intuitive thoughts are more likely to be fallible than infallible. In philosophical terms, this is to contrast an idealist view of intuition with a pragmatic one.

The most common way of discussing intuition is to show it as an element of personal knowledge and a tacit aspect of practical knowledge. This is how intuition appears in dramatic acts, and it is the view we adopt here. How is intuition part of personal and practical knowledge? The answer can be confusing because both the nature and function of intuition are highly complex.

The result of intuitive thought is insight. Intuition and insight are important factors in our personal knowledge. An intuitive thought appears without a moment's notice, without our being aware of it before it happens. Suddenly "it is" – and the result is that we know something. We have gained insight into the nature and condition of things.

How far are intuition and insight conscious or unconscious? Until intuition appears, we are not conscious of it; indeed, we usually infer that its workings are unconscious. Consciousness depends on an abstract theory being formulated in words and actions. We experience the theory, talk to others about it, and discover that they too experience it; and we continue to experience it while awake. Intuition, we assume, continues its operations covertly in the unconscious until such time as its results burst upon us. This may happen in many ways. One of the most common manifestations of intuition is an insight that solves a problem, either a problem we knew we were addressing or one we were not conscious we had. It may well be that intuition is linked directly to the solving of problems. Some of us go to bed and "sleep on" a problem (or "put it on the back burner"); in the morning we may discover that we have solved the problem unconsciously, through intuition. Intuition is similarly related to conjecture, hypothesis, hunch, and inference, forms of intelligent guessing fundamental to the conduct of life. Intuition and insight might also explain curious forms of coincidence; famous cases of mental telepathy, feelings that predict events, and ESP are often accounted for in these terms.

Intuition plays a significant part in our practical knowledge, or "know how"; often it underlies our ability to execute a task. We experience it suddenly – "it just happens" – and then, by marrying the insight with our explicit knowledge, we act. Our intuitive abilities help us to develop particular skills – typists type, teachers teach, fishermen fish – so that we work with practical knowledge. Some cognitive psychologists claim that when we do such things well it is merely a case of our being able to do some things better than others. However, only in some instances does intuition result from inherited or learned dispositions. In others, it may result from skills being learned well. In other instances, probably the majority, intuition and insight cannot be accounted for in such simplistic ways.

Clearly intuition is the kind of thinking that any progressive society must cultivate. Highly skilful practitioners in the creative arts and in education are not inclined to give much credence to abstract and theoretical statements about their activity. They claim simply to know what is of value and what is not. Artists say they engage in intuitive more than reasoned thinking; and it is the practice of their art (their skills in, and sensitivity to the process of, creating it) that validates their intuition.

Our research shows that most professionals in drama and theatre hold this view vehemently. Some thirty major directors of theatre, film, and television in North America all cited intuition as their major criterion in choosing a script. Teachers of educational drama in schools make various claims one cannot ignore: that their hands-on experience of dramatic action, and their practical reflections upon it, provides them with a unique perspective and way of teaching; and that their continuous "as if" experience gives them the practical knowledge that makes them experts in their field. Acting teachers working with adults can use widely different techniques of instruction; all agree, however, that technical mastery can only take actors so far and that intuition is the criterion by which, in the final analysis, they will be judged.

A teacher of playwriting experimented by emphasizing dramatic structure in one of his classes for a whole term. At the end he found no difference in the structures the students consciously created and those created in another class; he did find that the students in the experimental class worked intuitively to change model structures, through they were not conscious of doing so until it was pointed out to them. Although such arguments may appear somewhat naive to philosophers and psychologists, the intellectual position of drama practitioners is coherent and rational because it derives from practical knowledge. Like artists and creative arts teachers, most people working in drama do not regard explicit knowledge as being of great significance to the practice of their field. "I read a lot of plays and theatre history," said one, "because it helps me gain background. But I hardly ever consciously use any of it in theatre or creative drama. What I have read may appear intuitively as I direct a play – or it may not."

THE ORIGINS OF INTUITION

So far we have been concerned with descriptions and examples of intuition. What about how it occurs? To relegate the process to the unconscious, which is what most of us do, is to avoid the question of origins. Modern neo-idealists who follow Croce assume that intuition is the undifferentiated unity of the perception of the real and of the simple image of the possible. That is, perceiving and imaging are one unified process, whether based on the actual or the fictional. Phenomenologists who follow Merleau-Ponty argue similarly. To them, the whole thinking process occurs in perception itself, instantly.

These two views must be placed in the context of the functional operations of mind. We have seen (see p. 51) that the highly complex, even mysterious, phenomenon of perception is normally transformed (dramatized) by the mind into subjective experience. What I see is transformed into what I image, and seeing and imaging have very different mental functions. This fundamental process accounts for a great range of mental activity from reasoning to creating paradox. But we cannot in such a way account for intuition except by consigning the process to what is unknown, namely the unconscious. However, the two undifferentiated views (the unity of percept/image or of percept/thought) can be seen, at least in the abstract, as possible alternatives to a view that distinguishes percept and image, alternatives that might account for intuition. That is, with intuition the electric circuitry of mind can work on a fast track. This bears close resemblance to our experience. To us, intuitions and insights are immediate, and they are varied: from vague feelings to flashes of insight, from hunches to precise solutions. In the abstract we can say that these variations are paralleled by different thought processes: percept/image; percept/image/image cluster; and percept/image/imagining.

But the philosopher's unicorn shows that matters are more complex. When we think of a unicorn we combine previously attained images of a horse and a horn, which then, as one entity, operate "as if" they have been created from perception. That is, created mental entities (fictions) can operate in the same way as perceptions. We continually meet such mental entities in dreams where two existing images have been combined in various nonlogical ways to operate as a whole. Intuitions with similar characteristics sometimes appear in our waking state.

Although they bring forth cognitive solutions to problems, intuitions are characteristically aesthetic. They are founded on feeling in the background of deeply rooted knowledge that Kant calls a priori. Feeling occurs before experience, and it includes the initial ideas ("protoconcepts") of time, space, and causality. Here, the foundational modes of operation are active prior to cognitive, affective, aesthetic, or psychomotor thoughts, sensory organization, perception, learning, memory, classification, etc. Looked at developmentally, a priori intuitions arise in the first days of life as a baby begins to differentiate; and they continue to grow throughout life. What are the modes of this kind of operation?

The prime mode is that of *similarity,* to which we can now return, but in a different context. As an a priori operation, we associate similar or identical elements. *Transfer* is the application of similarity at the level of learning; this is extended to an acquired response. Much of basic mathematics hinges on similarity. For example, the concept of 2 is based on seeing two items as distinct entities, but acknowledging that they are similar. In much the same way, in dramatic acts we see two persons as distinct but similar. That is, if two mental representations (numbers, persons, etc.) have one or more characteristic in common, the appearance of one tends to elicit the other. To Kant, this was the nub of human creativity.

From similarity arise two closely related modes: the contiguous and the part/whole. in the first, if two forms of sensory data are experienced together (contiguously), they may produce a single effect on the mind and, if so, they may be reexperienced together. Thus when I think of my grandfather I may also think of the house in which he lived, which I visited in my childhood; or when I think of dawn I may also think of breakfast because that was the time I always had breakfast as a child. Contiguity occurs in certain dramatic acts, for example, "a crown for a king." Part/whole, the second mode, is mainly built on similarity but can be built on contiguity. Thus the idea of my grandfather may stand for my whole childhood and bring back memories of it. In much the same way, a fragment of an event may evoke the total event. Part/whole parallels certain dramatic acts, for example, one in which a king represents his people. Interestingly, whole/part appears to be the origin of metaphor, contiguity the origin of metonymy.

Thus we can say that intuition is a mental operation producing quick, intelligent guesses through insight. Characteristically these are dramatic and creative, telling us what is and what is not. Intuition supplies us with the identities of ideas, people, and things, and it permits us to make inferences. Whether we have good or bad insights depends on whether our intuitive processes work well or badly.

DRAMA AND COMMUNICATION

Our studies of artists and arts educators show that their intuition is related to mental clustering; ideas appear to be "lumped" in the right hemisphere (compared with the "splitting" that occurs in the left) and show "a kind of internal dialogue between whole and parts, between image and sequence."[6] Most intuition is dramatic, just as many dramatizations are intuitive, likely because the origins of both lie in identification and similarity. Adults' intuitions function as "whole" operations (mainly whole/part using inner dialogue) that grasp a total event through intuition's image-making power; as rapid and complex syntheses drawing on combinations, amalgamations, and generalizations of imagery; as aesthetic operations grounded in feeling, qualitative criteria, and independent choice; as cognitive operations recognizing and interpreting emotional cues, and using their own inner logic to create hypotheses. Many of our subjects used intuitions similar to those of Einstein, whose "toying with concepts" was intuitively related to visual imagination, metaphorization, and inner dramatization.[7]

We conducted a series of practica with a group of 17 mixed (boys and girls) senior-high students who were creative and intellectually gifted. Each practicum was a whole-class activity. That required group problem solving, associative and creative thinking, social interaction,

PRIMARY DYADIC COMMUNICATION SYSTEMS (two players)	
Model System	S —— O
Internal Systems	S —— S S —— SR
External Systems	S —— OS S —— OR SR —— OS SR —— OR
SECONDARY COMMUNICATION SYSTEMS	
	S —— O —— OP S —— O —— OR A

Legend: S = self; O = other; SR = self in role; OS = other's self; OR = other's role; OP = other players; A = audience

Figure 5
Communication in Dramatic Action. The model system can be extrapolated to other dyads or, through secondary systems, to other players and/or an audience.

and an outcome. We discovered that it was difficult to distinguish the creative imagination from intuition, metaphoric thinking from mental dramatization, and dramatic action from action in related media (dance, speech, languaging, sculpting). That is, when human beings are working up to their potential, as did Einstein and these students, the dramatic process infuses all that they do; imagination, intuition, metaphorization, and dramatization are closely linked.

Paradoxically, our subjects showed less ability to communicate intuitions in everyday life than when they shared a verse by an obscure poet. We compared the use of various media and found that partial isomorphism occurs more often between people dramatizing than between those using less dramatic and more explicit media (for example, games with rules) and those in other creative arts. True, increased isomorphism occurs among those "whose style of thinking is similar,"[8] but this does not account for the effectiveness of dramatic activity. We hypothetically attributed this to the generation of meanings that are global, holistic, cultural, and based on similar experience (self-presentation, etc.)[9] As dramatic activity is mostly tacit, to be communicated it must reach the receivers on a personal level. Information from modern studies in

DNA[10] shows that there are genetic structural patterns for dialogue as envisaged by Buber.

There is a commonly noted gap between what teachers say they intend to do and what they actually do. Though explicit aims can hide tacit intentions, we devised methods to discover the latter by comparing teachers' use of spoken metaphor, body language, and attitude to artistic form. One elementary drama teacher said of her students, "They need careful nurturing," unaware of her comparison between teaching and mothering or gardening: Her explicit aims contradicted the metaphor, and her procedures took little account of it. Some tacit levels of a teacher's intention can be revealed by body language and dialogue; to check these we used variations of the methods of E.T. Hall and Ray Birdwhistell.[11] If, as Robert Witkin says, creative arts teachers address the way in which "expressive form realizes and articulates qualitative feelings" that "demand objectivity," then they must engage the intuitions of their students.[12] Players learn the skills of communication and interaction, particularly those of negotiation, while playing. Negotiation is a two-way street; it not only involves "reading" other people but also communicating with them intuitively. The self/role doubling makes the various levels of communication highly complex. (see figure 5).

PACE AND TIMING

There are many aspects of intuitive intelligence, far more than can be adequately dealt with here. Thus one will be chosen as an exemplar.

The homology of dramatic action and intuition is nowhere better exhibited than in pace and timing. They are interlinked: We each have our own pace in life, and we each have personal rhythms based on our own heart beat. We relate to natural rhythms in a unique way. We learn the basic skills of pace and timing in everyday life. We can learn further from experience in educational drama and from the theatre. Theatre performers use others' everyday pace and timing as data for their representations. This relationship of life to theatre is complex and ambiguous: The player incorporates someone else's pace and timing – one form of intuition is absorbed by another.

Life and Theatre

People in both life and theatre live in process. We live in the present tense, spontaneously creating our responses to events; we improvise what happens next, functioning intuitively like an acrobat on a high-wire, trying to keep our balance as we go along. Similarly, whether we act as ourselves or in a role, we work in our "here"; we cannot function in a space that is "there." Pace and timing are ways we function in the "here and now." They are intuitive conditions for all kinds of human performance. To function effectively as human beings we need appropriate pace and timing; these give us our individual vitality and level of performance energy.

Pace and timing are vital to theatrical success. An actor may have received all the possible technical instruction in speech, gesture, stage movement, sytles of acting, and the like, but without good pace and timing the stage performance will fail. This is most obvious in reverse: Some famous popular singers may not have good voices, but their superb pace and timing make them top professionals. While some who had good voices when young may find the talent failing them with age, other singers maintain amazing pace and timing in later recordings (Bing Crosby, Frank Sinatra, Enzio Pinza, Victoria de Los Angeles). Great theatre performers are experts in pace and timing. Laurence Olivier, for example, whose body had been failing him for some years, achieved some of his most remarkable work in later years, for example as the Nazi doctor in the film *Marathon Man* and as Lear on television. His great voice disappeared and offstage he may have had to be helped to his dressing-room. But his pace and timing were perhaps even better in old age than when he was at the height of his physical powers.

Although intuitive, pace and timing are learned through experience. In the playhouse both actors and directors concentrate on pace in planning overall events and on timing for segments of events. Pace is the total patterning of rhythm, in life on the one hand, and on the other in a play, an act, or a scene. Pace is the ebb and flow of tension and relaxation. It has the following variables:

Cosmic rhythms: night/day, light/dark, sun/moon, good/bad, etc.
Natural rhythms: winter/summer, spring/fall, birth/death, earth/sea, etc.
Social rhythms: city/country, kings/slaves, owners/workers, love/marriage, public life/domestic life, etc.
Personal rhythms: happy/sad, success/failure, job/leisure, status/temperament, etc.

These vary between tension and relaxation.

Plays vary considerably in the kind of pace they require, and actors must learn the skills of each. Tragedy is likely to be primarily cosmic but with an underlying natural rhythm. Comedy is likely to be primarily social but also with underlying natural rhythms. Part of the tension in both genres is the contrast between the predominant rhythm of the play performed and the rhythm of the persons involved. In the most general terms, tragedy has a slow pace and a protagonist at a different pace, while comedy is fast and usually has at least one major character whose rhythmic pattern is slower. One play will require a slower pace than another; actors must adjust the pace of their character to that of the play. Most often, this is achieved intuitively.

It is the stage director's job to set the appropriate pace for a specific play. He or she must, therefore, have a particular kind of expertise – the ability to establish the correct pace and communicate it, through the intuitions and negotiations of the players, to an audience. This requires considerable knowledge of human interaction and great skill in translating that interaction to the stage so as to affect the audience. But any good director knows that there are no hard-and-fast rules about pace. This is easiest to see in film comedy, which is comparatively quick. Yet the "slow burn" of Jack Benny is totally different from the hectic pace of Mack Sennett or the mayhem of the Marx Brothers. Thus, on stage a French farce requires a much faster pace than, say, an Oscar Wilde comedy of manners, which requires a leisurely rhythm but extremely quick timing through the catching of cues. Comic rhythms are particularly various – compare the romantic comedy of Shakespeare *(Twelfth Night)* to the intellectual comedy of Bernard Shaw *(Pygmalion)*. Comic satire varies its pace subtly depending on its type: political (Aristophanes), social (Molière and Ben Jonson), or concerning human foibles (Goldsmith and Sheridan). Vanbrugh's *The Relapse* is exceptionally difficult because it varies its satirical level (and thus its pace and timing) within scenes. Each of these comic dramatists demands different rhythms from the stage actor. Some, like Shakespeare, require one pace for one play and quite another for a different play. Directors seek such effects indirectly through players' intuitions.

As *The Relapse* suggests, a play can also vary its pace from one moment to the next. An obvious example is Shakespeare's *Love's Labour's Lost*. Most of the piece has a double pace with a subplot echoing the main plot. The main plot, radiantly happy, is set in a fresh countryside to the rhythms of young and witty courtiers in love; this plot is echoed by a slower one concerning a group of rustics. Then suddenly the mood changes. A messenger arrives to tell one of the young courtiers, the Princess of France, that her father is dead. A melancholy shadow falls over everything, the pace slows down as the characters wander away, and the final curtain gently falls. No other Shakespeare play has exactly this kind of pace.

No two human lives have the same kind of pace either. Your "play" differs from mine, just as mine differs from yours. What we learn intuitively from the theatre is that life's major rhythms underlie our own pace. The rhythm of existence varies with who we are, the people we are with, the context in which we live, and the events that occur. Theatrical rhythms help us to understand those in life and vice versa.

On a stage, timing is the detailed way in which the overall pace is achieved. Each performer has his own intuitive timing. We can see this most obviously in ball games: Some of us can time our actions with finesse, others cannot. Drama teachers often demonstrate this to senior students by having individual bounce balls. The same applies to our timing ability in human (social and theatrical) negotiations. Each actor differs, each ensemble has its unique form of collective timing, each change of lighting and the rise and fall of the curtain affects timing.

A player's timing is the individual rhythm of a negotiation. Claude Rains used to prepare his moves and speeches meticulously by a counting procedure, allowing intuition to come into play later. In contrast, the caricature of "the method" actor is the person who can act only if s/he "feels it" – by sheer intuition. Most theatre performers fall somewhere between these two extremes, as people do in everyday roles. For example, the famous little grunts of Cary Grant enable him to adjust his timing to that of the script. How many of us unconsciously use idiosyncratic verbal or physical habits to time our negotiations? In recent productions of Ronald Harwood's *The Dresser* in London, New York, Edmonton, and Toronto, the directors aimed at more or less the same overall pace, but the varied timing of the performers in fact resulted in different paces and therefore in different nuances of meaning. We can think of famous film examples. The pace that John Huston achieved in *The Maltese Falcon* depended on the timing of not only Bogart but also Sydney Greenstreet (Gutman). When Huston came to cast *Beat the Devil,* a comic satire on movies like *Falcon,* he used Bogart again but, as he could not cast Greenstreet, he used Robert Morley. Morley's timing was very different from Greenstreet's, and so the pace of the two films radically differs. The brilliance of Alec Guinness in the Ealing comedies often lay in the tension created by his slow timing amongst performers whose timing was quicker or vice versa.

There are parallels in everyday negotiation, most obviously in small-group decision making. Change one member of a group for another and the group's timing differs. More subtle are the changes in pace and timing in a family conversation when one member leaves and another arrives. A high proportion of these changes are intuitive.

In live theatre timing is specifically related to the individual audience. Performers often characterize an audience as warm (they respond quickly) or cold (their response is slower). The actor must consciously alter his own timing accordingly. While this is most evident in farce (throwing a custard pie before a warm audience requires totally different timing than before one that is cold), it affects all kinds of performance to one degree or another. For example, we have all had the experience of telling a joke twice and discovering that the first time it resulted in guffaws of laughter but the second time it fell flat. Some of us intuitively learn to adjust our timing to our audience. Some do not.

This is different from film, where the performer's timing can never alter. It is fixed. A great comedian like Chaplin times his performances to certain universal human denominators and thereby retains his popularity through the ages. Comics who do not do so become mere names to film buffs. Abbott and Costello, top box-office draws in the mid-1940s, are today relegated to one-star events on late-night television. Such fixed timing is not part of normal human negotiation. Thus we learn from the theatre that timing is individual rhythms within the pace of a total event; that the timing of total events varies, as does the timing of individual players within an event; and that timing is the unique result of carefully planned skill on the one hand and intuition and spontaneity on the other.

Education

How do we learn such skills? In most instances, schools give no thought to educating students in pace and timing. If these are taught, it is by chance. Yet pace and timing are significant factors in the conduct of adult life. They are necessary skills for success in work and leisure. Schools should educate students in the generic skills of pace and timing. Students need to learn pace in order to identify and carry out group tasks; to vary pace according to the nature of a task; and to relate the pace of that task to the rhythms of those who must perform it. They need to learn timing in order to relate their personal rhythms to the pace of a total task; to vary timing in relation to the context of the task and to the timing of others engaged in the task; and to consciously alter their timing so as to complete a range of tasks. Having then learned timing, they need to trust their intuitions about it.

These issues are not being addressed in normal academic curricula. Most students are so concerned with acquiring information (the facts of social studies) or training skills (computation in math) that such issues can only be addressed tangentially at best. The ability to develop pace, timing, and intuition is the domain of play and educational drama in particular but also of music, dance, and physical education. Classroom activities based on play, improvisation, and creative drama require intuitive skills in pace and timing; through these, students can learn. Such skills are codified in theatre, but theatrical activities are only a small component of educational drama in most schools in the Western world today. Music programs have direct relevance to pace and timing. When the human skills of spontaneous and creative music are emphasized (as opposed to the technical skills of an instrument or orchestra, which stress timing) then both pace and timing assume considerable significance. In spontaneous and creative dance and movement, both pace and timing are extremely significant; they are also important in more formal styles of dance (ballet, tap, jazz, etc.). Physical education requires the learning of intuitive pace and timing in bodily development. While physical and athletic training stress these skills, the subject matters, like the arts, are often regarded as frills. More stress is placed on the basics, the 3 Rs. But pace and timing are basic to the basics. To prepare students for their role as productive citizens in the next century, a fundamental change in educational priorities is necessary.

THE DRAMATIC HYPOTHESIS

We have examined intuitive pace and timing in some detail to show how intuition and dramatic action are linked. Karl Popper has said that knowledge depends on guessing, that is, estimating or hypothesizing – both forms of intuition. This idea has support from a wide variety of contemporary research studies. For example, it is now suggested that the key skill in mathematics is estimating large numbers.[13]

We have examined the use of hypothesis by observers (see p. 91). The intelligence of actors also relies on intuition and takes the form of hypothesis. At the centre of dramatizing lies the "as if": I act "as if" I am a dog, or a doctor, or a space traveller, and in a variety of possible dramatic forms from play to theatre. In each case I engage in practical and tacit hypothesis. But to work well, hypothesis must feel right.

The first segment of an ideal model of a player's intuitive cognitive processing appears below. It is based on observations of and information from a variety of players in diverse dramatic forms. It divides the player's preparation into a number of assumed questions. The specific circumstances of the model are arbitrarily chosen. A ten-year-old boy, in free improvisation with two other boys and three girls approximately the same age, decides to play the role of a policeman. In role he asks the following (assumed) questions:

What's he going to do in the play? What is his place in the plot?	*Dramatic task*
How will he do it? How will he execute his task?	*Dramatic action*
How does he normally move? What will his body movement be?	*Occupational movement*

What clothes does he wear?	
How will that affect his movement?	
How does he normally talk?	*Occupational speech*
What will he say?	
How will he say it?	
What sort of person is he?	*Dramatic character*
Is he good/bad/neither?	
Is he type A or type B?	
If I try it this way, what happens?	*Trying out/proto-*
If he is type A what happens?	*hypothesis*
If I try it that way, what happens?	*Trying out/proto-*
If he is type B what happens?	*hypothesis*

By early adolescence, students have moved to dramatic hypothesis proper: "If I hypothesize my role as type A, I will act in way X," and "If I hypothesize my role as type B, I will act in way Y." In fact, the player does not usually ask such questions explicitly, only tacitly and intuitively. The questions are in model form; in practice, teachers apply them to a specific dramatic context.

Trying out a dramatic hypothesis in practice is something a player does and not necessarily something he or she talks about. Our studies show that adolescents need plenty of experience in practical, dramatic hypothesis prior to working with scientific hypothesis, which Piaget says develops in adolescence. Without this experience, the learning of scientific hypothesis can be difficult.

CONCLUSION

Intuition is clearly related to dramatization. Both are grounded in identification and empathy, mutuality and dialogue, association and metaphor, feeling and choice. Where they differ is that, while dramatization is both conscious and unconscious, intuition remains entirely unconscious until it appears like a flash. Both are related to sense perception. We directly apprehend the environment before we frame perceptions in the context of already-held concepts. Intuition works similarly by bypassing the cognitive. The painter works in two ways: first cognitively, as he plans a picture, second intuitively, using his field of vision and his paint directly and without conscious thought. The painter flips between the two modes until both are satisfied and it feels right. He does not need an intellectual explanation of what he is doing; indeed, he is likely to resist it.

Intuition is direct understanding. Its aim is to grasp meaning at once.

It does so through moments of insight, seeing through the clutter of mental activity like a searchlight. This is what Einstein meant when he described his own intuition as a feeling of direction, of going straight towards something concrete. Intuition and insight are related to spontaneity, which as Moreno tells us is "the readiness to act."[14] Intuition brings moments of insight that are primarily mental; spontaneity moves these towards action, which is dramatic.

Professional actors and directors inform us that in the final analysis their major criterion for judgment is intuition. Directors asked why they chose a particular play, and actors asked why they played a role in a specific way, typically said, "Because it felt right," or "I just knew." Similarly, drama teachers who had meticulously prepared a lesson plan often deviated from it almost from the beginning of the class. Asked why they did so, they replied that they spontaneously adjusted to the needs of the students. Asked how they knew to do so, they attributed it to insight, "reading" the students' needs or simply "feeling" that the deviation was right. What, then, was the purpose of such a carefully prepared plan? One representative teacher said, "The plan goes on the back-burner. I use it as I need it, moment to moment – by intuition."

CHAPTER EIGHT

Drama and Symbol

It is commonly said that a major factor of intelligence is the growth of symbolic thought. What are symbols? What is symbolic thought and how is it different from metaphoric thought? What is the relation of symbolic thought to dramatic action?

THE NATURE OF SYMBOLS

I have previously examined the nature of symbols in *Play, Drama and Thought,* so here I will relate their nature to cognition and intelligence. Symbols are a cognitive tool: they amplify meaning; they signify various things at the same time; and moreover, they mean different things to different people. Although signs and symbols are similar, they are not synonymous. All signs are symbols, but not every symbol is a sign. In the classical world a symbol was seen as two sides of the same coin. Today, however, symbols are regarded as more open in meaning: where signs are "univocal", symbols are "multivocal."[1] Symbol and allegory have wider meanings than metaphor, for they can be interpreted both symbolically and literally. Allegories and parables are sustained narration interpreted through a fixed key of correspondences. A symbol is not necessarily part of sustained narration and can indeed disturb it. Aesthetic and artistic symbols, although both context-dependent, are not synonymous. Aesthetic symbols work in the mode of feeling, choice, and qualitative decisions, while artistic symbols are medium-dependent, that is they only have meaning in the context of the work of art.

Not everyone holds this view of symbols. Some see signs as a subclass of symbols that convey more meaning than signs,[2] but others view sign and symbol as virtually synonymous.[3] For Umberto Eco[4] and most moderns, the symbolic mode occurs when neither the sender nor the receiver wants a definite interpretation – when a diffuse and ambiguous meaning is needed. This view implies that a higher level of intelligence is required to deal with symbols than, say, with simple codes. Eco distinguishes symbols from simpler tropes (for example, diagrams, which are maps and formulae based on precise codes and rules) and the images of dreams, which Freud searched for "correct" interpretations.[5] Symbols, then, have wide significance. Being multivocal, not all their inherent meanings are understood at any one time. Moreover, symbolic representation is cultural and occurs in the aesthetic mode.

Such a vague cognitive tool requires a high level of intelligence for its manipulation. This has been the case from the earliest times. The most significant symbols have always contained multiple meanings of two major signifieds: peoples' beliefs about the divine, and the divine's relation to humanity. The meaning of these major symbols, however, has changed in different contexts over historic time. Consider, for example, the differing attitudes to divinity symbolized by paleolithic hunters, ancient Egyptians, Jews, Christians, Buddhists, Moslems, etc. These major symbols have given rise to lesser but still important symbols that have also changed through time. Thus in earlier societies each colour had its own symbolic meaning, for example, yellow, which in the time of Shakespeare symbolized aspects of indecency but which does not today.

In tribal cultures no single thing is symbolic of another thing. Each individual thing is symbolic of existence as a whole. Among the Indian tribes on the Pacific Northwest Coast, for example, the design on a blanket, the shape of a mask, and the performance of a dance all symbolize total human existence, but from different perspectives. For the earliest times, symbols dramatized existential ideas in such all-inclusive and performative ways. Thus the earliest Homo sapiens spread red ochre over graves. This act was a knowing that had at least three levels of meaning. First, the red ochre was a representation of blood. Second it was a metaphorization (myth) and dramatization (ritual) of the corpse "as if" it were alive. And third, the whole act was symbolic of life after death.

Today we continue to realize our intellectual potential through representation, myth, ritual, drama, metaphor, and symbol; they remain cognitive and social acts whereby we grasp ultimate meanings. Contemporary Christians place flowers on graves much like the ancient tribes they called pagan. People in Western civilizations continue to express their understanding of goodness and plenty at Christmas time when they, like the silent mummers of medieval times, place presents beside "the winter tree" ("the tree of life," an ancient shamanic concept). Also like the ancient tribes, contemporary shamanic cultures all over the world unite religious acts, performance, art, and economy in one ritual performance that symbolizes "first times,"[6] that mythical period when the world was created. In these symbolic performances the players know existence and the cosmos: The past is brought into the present to affect the future; time is collapsed, and everything is a symbolic whole in the "here and now." For example, the earliest hunting tribes symbolically re-played the seasons, the heavenly bodies, the times the bison rutted, the weather, and hunting in dance, drama, music, and visual art.[7] The continuous inheritance of this tradition can be seen today in Arizona and New Mexico among the ritual performances of Pueblo and Hopi Indians,[8] for whom the dramatic world is the only way to grasp reality.

The earliest agrarian cultures also understood the world cognitively through symbolic performance, but in a different way. The Mesopotamians became herders and farmers somewhere before 3,000 B.C., followed by those in India, China, America, and elsewhere. The storage of vast quantities of grain and food led to human specialization and categorical thought. This changed the form of symbolism.

In all the great early agricultural civilizations farmers made the old total tribal symbols into complex and hieratic symbolic systems structured around the life of the gods, which was the mirror image of life on earth. Despite differences between cultures, they all shared some common symbolic meanings. Thus the gods Osiris, Damuzzi, Tammuz, Adonis, and Krishna had their differences, but the ritual-myths built around them shared the basic symbolic theme of the death and resurrection of crops, seasons, stars, gods, and human beings. This theme was enacted in the "sacred marriage," the ritual battle, acts of initiation, the "scapegoat," etc. Yet each culture's enactment was unique: Symbols had different levels of meaning related to the individual fictional world of stars, gods, human beings, the dead, and spirits. Each culture, that is, created symbols with cultural meanings specific to its members. For example, while Sumerian vegetation ritual-myths focused on the death and resurrection of the goddess Inanna, Egyptian death and resurrection ritual-myths did not permit the god Osiris to be fully resurrected – he became Lord of the Dead and his son, Horus became the chief god. And it was through such performative symbols that each culture re-cognized all aspects of their lives.

Near Eastern myths were ritualized until the invention of writing at Ugarit, which enabled myths to be compared with "objective" history. Then they were found not to be "true." When Homer created his oral myths they had lost the power of ritual; tragedy re-ritualized them and they influenced all subsequent Western civilization. Writing brought about literary symbolism and the idea of the objectivity of symbols. Things began to change in the Roman period:

Principally during the Lower Roman Empire, when the cohesion of the classical world was beginning to dissolve, Hebraic, Chaldean, and Egyptian elements

> began to ferment. Dualist Manichaeism and Gnosticism began to threaten the position of early Christianity. Among the Gnostics, the emblem and the graphic symbol were used for the propagation of initiatory truths. Many of the innumerable images were not of their own creation but were compiled from various sources, mainly Semitic. Symbolism veers towards the Unitarian doctrine of reality and comes to be a specialist branch of speculation.[9]

The medieval Church reinterpreted the Bible symbolically. Intellectually the Old and New Testaments were seen as parallel: The OT was the signifier and the NT was the signified from which meaning had to be cognitively grasped. As Eco puts it, the OT speaks of the NT while the NT speaks of something else.[10] There were four symbolic meanings (the literal, allegorical, moral, and anagogical) that were thought to provide the correct decoding of the Bible, even as late as Dante.[11] Augustine, who approved of symbolism as a method of teaching and learning, advocated a knowledge of physics, geography, botany, and mineralogy, using classical knowledge as "a syncretistic encyclopedia."[12] But medieval symbolism eventually collapsed as a result of Aquinas' *Summae,* which dictated a strictly coded allegory for the Old Testament. This eroded the ambiguity of symbolism.

In the Renaissance there was a decreasing interest in symbolism and a growth in allegory. It was a great intellectual game in the court of Elizabeth I to discover the correct interpretation of allegory and emblems – a cognitive activity carried to its logical conclusion with the multifaceted allegories in the masques of Ben Jonson and Inigo Jones. From the time of Descartes and Newton, when the universe and human beings were symbolized as machines, binarism became a fundamental way of cognitive thought while science turned to the quantification of evidence and the analysis of parts. The symbol, separated from science, became the domain of the arts. Thus the West lost much of the unity that characterized the earlier symbolic tradition and that continued in the East.

For Kant and the Romantics, *symbol* was virtually synonymous with *works of art,* and the term *aesthetic* appeared for the first time. Now artistic symbols had a specific intellectual purpose, an indefinable meaning that communicated, it seemed, the fundamental issues of Nature "as a prophetic language whose hieroglyphics are beings and forms."[13] For Goethe, symbols influences mental operations: "Symbolisms transform the experience into an idea, and an idea into an image, so that the idea expressed by the image remains always active and unattainable and, even though expressed in all languages, remains unexpressible. Allegory transforms an experience into a concept and a concept into an image, but so that the concept remains always defined and expressible by the image."[14] The Romantics had to learn that aesthetic symbols conveyed two kinds of cognitive messages:[15] those coded in a structure, and those implied in synaesthesia, association, awareness, and aesthetic transcendence.[16] Thus the symbol was cognitively ambiguous, as it was for Hegel, who understood it to be an analogue of four kinds:[17] the symbol proper, or the significance; a mental concept distinct from any context; the aesthetic experience, or the mode in which the concept is expressed; and a form of the sensuous, or a representation.[18]

Traces of many of these earlier ideas about symbolism linger in the twentieth century, but there have also been significant new theories of symbolism. Classic psychoanalysis[19] linked symbol to dream, thus removing symbolism from the sole realm of art and returning it to mind as a whole. More contemporary is the work of Ricoeur,[20] who states that symbols are not a code but rather opaque analogies bound to language and culture; they allow us to understand our past unconscious and how we can cognitively grasp the future. Today it is generally held that an artist expressed a personal vision in vague symbols, usually without a preestablished code, and that the work of art is open because ambiguity attends all artistic languages. At a particular moment in time, anything can be a symbol. Thus "the symbol is... a textual modality, a way of producing and of interpreting the aspects of a text... It is a modality of textual use."[21] We have already seen that Heidegger, Gadamer, and others consider that play symbols have something in common with those of art, which child psychologists regard as fundamental to human learning. But an aesthetic symbol is also a quality of mind. How we use it indicates the style of our cognition. How well we do so shows the degree to which we are using our intellectual potential.

SYMBOLS AND QUATERNITIES

Amongst modern views of symbol the theories of Jung[22] have been highly influential. He accepted the necessary vagueness of a symbol as an analogy, making a comparison between expression and content. To this he added the collective unconscious, in which symbols express a deep, innate layer in the human psyche where content and action are similar for all people.[23] Although various scholars have rejected the collective unconscious as unproven, Jung's ideas about symbolism are widespread.

Importantly, Jung says that *symbols are at one and the same time both empty and full of meaning.* That is, symbols are fundamental structures empty of meaning until their creator fills them with content; only then do they become powerful. Created symbolic meanings are cultural forms of archetypes (archaic types, or universal images) that can be expressed in the symbols of myth, dream, vision, and art; many of Jung's studies, therefore, compare the symbols contained in these forms. They are not signs but genuine symbols with ambiguous and inexhaustible meanings. Put in theatrical terms, *Much Ado About Nothing, Tartuffe,* and *The Broken Jug* all contain fundamental symbolic structures that Shakespeare, Molière, and Heinrich von Kleist filled with unique meanings derived from both archetypes and cultural content. Similarly, when improvisers use symbols they are structural, cognitive forms that the players, responding to an audience, "fill up" with archetypal and cultural materials. The idea that creator and audience fill up artistic symbols with new meanings is a view tangentially related to deconstruction and the work of Bakhtin.

As we have already seen, inherent in dramatic acts are quaternities, among the most ancient of symbolic clusters. Everywhere they can be found in prehistoric illustrations expressing a tribal knowing of existence. We have seen that the fourfold system is closely related to metaphor, but symbolically it is circular and spiral in motion. It should come as no surprise that there is a high correlation between the concept of quaternities, the Jungian psychology of individuation, and aesthetic thought, action, and learning, particularly in the contemporary teaching of visual arts. Nor should it surprise us that Greimas' quaternities can plot the *transformations* of dramatic acts. While quaternity structures are tacitly inherent, in Jung's view, in the human psyche, the mode of thought that we in the West are most accustomed to using today is directed and linear thinking – thinking in words in logical sequence. But this is a relatively recent human acquisition: "The tremendous work of education which past centuries have devoted to directed thinking… has produced a readjustment of the human mind to which we owe our modern empiricism and technics. They are absolutely new developments in the history of the world and were unknown to earlier ages.[24] [This contrasts with the] spontaneous, imaginative, largely non-verbal and nonlogical processes which can be said to form the raw material of all creative activity."[25] The two styles parallel the convergent and divergent modes of modern educational psychology,[26] and the planning of the improvisers on the one hand and their freedom to create on the other. The two mental operations are not mutually exclusive. Quaternities, thus, occur in both.

Jung shows the direct connections between the quaternity system and symbolization and suggests that these are inherent in cognition and intelligence. The quaternity is a fundamental mental process that relates the self symbolically to the eternal problems of existence. Similarly, the traditional figure of Christ is synonymous with psychic manifestations of the self, and, universally, the mandala and other quaternity/circle symbols are motifs for ultimate wholeness, or God.[27] Jung proposes that "the one against three" is the quaternity within a mental structure acting as a catalyst in the unification process; or in alchemical terms that sparks the spagyric birth ... For in the One, is the One and yet not the One, it is simple and consists of the number four. When this is purified by the fire in the sun, the pure water comes forth, and, having returned to simplicity, it will show the adept the fulfilment of the mysteries."[28] Whereas metaphorically there are close links between four with five (the quincunx), Jung indicates that with symbols there is also a continual vacillation between four and three: We unconsciously tend to round off the Christian trinitarian formula of the godhead with a fourth element, which tends to be "feminine, dark, and even evil." This fourth element "has always existed in the realm of our religious representations, but it was separated from the image of God and became his counterpart, in the form of matter itself (or the lord of matter – i.e., the devil)."[29] In alchemy there are three as well as four procedures, and three as well as four colours; while there are always four elements, three of them are often grouped together with number four in a special position. In psychological terms this indicates that every conscious act is precipitated by a startling event. Ricoeur[30] suggests that parables teach by means of *jolting the imagination;* they disorientate before they reorientate. On the semiotic square of the dramatic metaphor (figure 3), it is the fourth position (as with the adverbial phrase) that brings creativity, that enables a new square to be formed. Similarly the improvisation leader provides "overload" to the players, who, jolted into a new plane, move the action forward.

For Jung, the circle is the symbol of wholeness and fourfoldness is the divine's way of surveying the circle. Brahma, standing on a huge lotus, turns his eyes to the four directions before his work of creation. This action not only parallels "the divine quaternity" of Christianity, it also reflects the same concept in the fourfold function of consciousness: thought, feeling, intuition, and sensation. This concept is followed by many in creative drama, specifically Brian Way. Brahma's action and the Christian quaternity are not just metaphors for the four qualities of consciousness; they are also symbols of the necessary integration of these four functions that human beings must strive for.[31] For the same reason, the four- or eight-rayed circle of mandalas and yantras symbolizes wholeness as such. Because the quaternity symbolizes the nature of consciousness it can have even more meaning than double similarity.

Though we do not have the space to examine quaternity symbols in tragedy and comedy, it should be pointed out that Jungians have shown Tibetan mandalas to be constructed with the use of directed fantasy, accompanied by masked dramatic rituals. Mandalas always have power, even those in European Christian art: "Some of the most splendid examples are the rose windows of the cathedrals. These are representations of the Self of man transposed onto the cosmic plane ... We may regard as mandalas the halos of Christ and the Christian saints in religious paintings. In many cases, the halo of Christ is alone divided into four, a significant allusion to his sufferings as the Son of Man and his death on the Cross, and at the same time a symbol of his differentiated wholeness."[32] All mandalas, like the sand paintings of the Hopi and Navaho, try to restore the harmony of the self and the cosmos. Mandalas give expression and form to something that does not yet exist; they demonstrate that something is like something else (metaphor), but they do not state what either thing might be. All quaternities are based on metaphors: They create double meanings and function in ways antithetical to the binary mode spoken of earlier. But a mandala goes beyond the quaternity/metaphor to create a symbol, and a symbol has multivocal meanings. Intellectually, a mandala is a symbolic tool that creates meaning but in a cognitive style different from that of linear thinking.

How far does this affect dramatization? The quaternity symbol in the mandala shape, as described by Aniela Jaffe, is dramatized as the plan of both secular and sacred buildings in nearly all civilizations. Furthermore, the founding of Rome was dramatized as having the power of the quaternity. Plutarch tells us that Etruscan experts instructed Romulus in the sacred rituals, to be used "as in the Mysteries." They dug a round pit (called *mundus,* which also meant "cosmos") for the symbolic offerings of the fruits of the earth. The pit linked the city to "the other reality" (the land of the dead and the ancestors, which like the Hopi *sipapu* was "the centre of the world"), and it was covered by a great "soul stone," which when removed allowed the spirits of the dead to emerge. Round the pit they drew the boundary of the city with a plough drawn by a bull and a cow, an ancient land ritual, while a ploughshare was carried over the threshold wherever a gate was planned (a ritual for centuries in later agrarian Europe). Thus Rome was both circular in shape and known as *urbs quadrata,* "the square city," because the circle was divided into four parts by two main north-south, east-west arteries that intersected at the *mundus* (the quincunx). Thus the city was symbolic of the mathematically insoluble problem of squaring the circle, which preoccupied the ancients and the alchemists. The mandala became a living and dramatic symbol in architecture through the dramatic transformation of the city into an ordered cosmos – a sacred place bound by its centre to the other world. The symbolic shape of Rome was the externalization of the dramatic world in architecture, that is, it expressed the way the Romans understood and intellectually controlled the external world. We should not dismiss this as simply an ancient and outworn form of magic. Rome became a model for many later towns and cities, including Washington, D.C.[33] These cities, dramatizations of the quaternity symbol in the mandala shape, demonstrate the practically of symbolism as an aspect of the human intellect.

FIGURES AS DRAMATIC SYMBOLS

How does symbol, expressed in dramatic action, reflect and improve cognition and intelligence? This issue is complex because, first, we must make a distinction between the intelligence of the players and the audience, and second, it is not always possible to separate signs, metaphors, and symbols in the dramatic process.

Signs, symbols, and similar figures operate the same way in dramatic action as in other media, although there are differences. A symbol represents something else, even when that something else is missing. Thus, even if Sandra is abroad, when we use the word *Sandra* we all know we are talking of that particular person. The word stands for that person; it symbolizes her. Whereas the word *Sandra* symbolizes her when she is abroad, dramatic acts symbolize for more, including whole aspects of the action that are symbolically off-stage. Attic tragedy gives us the classic instance of this. Because of the strict limitation on the number of actors, a Messenger brings news of off-stage events that carry various symbolic meanings. There are some dramatic symbols whose meanings cross cultures and that have deep human implications. Take, for example, placing the forefinger on the cheek and turning it. This is a common symbolic gesture in both the Near East and the Balkans, though it is empty of meaning: Each culture provides it with a unique meaning. The meaning conveyed by acts can include signs, metaphors, and/or symbols, but it is the meaning of symbolic acts that influences and shapes reality as we and others know it.

When these figures (signs, metaphors, symbols) are externalized through dramatic action, *each can be transformed into symbols.* This occurs in degrees of intensity from the least symbolically significant to the most. In theory at least, it is irrelevant which kind of figure is used; in dramatic action, a sign transformed into a symbol can be more significant than a dramatic symbol proper. In practice, however, symbols are usually more significant than other figures. In the film *Richard III,* for example, Olivier constantly surprises us by elevating a plain sign, usually physical – a small hand gesture, a look or the turn on a heel – into an extremely powerful symbol. The transformation of figures into symbols is an instance of *deixis,* the deliberate choice of the player (or, in the playhouse, the director) to point to a specific element in the performance, giving it more power than other elements. Such choices, like C.S. Peirce's indexical signs and their degrees of difference, are recognized cognitively (consciously or unconsciously). But *deixis* creates many problems for the observer: What is a highly significant symbol at one dramatic moment can become unimportant in the next. It is here that semiotics comes to our aid.

From a semiotic perspective of dramatic action, we need to know the generic nature of the signifier (is it a sign or a symbol?) as well as its relative importance in present action (is it symbolically significant at this moment?). These questions tax our intelligence variously: Some signs have a specific character at a particular moment in history; others change over time; still others are treated differently in the dramatic "here and now." For Hippocrates, a sign was a symptom while a word was a name; for Parmenides, a sign was evidence while a name was both reality and the concealing of reality. Aristotle distinguished symptom from sign and said that there were two kinds of sign, that providing evidence and that providing only probable correlation. We might agree with the highly complex semiotic system of the Stoics, claiming that signs and symbols were not direct evidence but rather inferences from dramatic statements that only emerged when signs and symbols were expressed. According to Augustine's remarkably modern view, signs and symbols were the genus of which expressions in media (drama, language, etc.) were species. Only in recent times has semiotics returned to this idea, considering inference (rather than simple equivalence) to be the process underlying figurative signs.[34] From a Peircean perspective, however, the sign/symbol is something that stands for something to somebody in some respect or capacity.[35]

Dictionaries show various common interpretations of symbol as being signs from which inferences can be made about what is latent; gestures intended to communicate; units of communication rather than of language; or signs that can be identified with the idea of the subject of the sign.[36] Other definitions, with which we would not agree, call dramatic symbols abstract formulae, or linguistic signs, or sequences of a performed speech act, or signifieds existing in the text.[37] This study follows the view of Eco that a figure is "not only something which stands for something else; it is also something that can and must be interpreted. The criterion of interpenetrability allows us to start from a given sign to cover, step by step, the whole universe of semiosis."[38]

The key question is not what the figure is in abstract, but *what it becomes in dramatic practice*. It may, perhaps, be startling at first blush to note that signs and other figures are not permanent, that drama creates them. The figures of dramatic action are in constant flux; they are not objects but dynamics. Metaphors, for example, change their nature under dramatic conditions. In the script, Ben Jonson's character Volpone is a metaphor of a fox: He is a false shape-changer who acts "as if" he is a fox. But Jonson knew, as do all good dramatists, that when the character is given flesh and blood by a player and appears on the stage in the context of other players, his nature changes. When Volpone is played in the "here and now" the player *is* a fox – a symbolic fox with dimensions unrealizable in a mere reading of the script. In this particular dramatic process, metaphor has become symbol.

CODES AS DRAMATIC SYMBOLS

Most dramatic actions are not codes, but some are. The most obvious are charades and various other mime activities where we agree that *this* action stands for *that* meaning in all instances. With codes, a convention is created. In theatre some symbols have such a direct relation to their referent as to be almost codes. For example, as the curtain rose on John Gielgud's *Cherry Orchard* there was no one on stage, but the door was open and after a pause dry leaves blew in from outside. This was not a code, but it nearly was. It was almost a sign for a stock response.

Codes are commonly thought to be one-to-one relationship, one sign equivalent to another sign. But we have many variations. For Aristotle, there were strong and weak codes – a diagnostic sign (for example, birth is linked to intercourse) and a prognostic sign (a wound is linked to death). Signs were also linked to the concept of cause and effect; a necessary cause (for example, oxygen is a necessary cause for combustion) applied to all cases, while a sufficient cause (striking a match for combustion) did not. In dictionaries and common parlance, types of code include the referenced, which tells something else; the institutional, which refers to a body of laws; and the correlational, which refers to a specific system such as the Morse code. In contemporary semiotics the term *code* is understood as one of two systems of communication: that which transfers information between two systems,[39] and that which provides a formal correspondence betwen two systems.[40] For Eco these two systems, being complementary, are relatively useful.[41] There are dramatic examples of both, but in all instances they relate to a specific action in a particular context.

Most interestingly, there are many instances of codes transformed into symbols by dramatic acts. Examples of the transformation of all the above usages for codes can be found in a specific case of improvisation, as follows:

Creative drama class (31 boys and girls, grade 4, 9 years old), Adelaide, Australia, 1979, 1 hour

The main block of time (45 minutes) was spent in the preparation and performance of improvisations (in 5 groups) of the first white people setting off from Adelaide and traveling inland across the desert, where they met some aboriginals for the first time The players were to experience dramatically what it was like to:

- live in Adelaide at that time;
- travel across the desert;
- be white people meeting aboriginals for the first time;
- be aboriginals meeting white people for the first time;
- find possible solutions to the meeting.

During the improvisations, among the many individual dramatic acts the following were observed:

- The white settlers could find no work in Adelaide because they were ex-convicts *(diagnostic sign).*
- One died of thirst in the desert *(prognostic sign).*
- The travellers had to hunt, kill, and eat a kangaroo in order to survive *(necessary cause).*
- One group shed clothes to survive the heat *(sufficient cause).*
- One group of aboriginals spoke their own language, which the white people did not understand *(referenced code).*
- Another group of aboriginals shared what little food they had with the white people because that was what they did in their society *(institutional code).*
- Some aboriginals used sign language *(correlational code).*
- Whites and aboriginals made various attempts to communicate which each other using varieties of mime *(communication system that transfers information between two systems).*

In each of the above cases, the dramatic meaning conveyed by the code was not strictly that of a code (sign 1 = sign 2) but had been transformed into the symbolic mode; that is, it conveyed a complex of meanings and appeared to have significance. Each meaning contrasted with codes that were not transformed dramatically, like those of information theory where there is a sharp distinction between the meaning of a message on the one hand and information (as the statistical measure of the equal probability of events at the source) on the other.[42] The concern of the information theorist is not with meaning but rather with the most economic way of sending a message without ambiguity.[43]

TRANSFORMATION AND MEANING

It is the nature of dramatic action that it bestows symbolic meaning on any linguistic or other item that might or might not be symbolic in another form. This was acknowledged in the Russian and Prague schools of semiotics earlier in the twentieth century, and not only in terms of figures. For example, Petr Bogatyrev showed that the theatre radically transforms all objects and bodies within it and bestows upon them a signifying power which, in other circumstances, they lack.[44] Jiri Veltruvsky said, "All that is on the stage is a sign."[45] In other words, theatre demonstrates a transformative power whereby it can create symbols for any specific enactment.

Not only in theatre but also in other forms of dramtic action, such transformation is subject to the conditions of significance, context, interpretation, inference, ambiguity, and Being. In a general sense, all that is played is symbolic: The total dramatic action, from beginning to end, is certainly deliberate. From the myriad elements of the actual world, aspects are chosen to be transformed into the dramatic event – aspects that must have potential for significance in order to be chosen. In theatre, these aspects are the subject of much reflection before they are finally chosen, for example, in the dramatist's rewriting and rehearsals. But in improvisational forms less time is available for reflection, and many symbols are spontaneously created in the "here and now." The value placed on the degree of significance depends the social and cultural context, the nature and genre of the dramatic act, and the intention of the players (or the players and audience).

A symbol has no meaning without a context. In life, a flag elicits feelings of patriotism only when it represents a country. A culture structures a symbol so that people share it; yet, at the same time, individuals contribute to it, maintain, communicate, and change it. As we live through dramatic action, symbols can be difficult to recognize consciously. The dramatic context in particular is fleeting – undergoing continuous change in action and story line because it exists primarily in time. Additionally, in all and any circumstances, a received meaning is not always the same as an intended meaning. In dramatic events this problem is particularly acute when so much of what is played is significant and therefore ambiguous. The clearer and more precise a meaning, the less ambiguous it is, and the more significant the meaning, the more it is ambiguous. Drama, whose creators intend it to be highly significant, is also therefore highly ambiguous. The dramatic is not only inherently symbolic but also inherently ambiguous.

This can be understood most simply in terms of theatre. When Bernard Shaw said that the greatest plays of humanity were Sophocles' *Oedipus Rex,* Shakespeare's *Hamlet,* and Pirandello's *Six Characters in Search of an Author,* he was describing three scripts which, because of their high degree of complexity and ambiguity, have been constantly reinterpreted. We need only think of the many Hamlets – Gielgud's, Olivier's, Redgrave's – all of which were different, and different from any others performed in that generation. In other words, no two performances of *Hamlet* are the same.

If for no other reason than dramatic ambiguity, therefore, the most appropriate method for critics and researchers in describing, analysing, and interpreting dramatic data is perspectival and, thereafter, comparative. The symbolic meaning of dramatic action varies in each instance, so how can we capture the essence of any given performance except in a perspectival way? We understand symbolic meaning through inference. Inference leads us to create meanings beyond the original sign; thus the word *father* (signifier) implies, among other things, both *child* and *mother* (signifieds). An act (signifier) is also that from which we infer the player's cognition and intelligence (signifieds). Yet, although some inferences are similar to those of the intended expression, others are different. Thus: "The sign is the instrument through which we are constantly made and remade... It tells us who we are and what (or how) we think."[46] This also applies to artistic signs. A painting is a sign containing other signs, each of which can be interpreted similarly to or differently from the intended expression; the painting does not have the meaning "in it." The artist creates meaning 1 when he paints; a viewer creates meaning 2 when he observes, another viewer creates meaning 3. The fact that in many cases a gap exists between different symbolic meanings is to be expected, for "the medium is the message." Theatre is more complex than painting, not a static entity but a process giving out symbolic meanings as we live through it. Some of those meanings we catch, some we do not. When we make inferences about the symbolism of theatre and other dramatic actions, therefore, we are dealing with an issue of the utmost complexity, and we must acknowledge that our data represents one specific perspective. If we apply cognitive reasoning to the data, therefore, we must ensure that it has logical and intellectual rigour (see chapter 6).

Symbolic meaning in dramatic acts is imprecise and multifaceted. It contrasts with abstract meaning, which can be precise. Drama provides meaning in a way similar to life, for we live through the dramatic experience in the "here and now." People in the actual world and living personages in the dramatic world understand and work in a particular milieu, perceiving themselves in, and reacting to, that environment.

They do so in the mode of time and, in terms of what they do, persons are *actualizing,* players are *virtualizing,* and both are *realizing.* But where dramatic events are highly symbolic because people have made them so, life actions are not. As we have seen in the case of *Volpone,* dramatic symbolism carries many meanings: We in the audience witness the player as a metaphor of a fox and the personage as a symbol of a fox at one and the same time.

Symbolic meaning in dramatic events derives from the major questions of human existence with which drama deals: Who am I? Who am I for other people? In early tribal cultures, "whole symbols" were concerned with the issues of the greatest concern to Being – life and death, marriage and birth, and the relation of humanity to the divine. But as Bakhtin has shown,[47] the development of civilizations increased differentiation not only of occupations, economics and the like but also of forms of symbolization. Contemporary symbols, as a result, are highly fragmented. Even so, they indirectly convey similar existential meanings. Highly significant to the dramatic representation of Being is the fiduciary contract, the assumed contract of trust between two players (see p. 32). A player projecting a dramatic world (a fiction with its fictional objects) outside the self effectively sets in motion intersubjective behaviour; the fiduciary contract, however, procedes the intersubjective relation. Dramatic symbolism derives from the contract. Establishing it is a matter of confidence in others, in oneself, in both. Confidence may be well grounded in the self or it may not; and it may be either spontaneous or based on repeated experience, but whichever is the case, it is the foundation of dramatic symbolism[48]

FACTORS OF SOCIALIZATION

The capacity to understand symbolic meaning develops with maturation, as continuous observation of dramatic activity with children and students reveals. The baby works with icons, or undifferentiated double meanings. These are protosigns and protosymbols, that is, partially formed significations primarily understood through emotional and feeling states. Signs, metaphors, and symbols emerge from icons and develop in many ways according to the individual and the culture. In Western societies, they are normally begun unconsciously at birth, and deliberately by the end of the first year. They are usually well established by adolescence. From preadolescent learnings of concrete signs, metaphors, and symbols, children begin to experiment with abstract signs and codes. The adolescent learns abstract signs (algebra, etc.) that are languages of complex abstract systems, or games. Thus the student learns the many ambiguities of dramatic symbolization progressively.

Symbols contain three simultaneous meanings: that of the player, "the personal, subjective relevance and internalized normative value";[49] that moulded and communicated by media (for example, by the costumed player communicating with others); and that of culture itself. Their unity creates "a communication currency."[50] Social symbols like the cross or the swastika have quite simple forms and communicate with great economy and generalizing power. Yet they are also multivocal and complex in what they convey. They synthesize many meanings and collapse them into rich clusters from which we construct reality, both our fictional worlds and our social worlds.[51] We construct reality from an aesthetic quality of likeness (similarity) between symbolic form and its meanings, and from a felt objective quality – the shared cultural code that gives external existence to symbolic meaning.[52] For many modern anthropologists, when symbolic meanings are communicated they are polarized into the conceptual versus the experiential,[53] or the normative versus the affective.[54] When the normative and conceptual become dramatic symbols, they contain organizational and moral meanings and principles groups together as ideologies (world views).[55] But when the sensory and affective are dramatic symbols, they contain physiological and biological meanings; then norms and values are highly emotional and thereby ennobled. Symbolic meanings of these two kinds appear to be autonomous and objective, but for adequate societal development, the interchange between symbolic poles must be balanced. Although we may find such symbols in spontaneous dramatic forms, any major theatrical play contains all of them, appropriately balanced.

Collective symbols, with their assumed objective quality, provide social information, knowledge, or ideas as feedback to the mind. Although social symbols are empty and we fill them with meaning, *once they return to the mind, they are established as mental entities and become highly active.*

This is how we normally meet them in dramatic action. Active symbols act on their own. They are not preprogrammed. Rather, they float freely in the mind, one cluster linking with a second and then, at another time, with a third. Symbolic cognition (in the limited sense) appears to be the result of deep inner processes that are less rational than irrational, intuitive, and even paradoxical. We can infer this from spontaneous improvisation. However well the players plan, in the process of acting together they "spark off" each other spontaneously, introducing active symbolic meanings they have not prepared for; one symbolic cluster activates another within the action. The connection, or link, is often parallel: One symbol set elicits a second by an element similar to an element in the second. Our real intellectual power is that we use symbolic clusters to dramatize a variety of plausible futures.

CONCLUSION

Dramatic symbols belong to a network of correlations between two levels of signifying reality, the actual and the fictional. The actual world of common sense is made up of mobile and immobile objects. This allows us a posteriori to establish equivalences between things on the one hand, and between signs that refer back to things other than themselves on the other hand. This relation of reference can be articulated in a variety of ways, one of which is dramatic. In abstract, the referential relation is obtained by two reductions: first, the reduction of all occurrences (of, say, the dramatic context of master/slave) to an invariant or prototypical one; and second, the reduction, or bracketing off, of all ancillary functions of the context. Such reduction results in an abstract dramatic figure, one of many that make up a corpus of dramatic signs. Each figure becomes special in a particular way; that is, dramatic action has elevated it to symbolic status.

In dramatic acts symbols become felt realities – fictional entities of significance in the players' doing and Being. Symbols then become cognitive elements available to our intellectual potential. Whether we fulfil this potential or not depends on the quality of our performance, which is the subject of the next chapter.

CHAPTER NINE

Drama and Performance

The issues we have discussed so far in this book can be reframed in terms of human performance to provide us with a new cognitive perspective. Performance can range from the informal and spontaneous, as in dramatic play or happenings on the one hand, to formal and carefully prepared actions, as in ritual and theatre on the other. These are general categories; many activities fall somewhere in between them. What kinds of cognition and intelligence do these categories reveal?

DRAMATIC AXIOMS

Practical dramatic actions in informal and formal performances share some uses of intelligence but not all. The dramatic is the aesthetic genus of which theatre is the artistic species. All artistic performances are aesthetic, but not all aesthetic activities are artistic. At the level of surface meaning there is a continuum from drama to theatre, but not all differences are precise. For example, the drama of improvisation can be directed to an imagined audience. At the level of deeper meaning, there are further differences of considerable importance to the development of intelligence.

1 *Performance is primarily aesthetic.* Aesthetic thinking is a tendency of thought as a whole. There are aesthetic qualities to all thought, just as there are cognitive, affective, and psychomotor qualities. Though some behaviourists would disagree, no thought is purely cognitive, affective, aesthetic, or psychomotor. In practical and creative workshops, for example, "1 + 1 = 2" can be the first line of a poem. Feeling is holistic and impinges on other domains: It relates to the affective in that emotions are total and immediate (aesthetic feelings are discriminatory); it is cognitive because it provides tacit

knowing; and it is the basis of moral judgment and personal choice. Feeling is different from emotion, although the two overlap. Its cognitive aspect is "the intelligence of feeling,"[1] which approaches the core of consciousness in the form of a performative response to an external or internal stimulus. In addition, there are some thoughts in which the aesthetic is the predominant mode. Aesthetic thought is clustered around imagining and feeling, choice and judgment, metaphor and symbol. But feeling is what forms the ground of aesthetic thought. A personally embodied experience feels "good" and "appropriate" in performance. Through feeling one relates to "the inside" of another's performance. Then there is "a feeling *for*," a response that develops from, and is closely akin to, identification and empathy. It relates to what we value and how we value it. Performance is discriminatory: We come to value *this* rather than *that* and, eventually, to distinguish what we like from what we appreciate. It has to do with intelligence – the understanding of the self, and the understanding of the self in relation to others. Performance is deeply involved in the creation of both personal and social worlds. It is always dramatic, often liminal, and mostly tacit. It is aesthetic. Moving from self-presentation to the presentation of self in role, the performer centers on fundamental questions of Being: What is the meaning of life and death? Who am I? Dramatic action links feeling to knowledge and belief. It creates tacit knowing. Although it is unnecessary for mind to know *how* tacit knowing occurs, it is necessary to know *that* it happens, because this is what leads to an increased control over feeling.

2 *Performative thought and action are imaginative.* Aesthetic thinking works with the imaginative "as if" and thereby has an inherently dramatic character. Our thoughts project out from the self to become dramatic acts in performance, impersonation, social drama, and ritual (specifically, in play, creativity, liminal periods, ceremony, festivity, learning, and art). Performance is what imaginatively created the ancient labyrinths as metaphoric models (signifiers) of the polydimensional meanings of death and resurrection (signifieds). Similarly, the pavement and turf mazes of medieval and Renaissance times dramatized aesthetic fictions revealing the paradox of the seeming simultaneity of life and death. Imagining is the state of Being where images interconnect to conceive possibility, to order situations so that inquiry can begin, and to comprehend the dynamic relationships between two concepts. Human performance develops from the imaginative ability to see things from another's point of view. It involves the "as if," allowing us to create the double of reality and to relate subject and object. As performance is based on imaginative possibility, its cognitive aspects cluster around trial and error, hypothesis, and informed

guessing of all types. It hinges on our ability to choose – to make judgments of all kinds – during performance. Do we make appropriate judgments as we live through our experience in the "here and now"? Freedom within cultural limits is implied. We impose order on the chaos of the environment when we operate through the double and create mental worlds. Mind dramatizes the actual in order to create the fiction of the dramatic world, the basis of human performance.

3 *Performative thinking and action are metaphoric.* Metaphorization *is* consciousness. Metaphor as a double notion originates in our earliest differentiations between self/not-self, here/there, this/that, inside/outside, subjective/objective, whole/part. Its proto-symbols (icons) create parallels between two parts: percept/image, actual/fictional, etc. Icons lead to fundamental structures: polarity, similarity/difference, etc. From these origins is created the thought structure of metaphor, two concepts in one notion, that can be viewed separately and/or together. Thought oscillates between the double meaning. Metaphoric thoughts are linked by four forms of association: similarity, opposition, contiguity, and differentiation – the metaphoric quaternities of the semiotic square, which also relate to the axiological bases of performance and the tacit bases of belief.

4 *Performative thinking and action are creative.* The metaphorical thought, a leap of creativity, propels dramatic action into performance. We play and re-play with mental relations, and in turn, we are played by them. The creative leap takes place between one logical class and another (dogs/animals), or from the "negation of a negation." It is open-ended and the source of creativity. It generates another structure and is capable of virtually unlimited variety. Performative creativity functions like adverbs in linguistic constructions, or like "knight's move thinking," bringing about dramatic transformation; freedom is a quality of aesthetic creation. The dramatic metaphor has ontological meaning that provides us with cognitive frameworks, for example, Descartes' view of people and life as a machine, and the *Theatrum Mundi*'s view of the world and life as a theatre. In performance these are active "root metaphors," lenses through which we examine human performance. As metaphor and drama vary from culture to culture, so do performances and the realities they define.

5 *Performative actions are symbolic and vary according to culture.* When we think and act we use symbols with multifaceted, imprecise, ambiguous, and even paradoxical meanings. Symbols are structured by society, they integrate cultural meanings, and they are vital to social and cultural learning. All key symbols are understood intuitively, they are grounded in feeling, and they signify feeling states that may not be fully explicable in words. Key symbols, which condense experience,

are summary notions that affect cognition and intelligence. They allow us to develop and elaborate concepts and ideas in new and creative performances. Symbols used in dramatic action have various effects. They develop the concept of the self – a personal self and a series of social or performative selves ("the mask and the face"). These concepts enable us to perform in dramatic relation to other selves symbolically, and they affect our memories by supplying feelings that are easily recalled; they tacitly reveal and clarify reality; they structure imaginings and the way we act; and they provide a societal framework in which performatives can work. They are closely tied to all forms of tacit and personal knowledge and, performed in our social dramas, they create a social world. The power of symbolic thought lies in two things, its existential meaning and its ambiguity. Symbols give a deep existential quality to aesthetic thought and the performances that thought generates. In early cultures, symbols clustered around life, death, marriage, birth, and the relation of humanity to the divine; contemporary symbols may be more complex and fragmented, but indirectly they convey similar types of meanings. The ambiguity of symbols gives them considerable ideological and performative power, and they are liable to underpin belief systems.

6 *Performative thought and action are basic to knowing and cognition.* Drama provides the player with more tacit than explicit knowledge, and the audience with more showing than telling. It is a kind of knowing we perform rather than a knowing ABOUT. Performances are "re-experiences"; when we re-play original experiences they become signs that, in referring to and illustrating other signs, are part of an indefinite and ongoing knowing. Sensory experience is condensed (abstracted) to fit an unconscious structural grid that provides a filter. By interacting with the environment in performance, we create a tacit hypothesis about the world, adjust subsequent performances to fit this hypothesis, and gain implicit knowledge. Re-play is recognition. Tacit knowing has to do with each person's intention, needs, logic, world view, language, and culture, all of which are in a state of continual change. Performance does not, therefore, provide absolute truths. The kind of knowing it teaches is prior to knowing ABOUT, or discursive knowledge. Some knowledge mixes both styles: in experience we gain tacit knowing, but on reflection we gain discursive knowledge that requires a foundation of tacit knowing. Tacit knowing exists in time, in the living performance, in the "now." Discursive knowledge exists in space, through speaking and writing; it is fixed in an abstract "then." We can map dramatic knowing as a quaternity of tacit/discursive and actual/fictional. In performance, much of our cognitive activity is tacit and fictional as it oscillates between simi-

larities (whole/part) in what Derrida has called "trace" – the energetic quincunx between quaternities. Similarly, holistic knowing comes through the trace that lies between actual/fictional and between digital/whole part.[2] Such knowing provides the intuitive foundation for ontological and epistemological thinking.

7 *Performative action provides the foundation for belief.* The fundamental tacit understanding of who we are (being/seeming) and of feeling (good/bad) is "the deep structure" (fundamental semantics) of belief. Fundamental semantics are projected upon various aspects of human experience (narrative semantics) by performance. At the practical level of belief (discursive semantics) projections are made actual in terms of themes (practical beliefs) and their manifestation in figures, or persons. Through these manifestations the believer acts "as if" the belief is true. Then the fundamental quaternity of being/nonbeing and seeming/nonseeming becomes the discursive quaternity of truth/falsity and simulation/dissimulation.

THEATRE AXIOMS

Artistic performances are a small but vital part of dramatic activity. They are like the tip of the iceberg; they codify dramatic meanings in artistic form and thereby heighten specific meanings.

1 *Theatrical action is a particular mode of dramatic performance.* There is a difference between creating and appreciating theatre. Artistic thought is expressed in performance, in the practical and concrete experience of creating theatre. Performance is a particular mode of dramatization dominated by imagining and feeling, while also clustered around choice and judgment, metaphor and symbol. It is dramatic in that it projects the self into the work and tries to view that work from the inside, providing tacit, metaphoric, symbolic, and artistic knowledge. In contrast, discussions about theatrical performance take place in a metalanguage and are logical. They become increasingly abstract and explicit, condensing the mental structures upon which they are based. However, unconscious homologies function as tacit beliefs. The knowledge that discussion provides may be aesthetic, but it is equally cognitive, linguistic, and logical.

2 *Action in theatre constitutes a specific sign system.* Any art form, like any language, is a unique sign system that mediates between the self and the environment.[3] Theatrical performance creates and operates a sign system that presupposes dramatic thinking. It is, however, excessively complex. Even Aristotle was forced to regard theatrical performance as "a mixed form" based on literature, an idea that

influenced criticism for generations. Here it is viewed as a single, unified form, the art form of the life process.[4] There are differences, however, between the meanings given by the performing artist, the work, and the critic. The artist and the critic both use logic, but in different ways. The performer expresses and endows imagining and feeling with homologous, unconscious, paralinguistic, and cultural meanings, in concrete situations using a theatrical medium. To the critic, the meaning of theatre lies in our feeling-response to it; yet theatre as performance also carries a world view that is largely implicit. The critic engages in explanatory thinking, presents alternative thoughts, views, or propositions, and juxtaposes two or more messages about the performance.

3 *Thought and action in theatre are metaphoric in their structure.* Theatre performance is an external representation of the dramatic metaphor, and like any other art form, it brings about a self-contained and self-sustaining world. A world is born with each individual theatrical event. An art work is the signifier, its metaphors are the signified; a theatrical performance centers on the existential metaphor of being/seeming in the "here and now." To the audience, the creation of an artistic world is a powerful metaphor of existence, a root metaphor.

4 *Theatre performance becomes symbolic in action.* Dramatic action manipulates, examines, and organizes metaphoric thought into the socially symbolic. Theatre performances, like all works of art, are complex symbol systems and operate as representations of thought that permit the clarification, systemization, and comprehension of events. Symbolic meaning not only elaborates the performer's perceptual knowledge but also constructs autonomous symbolic representations. Theatrical images and symbols exist at a deep level and are related to a performance's surface structure in a homologous manner.

5 *Performative thought varies with the medium used.* There is a difference in creating works of art according to whether they exist primarily in time or in space. Speech and the arts of performance emphasize time, process, the whole, the less discrete, and the more complex. In contrast, writing and the static arts (painting, sculpture, architecture, etc.) tend to emphasize space, boundaries, categories, distinctions, and classes. The temporal arts are nearer to Being than the spatial arts. Theatre focuses on the performer as the costumed player in the "here and now" – as near as representation can get to Being. Other performative styles, like dance and music, are variants of theatre. Thinking, discussing, and writing about the arts are at a different level from performance. Creating art is generally nondis-

cursive and holistic. To criticize the arts, however, is to function in a metalanguage that is more analytical and objective.

6 *Theatre activates knowledge, cognition, and intelligence.* The tacit knowing that results from aesthetic thought is also basic to theatrical performance. Artistic intelligence is represented by the degree of skill in an artistic medium. Performative intelligence is a form of practical knowledge, or "know how." The skills of great artists are largely tacit – "they do it without thinking." These tacit skills vary with the medium used: In theatre and the performing arts they are mainly performative and temporal; in the visual arts and architecture they are spatial; and in some arts (film, television, multimedia, etc.) they can be both. There is a quaternity of knowledge functions in performance: expression (creator) versus connation (addressee), and representation (content) versus aesthetic (the feeling message). Conceived as an aesthetic object, a performative work of art operates at the "trace," or quincunx: It oscillates *between* the subjectivities of all involved. Theatrical performance brings a multivalent knowing. It tends to stress symbolic thought of two kinds. First, each performance contains a symbolic quaternity of artistic knowings (signifier-signified/creator-perceiver) and two styles of meaning (part/whole). Although the symbolism of performative knowing is culture-bound, the signifier/signified relationship can be freely changed by the creative artist. Second, in performance there are also secondary and specific kinds of knowing. For example, theatrical symbols provide selection, polysemy, self-reference, social reference, and subjective/objective variations. But these are closely related to performative social knowing. For instance, *deixis* is a key factor in the audience's knowing that results from both theatrical and social interaction in any culture. In other words, there is a continuity in dramatic and performative ways of knowing.

PERFORMANCE

We have probed the question, What kinds of intelligence are revealed by informal, as compared to formal, performances? Both are types of mediation: The child uses play as a medium, just as the adult uses dramatic performance in life and theatre. Do their characteristics as media affect our cognition and intelligence?

In semiotic terms, aesthetic mediation is a relationship between signifieds. Artistic mediation, however, is a relationship between signifier and signified. We must distinguish between the two. The word *medium* is used in two ways. First, in aesthetic terms, it denotes that which relates inner/outer, consciousness/the world. Mind interacts with the world through mediation. Interaction evolves from the use of "mediate objects"[5] through play to the arts. Like mental structures, meaning, and learning, aesthetic mediation moves progressively from relative simplicity to complexity. Second, in artistic terms, a medium refers in a commonplace way to the materials of the form – paint and stone for visual art, sound for music, etc. Yet, at the same time, artistic media can be viewed as aesthetic media. For example, while paint is a physical medium, philosophically it relates inner and outer. In both types of medium progression, or learning, centres on the medium itself. In play, we learn about the medium in two ways, as a double relation. First we learn the aesthetic qualities of media as (a) our inner feeling-response to the medium, which is a relationship that must primarily satisfy the self; and (b) the meaning we receive from the work of art in the feeling-response and which we incorporate. Second we learn about the nature of media themselves – in the arts, how to manipulate media (paint and stone in visual art, or the inner workings of performance in theatre), and the *how* and *what* of all media, artistic or not.

But our cognitive attempts to improve intelligence are not simple. The meanings inherent in media are multivocal, and we learn the ambiguities and paradoxes inherent in aesthetic relationships. Both feeling-responses [(a) and (b) above] exist seemingly at the same time, while in addition, a work of art can exist both physically and conceptually as an art object. Thus, for example, as a member of an audience I may have a positive feeling-response to the theatrical medium but a negative response to this particular production, even though it is mounted beautifully and has been critically acclaimed. All works of art are different, yet they share aesthetic qualities; and the resulting oscillation between difference and similarity leads us to expect the unexpected, a metaphorical meaning. I may find the plays of, say, Harold Pinter difficult in the playhouse (perhaps their differences are outweighed, at least in my mind, by their remarkable similarities); yet I continually expect something else to happen. With increasing awareness of aesthetic media we grow more critical, while at the same time our philosophic assumptions become contradictory. For example, with increasing experience of educational drama I discover I can understand student improvisation better, but I also find that actions which ten years ago I thought were highly original are not all that original. Meanwhile I move from idealist assumptions to relative ones. What is the connection between the two events?

There is an irreconcilable tension between pervasive aesthetic qualities of art (the so-called universals) and the fact that my appreciation is a question of free judgment. This may lead me to irreconcilable dichotomies. For example, I may believe that art concerns itself with the beautiful and yet be fascinated by a production of Gorky's *The Lower Depths*, which is ugly, sordid, and in places, revolting. While art in oral cultures mirrors the spiritual world, in literate cultures it both mirrors and contradicts the natural world. Take another example: I may well be puzzled by the similarities and contradictions between two performances in British Columbia: possessed Indians dancing in a longhouse on a Saturday night, and on Sunday, a professional production of Wilde's *The Importance of Being Earnest* in a playhouse. While art works are the result of artists' invention and originality, no thought is ever entirely new,[6] and the knowledge carried by signs is always dependent upon prior knowledge.[7] Thus Stanislavsky's naturalism, thought revolutionary in its time, can be traced back at least to the Saxe-Meiningen company and, perhaps, to Tom Robertson; and Brecht's epic theatre, also considered revolutionary, derived from the experimental theatre of Erwin Piscator and others earlier in the twentieth century and, perhaps, from Shakespeare's *Henry V*.

Ability to work with paradox is one sign of intelligence. The reader of a novel, the viewer of visual art, and the audience member all learn over time, that what they are doing is paradoxical. But aesthetical awareness is a particular case of general awareness: "Consciousness is consciousness of nothing outside its interaction, past or present, with the context of the physical world. It is an error, then, to talk of the interaction of two 'substances': consciousness and the physical world, or mind and body. We must, in contrast, distinguish between two different forms of interacting states."[8] Our minds learn to interact with the environment by means of feedback channels: "What is transmitted around the circuit is transforms of differences," as Gregory Bateson put it.[9] Yet "difference," Merrell shows,[10] lies in the medium, not the message. We learn to *appreciate* art as media through cultural norms, and through the increased awareness of difference interactions. Reading a novel, for example, involves constant oscillation between the reader and the text ("the willing suspension of disbelief"), the cultural worlds of both the reader and the novel, and the linguistic units and the whole work, etc. We learn to deal with oscillation. A reader who appreciates a novel learns that his reading involves both identifying with and standing apart from the novel; he or she can then perceive the oscillation process from the larger context of comparative differences. In terms of media, we improve our cognitive abilities and intelligence through performance – through interacting with connected sign systems that are capable of continuously developing meaning, of constantly revealing new problem situations and inconsistencies. In the final analysis, the human quest for meaning is an unending performance.[11] Nowhere is this more evident than in dramatic action, where the illusion within the illusion (the play within the play) provides a myriad of meanings, actual, metaphorical, and symbolic.

Is there such a thing as performance logic? We use logic to make judgments about playing and performance. In drama, as we have seen, we use two kinds of logic: experiential logic, exercised as we live through the dramatic experience, and if we are members of an audience, exterior logic. In a general sense, all performers and audiences use these two kinds of logic. There is a particular quality to modern logic that affects our judgments, for we incorporate into them our inherent beliefs and assumptions about life and human beings. Our judgments bring a specific perspective, even a unique flavour, to our use of logic. This is understandable when the model for meaning is a labyrinth-net-rhizome, and when there are moral and interpretative reasons as well as inductive and deductive ones. Indeed, the pictures presented of human performance by, say, the psychology of B.F. Skinner and Abraham Maslow[12] could almost be pictures of different species.

While the pictures presented of theatrical performance are not so extreme, the basic assumptions of, say, Stanislavsky and Brecht[13] are far apart from one another. Indeed, a plurality of theatrical forms exists at the end of the twentieth century, each form with its own inherent logic. The situation is similar with other forms of dramatic action. In educational drama, for example, the differences between the theories of Brian Way and Gavin Bolton are well documented.[14] Professionals in various dramatic fields must be cognitively aware of these differences and the logic used to justify them. Under such circumstances, they must also be clear about what the logic is being used for. Essentially, they use reason to understand the whole complex of players' performances, but in terms of three elements: Being, knowing, and doing. Human ontology and epistemology are created in dramatic acts and form the ground for intelligence.

But the concept of Being has been treated in a variety of ways. Much depends on what we are talking about. Here, Being includes both consciousness and reflexivity (self-consciousness). It means both *what we do* and *what we talk about* when we are concerned with the self; it is the "I am" related to the world. It is encapsulated in the theatrical vaunt. For some, Being is soul. Mind is how we think: It includes the total physical self (the body) as a sign or metaphor, and refers to cognitive, affective, aesthetic, and psychomotor operations. For some, indeed, mind includes all matter and thought, even the cosmos. Motives are those attitudes we signify in doing or not doing; they are inherent in human intentions. Thus Being, mind, and motives are not signifiers of discrete entities but are words for overlapping and linked functions. At the nub of Being lies a *relationship,* between consciousness and the world. How A relates to B, and how C relates to D, is not a cause-and-effect relation; it is an awareness of the tensions between parts, or between parts and whole. One set nests within the other. This awareness enables us to discover the power of human consciousness, whether in the satisfactions of harmony or the dissatisfactions of discord. It is the necessary precondition of all learning and intelligence.

The relationship between parts, or between whole and parts, functions in different modes, in five states of being: remembering, living, dreaming, fantasizing, and imagining. These states are not discrete entities but rather functional modes that mix according to the needs of the organism. Each state works with mental images; it is the use that individuals make of them – how they are transformed into intelligent acts – that differs. Transformation is largely (but not entirely) controlled by feeling: It gives meaning to the state of Being. In this sense we can say that Being is an aesthetic meaning-giving activity in the creation of mental worlds.

What are the differences and similarities between these states? Dreaming, remembering, living, and imagining interact productively and contribute to each other. Fantasy works alone, drawing off energy that could be used by other states. Three are states of time: remembering the past, living the present, and imagining the future. But dreaming and fantasizing are not states of time; both use images formed in the past, yet as states they are suspended in time. Remembering works with the signs of consciousness; it brings back images and concepts previously created through dramatization. As a result, it is constantly used by other states. But recall does not simply bring back facts. It places past images in the context of the present. In other words, memory is another form of replay: What we recall is re-created according to the needs of the present. Living is our workaday state. It has (falsely) all the appearance of being objective: It uses sensory data as signs and tries to analyse them rationally and/or empirically. Although the living state has more objective signification than dreaming, remembering, and imagining, it places the objective in a subjective matrix. It is set within felt-time and felt-space, so that Being is what provides reason with meaning. Dreaming uses the undifferentiated signs and symbols of consciousness and connects them in metaphoric ways. Dreams work poetically or, as Hadfield would have it, like a drama,[15] relating different images by association – inner to outer, past to present or to future – with a unique logic that symbolically signifies the individual's worries and concerns. Within a dream, however, the self cannot distinguish between subjective and objective signs or symbols. Fantasy is a dissociated state; it exists for itself. For most persons, fantasy lodges in the daydream, but it can become the dominant waking state for some disturbed persons.

Imagining is the uniquely human state. Human beings can suppose, postulate, create designs, invent theories, and test them out, even rejecting them if they fail. In the abstract, people can compare the possibilities of signs and symbols. And possibilities lead to probabilities. The major characteristic of imagining is "as if" thinking. In the living mode, we can imagine that something is fictional. The real and the fictional coexist. Imagining allows us to create a double of reality. We assume that we are working in two realities at one time, while in fact our attention oscillates between the actual and the fictional in such a way that they appear (falsely) to be simultaneous. There is a leap between one logical class and another that relates the actual to metaphor, metonymy, play, and creation. Imagining relates subject and object through the possibilities of media; it takes signifiers from the environment and, via media, re-creates them subjectively; it is thus the foundation of all root metaphors. The other states of mind work with the results of this process. By casting the objective as fictional, imagining is the foundation of symbol formation. In imagining plans for the future, we set up possibilities and try them out in action, overtly or covertly, and we use eclectic elements from the other states, unifying them into new significations. By focusing on possibility, bringing about actions that are future-oriented, imagining also re-creates human meaning.

Imagining creates meaning in a unique manner – through transformation. It does so in various complementary ways. We transform our perceptions of elements of the environment into images with which we can work. Then we activate a second transformation in two parts, grouping images into imaginings and giving these imaginings new meaning through metaphorization. The oscillation between part and part, or between part and whole, focuses the energy of imagining, creating the double. In this way we create not merely meaning but also the internal signs that carry meaning. We also convert imaginings into actions – internal or external, indirect or direct.

CONCLUSION

We should also remind ourselves that it is performative imagining that allows us to create metaphors and symbols, root metaphors, models of learning, and models of the mind. Imagining, by focusing the tension between oscillating elements, leads mind to explore, learn, and master through performance. Human competence depends on the skills of performance. Imagining requires the satisfaction of self-actualization – safety, love, esteem, curiosity, etc. Without the ability to imagine, these human needs could not acknowledged or signified. Of course, physiological needs still have to be satisfied. But human dynamism and intention originate in imagination, and it is here that the most basic potential for intelligence lies.

CHAPTER TEN

Drama and Human Learning

Learning is change, it is said. That is, learning is exhibited by a change in actions. From the perspective of this book, learning is a change in the imaginative/thinking process that becomes externalized in dramatic action. Change within the learner (the signified) affects the signifier. Learning is a signified that affects all subsequent actions. Those concerned with the improvement of cognition and intelligence focus their interest here. Aesthetic learning is a change in feeling, choice, and judgment, and the ability to work with the actual/fictional. This is a paramount process in cognition and intelligence. It distinguishes our species from others; while the upper primates appear to engage in cognitive, affective, and psychomotor learning, none so far as we know work with the aesthetic mode.

The issues that concern us here are the following: How does learning relate to knowing? How far does human intelligence measure up to its potential? What are the major contemporary perspectives on aesthetic learning? How does dramatic learning improve intelligence?

LEARNING

If learning is change, we can say that we have learned something after acquiring knowledge that brings about a change in our thoughts and actions. We have seen that knowing is to so grasp ideas that they become part of our inner self. Our knowledge depends on our mental structures and reflects our beliefs, assumptions, attitudes, and motives. Knowing and learning are built on dramatic action. Actions interface with the environment, creating meaning for ourselves and for others. Acts, and the media they use, are signifiers. We gain either *signifier knowledge* (learning that changes actions) or *signified knowledge* (learning that improves knowing and the ability to think). The second depends on the first: What we do affects who we are. Signifier learning is paramount and can be called learning to learn.

Most mechanical research tells us very little about how we learn. In the vast empirical research literature about reading, there is hardly anything about the "Aha!" moment when we learn to read, but there is a great deal about remedial reading. Much of this can be attributed to the fact that the issue is extremely difficult to address by mechanical, empirical methods, which are relatively unsophisticated.

There is no one answer to the problem of how human beings learn. During studies in a variety of cultures,[1] we found that there were three general factors in learning. First, different people learn in different ways, although there are some ways that are more common than others. Common ways exist more within a single culture and/or related cultures than they do across diverse cultures. Second, it is generally easier to learn simple things than complex and ambiguous things. Third, basic concepts and thinking skills are acquired more through practical experience and discovery than through direct methods of instruction; for example, language and related areas are best learned through practical immersion rather than in isolation from the linguistic context. More sophisticated thinking skills are learned both ways, through direct and indirect instruction. These three general factors are tempered by a variety of variables, the most common being personal conditions (maternal bonding, maturation, nutrition and health, intrinsic motivation, physical and/or mental handicaps, personal disposition/attitude, and anxiety); social conditions (language, child-rearing practices, parental attitudes, quality of teaching, parent/peer/teacher expectations, social norms and codes, availability of models, the social value of learning, the level/degree of acculturation, class, poverty, sex, colour, race, and other power relations); and learning conditions (transferability, concentration, perseverance, opportunity for activity, the degree/style of stimulation, and the size of the instructional group). With any one individual, learning may occur through one or more of the three general ways, tempered by several variables.

The kinds of learning achieved by dramatic activity are intrinsic, extrinsic, aesthetic, and artistic. Intrinsic learning is when dramatic activity enhances the learner's inner qualities. One study identified the following factors: perception, awareness, concentration, variety of thought-style, expression, inventiveness, problem identification and solving, confidence and self-worth, social learning and negotiation with others, and motivation and transfer of learning.[2] The literature identifies these factors as being important for psychological health and for personality development, coping with existence, "thinking on the feet," and life/interpersonal/social/cognitive/generic skills. Extrinsic learning is when dramatic activity enhances the learner's potential and ability in activities other than drama (language, math, science, social studies, etc.). Dramatic activity increases the learner's inherent motivation to learn nondramatic content, and this produces a transfer of learning to other fields. It was Joseph Lee who said in 1915, "When at eight years old you have acted the role of Christopher Columbus, you never forget it was *you* who discovered America."[3] Aesthetic learning is when dramatic activity enhances the learner's feeling, judgment, and choice. Studies have indicated that, through spontaneous drama, the player learns to refine raw emotion into feelings that can be controlled and expressed productively.[4] Contemporary educational drama is specifically designed to promote aesthetic learning. With very young children, the teacher provides the *What?* but the students choose the *How?*[5] With maturation and an experienced teacher, students are provided with a wide variety of choices, which through dramatic discovery and trial and error become the basis for their later judgments. As for artistic learning, its elements in spontaneous drama and theatre coincide: the realization of personages, sound and dialogue, gesture and movement, human interaction, colour, shape, light, story, and contrasts (light/dark, sound/silence, movement/stillness, presence/absence, etc.). Dramatic play, creative drama, and improvisation teach in a manner appropriate to the age, ability, and aptitude of younger learners. They are the bases for later artistic and theatre education.

Learning of this sort changes how we think and act. Acts, as signifiers, indicate what we know. Knowing depends on the ability of mental structures to work flexibly and creatively with a variety of contexts and relations. Learning is the growing capacity to develop mental structures and dynamics. The more we extend the fourfold oscillation of our thought into further complex relations, the more we increase our ability to learn. This "learning to learn" includes all other definitions of learning, and it is fundamental to the acquisition of all types of knowledge. It also improves dramatic action, the signifier from which an observer infers that learning has or has not taken place. But how far does dramatic action go in fulfilling the potential of human intelligence? In order to answer this question we must turn to the theory of logical types.

HUMAN LEARNING AND LOGICAL TYPES

The theory of logical types is one way to examine intellect and its potential. First generated by A.N. Whitehead and Bertrand Russell, the theory was limited to logical systems. But its greater implications have occupied modern thinkers. Recently, it has received commentary by

Gregory Bateson and a series of semiotic studies.[6] The theory states that, in formal logic or mathematics, (1) *no class can be a member of itself;* and (2) *a class of classes cannot be one of the classes which are its members.* That is, subclasses within a class (cod, halibut, etc.) and the class itself (all fish) exist at different logical levels. "All fish" exists at a different logical level than "fish 1," "fish 2," etc. If this simple rule of logic is broken, said Russell, then paradox is generated and discourse is impossible. But there is a difference between the world of logic and the world of ordinary experience. In logic, if a paradox appears from a train of propositions, all previous discourse is reduced to nothing:

> But in the real world... there is always time, and nothing which has been can ever be totally negated in this way. The computer which encounters a paradox (due to faulty programming) does not vanish away. The 'if ... then ...' of logic contains no time. But in the computer, cause and effect are used to simulate the 'if ... then ...' of logic; and all sequences of cause and effect necessarily involve time. (Conversely, we may say that in scientific explanations the 'if ... then ...' of logic is used to simulate the 'if ... then ...' of cause and effect.) The computer never truly encounters logical paradox, but only the simulation of paradox in trains of cause and effect. The computer therefore does not fade away. It merely oscillates.[7]

In other words, a paradox may destroy an argument in logic, but it must be accounted for as we live through experience.

The theory of logical types has been extended by two distinctions: that between direct communication and metacommunication, which is about communication;[8] and that between direct language and languages about language, or metalanguage.[9] Metacommunication and metalanguages must *account* for change. Learning denotes change, and change denotes process; but processes themselves are subject to change and, indeed, any process "may slow down, or it may undergo other types of change such that we shall say that it is now a 'different' process."[10] Thus we should order our ideas about learning from the simplest level. In brief, the theory of logical types states that learning occurs in a hierarchy:

1 *ZERO LEARNING is through specific responses.* Zero LEARNING is the simplest form of learning. For example, the simple receipt of information from an external event may teach me that a similar event at a later time may convey the same information. I learn from a factory whistle that it is twelve o'clock; if the factory whistle only blows at twelve o'clock, my learning is not subject to trial and error.
2 *LEARNING I is through imprinting.* This type of learning is a change

from ZERO LEARNING. It introduces trial and error that is characteristic of all other learning to some degree or other. LEARNING I occurs when an error between two similar classes is revised. This causes an irreversible mode of action. As LEARNING I is subject to little or no revision, it can be said that behaviour is determined by external objects, acts, or events; thus LEARNING I includes all those behaviours normally called learning by experimental psychologists – habituation, classical conditioning, instrumental reward and avoidance, rote learning, and basic reinforcement. Here "every item of perception or of behaviour may be stimulus or response or reinforcement according to how the total sequence of interaction is punctuated... [But] the distinction which is commonly drawn between perception and action, afferent and efferent, input and output, is for higher organisms in complex situations not valid."[11]

3 *LEARNING II is learning to learn.* LEARNING II occurs through consciousness, self-consciousness, and the development of a world view. From the perspective of the holistic, organismic model of mind, therefore, learning in complex situations, including dramatic acts, exists at the next level. LEARNING II is variously known as learning to learn, set learning, transfer of learning, and deutero-learning. It operates at a metalevel with regard to LEARNING I. In terms of trial and error, LEARNING II occurs when an error between two similar sets is revised – a change from LEARNING I, because it corrects by choosing from a set of alternatives or it changes how the sequence of experience is punctuated.[12] In the animal world LEARNING II allows for alternatives (usually only two), but as animals cannot think about rules, they are incapable of changing them. With humans, however, LEARNING II leads to a dramatic increase in possibilities over time. The process involved is similar to Peirce's four steps that lead to action: consciousness of sensations; associations between sensations and creativity; the belief that certain things are the case under certain conditions (hypothesis); and the predisposition towards a particular mode of action in specific situations.[13] The result is a redefinition of the self, which leads to a general view (basic believing) about the way things are; we are not particularly conscious of how we think, what we do, or how we do it. However, through LEARNING II people are capable of developing highly complex conceptual frameworks[14] and world views[15] that can be applied to new situations, as in the current paradigm view of the sciences and in other metaphorical ways of understanding existence.[16] Some experimental studies in learning claim to have produced LEARNING I results, when in fact they have confused subclasses with classes, in Russell's sense.[17] LEARNING II includes learning that occurs in transactions between a person and the environment (mediate learning),

and learning that involves empathy, identification, and impersonation (basic dramatic learning).

4 *LEARNING III breaks normal bounds and leads to new ways of thinking.* LEARNING III alters normal rules and strategies. It leads to the creation of new classes and mental structures. By breaking down existing thought patterns and opening new systems, as well as combining and recombining sets and classes of relations, it provides a kind of metaperspective on all thought, action, and learning. It implies a radical reorganization of previous learning, although LEARNING I and LEARNING II are subsets of to LEARNING III. Selfhood, a product of LEARNING II, is no longer important in LEARNING III. The "I" and its role in relationship is no longer as significant as the perspective on self and its role. LEARNING III thus parallels the final stage of the moral development of Kohlberg.[18] The metaphoric view of LEARNING II moves on to the paradox and metaperspective of LEARNING III. In LEARNING III the individual might learn more readily to form the habits of LEARNING II; to close for him/herself the loopholes allowing him/her to avoid LEARNING III; to change the habits acquired by LEARNING II; to understand that s/he is a creature which can and does unconsciously achieve LEARNING II; and to limit or direct his/her LEARNING II. As LEARNING II is a learning of the context of LEARNING I, so LEARNING III is a learning of the context of those contexts.

But this presupposes the paradox. Mental structures consist of complementary characteristics that "nest" within each other. LEARNING III may lead either to an increase in LEARNING II or to its limitation and perhaps reduction, or to a greater flexibility in the premises acquired by the process of LEARNING II – "a freedom from their bondage."[19] Not all human beings resolve the paradox or acknowledge (with William Blake) that "contraries mutually exist." Nor do LEARNING I, II, and III correspond to many people's idea of levels of intelligence – at least in terms of IQ measurement. LEARNING III in particular encourages creative thinking and spontaneous action. It can therefore be seen as dangerous, and some contemporary educational systems discourage it, especially when genuine creativity and spontaneity present a radical, if positive and essentially democratic, critique of society itself. This is the case with the theatrical metaphor ("All the world's a stage") and the dramatic metaphor ("We are such stuff as dreams are made on"): Both are perspectives on perspectives and both are critical and inherently paradoxical. Indeed, all mental structures of LEARNING III have paradox built into them. One side of the paradox stands at a logical level different from the other side; it is simply that in LEARNING III (and dramatic action) the potential of both paradox and intelligence is realized.

DRAMATIC LEARNING AND LOGICAL TYPES

How does this relate to dramatic and theatrical learning? As a simple example, types of artistic learning are related to how we understand art: Through specificity of response we learn to distinguish art from nonart (ZERO LEARNING); through conditioning we learn to respond to particular content or form (LEARNING I); through metaphor we learn to respond to the symbolism of art (LEARNING II); and through paradox we learn to view art as a metaperspective of existence.

But dramatic learning is more than this. Interestingly, when we study the nature of dramatic learning, it is not usually content or subject matter that concerns us. Rather, as both McLuhan, in his phrase "The medium is the message,"[20] and Bateson, in his "Not the message but the code,"[21] have indicated, it is the form or structure that counts. A landscape is a landscape, whether it is by Hobbema, Constable, or Cezanne. The meaning, This is a landscape, is not our primary concern. The importance lies in the deeper meanings carried by the medium itself – the nondiscursive meanings inherent in a particular landscape and their significance for all landscapes and for life. If this were not the case, no landscapes would have been created after the first artist painted his.

With educational drama in schools, it is not the subject of the improvisation (mothers and fathers, space travel, applying for a job, etc.) that is the most significant feature. Rather, as Viola Spolin has always emphasized,[22] it is the inner workings of improvisation itself. The plot of *Hamlet* cannot be what most intrigues an audience: Most know it already, it is highly melodramatic, like many plays of its period it strains credulity, and it is excessively long. What interests us, and has interested human beings ever since it was first staged, is the existential matter it explores at great depth and in patterns that evoke deep responses in us. Metaphorically speaking, we look through *Hamlet* to ourselves and all humanity.

Dramatic and theatrical learning hinges, then, on structure rather than content, on how thought/action is put together, patterned, and shaped. Dramatic learning is achieved through relations between the more or less unconscious premises and assumptions of LEARNING II; through consciousness that is symbolic, metaphoric, and paradoxical (LEARNING II and III); and through immediate action.

There are nine basic issues to consider when discussing the nature of dramatic learning. First, when dramatic learning occurs in the "here and now," there is a heavy preponderance of unconscious learning; but conscious and explicit learning may also occur. Second, mind does not necessarily have to know *how* it uses tacit knowledge in the dramatic mode; but it is necessary to know *that* tacit learning takes place and that it is usually expressed, by both creators and percipients, as increased control over emotion and feeling. Third, dramatic learning is reflected in the increased ability to give meaning to symbols and metaphors shaped for dramatic and theatrical purposes. Fourth, dramatic learning involves improvement in feeling-response – in the oscillation between impulse and medium, and in choice, judgment, and the use of imagining. Fifth, as we learn more about the tacit and unconscious elements of dramatic activity, we are not necessarily able to distinguish between their multiple forms. Categorization, classification, and naming devices are discursive, not tacit, operations. Dramatic learning does not necessarily relate to the ability to describe events in verbal or written forms, although when activity is directed towards language, it can. Sixth, dramatic learning demonstrates an increased ability to communicate tacit and unconscious thought and feeling. Seventh, dramatic learning increases the skills of creation and/or interpretation. This does not mean that the creator is more explicitly aware of how he does it: "The skill of an artist, or rather his demonstration of a skill, becomes a message about ... his unconsciousness. (But not perhaps a message from the unconscious.)"[23] Eighth, dramatic learning is integrative and holistic. Consciousness is selective and partial, but the dramatic, based on unconscious similarities, is more integrative than other aspects of the human intellect. Ninth, dramatic learning increases the ability to work with the double. The tendency to work simultaneously with the actual/fictional (or seemingly so) increases to the point where, with high-calibre performance and plenty of experience, a person grows more aware of metaperspectives and paradoxes (as in LEARNING III).

Coleridge said that we respond to fiction through "the willing suspension of disbelief." That is, we respond to the imaginary world of drama or text "as if" it really exists. We do so by degrees, as we mature. We learn about the fictional as well as the actual. At the metaphoric level (LEARNING II), we learn to work with all objects within a fictional context "as if" they are real, whereas from outside the system they are "not really real." The models and paradigms of religion, science, myth, and ritual – part of our culturally embedded knowledge – are constituent parts of LEARNING II. But at the level of LEARNING III, fiction takes on the characteristics of paradox. Here dramatic fiction is the model of all metaperspectives, a factor that is essential to intelligence at this level.

LEARNING AND THE FUTURE

Because dramatic activity improves both LEARNING II and LEARNING III, it stands on the threshold of the future. Only dictators and fools are sure what the future will bring; futurists like Alvin Toffler give us "indicators" by extrapolating from current trends. LEARNING III (in many disguises) occupies many of the best minds today, and it is likely to be a pervasive method of teaching in the twenty-first century. Opening new systems of thought, combining and recombining sets and classes of relations, denying stereotypies, accepting others as persons like ourselves, adopting perspectival and comparative approaches and flexibility of attitude, recognizing our functional processes, radically changing learning habits, and working at metalevels – these and related factors are liable to be the major learning issues in the foreseeable future. The fact that dramatic action leads us from LEARNING II to LEARNING III is merely one indication of why it is increasingly successful in contemporary learning situations.

A progressive society develops and adjusts to change by educating its youth in the generic skills they will need, in work and leisure, to contribute to society and lead satisfying lives. But the increasing speed of change has left the Western educational system behind. Established in the nineteenth century to provide clerks for industry and cogs in the machines of the Western empires, it can hardly be expected, even with the various repairs by changing governments, to cope with the problems of postindustrial society. Today employers complain that students are not prepared for work, while adults are increasingly dissatisfied with their leisure. Contemporary research has shown[24] that the heads of Canada's major businesses rate as their top employment priority not the basics but the ability to negotiate. A salesman needs to negotiate with a purchaser, a bank manager with a customer, a foreman with workers on the shop floor, etc., and vice versa. Even computer operators need not only to send each other digital messages but also to negotiate with one another. Negotiation consists primarily of the ability "to see things from the other person's point of view," and a mastery of the techniques of cooperative persuasion. Those adults who are most dissatisfied with their leisure are also concerned about human interaction; either they lack the opportunity for it (as with so many of the aged) or they are disappointed in their own practice of it (lack of skill). What such people need is to learn negotiating skills through dramatic action.

There has been a continual search, at least in the past half century, for ways to train creative intelligence among youth and adults. This has only been partially successful, particularly when mechanical methods have been used. Different social scientists such as J.P. Guilford and Paul E. Torrance have evolved ways of identifying and testing various intellectual categories and cognitive operations, but the subsequent use of these operations in practical situations has not been as effective as checklists of adjectival descriptors (for example, that of Gary Davis). Yet the creativity resulting from creative drama activities has been discovered to be general, cumulative, and relatively permanent.[25]

There is an increasing demand for social justice in learning. The work of Paulo Freire, Henry Giroux, and others has raised this issue to one of increasing importance. Freire's attempt to achieve educational power for oppressed Brazilian peasants has assumed legendary status, and some of the educational disadvantages in the so-called Third World are of frightening proportions. But educational social justice is also required in postindustrial societies. Peter McLaren's *Cries from the Corridor* shows the social and learning needs of disadvantaged children in a Toronto suburban ghetto, and whole literatures now exist about the genuine learning needs of minorities – women, blacks, immigrants, etc. To increase awareness of the issues, many workers in education have turned to political action which, while it can have short-term effects, often peters out as circumstances change. Some, however, have realized the power of dramatic action to right such wrongs. Spontaneous drama contains an inherent critique of society which, while not primarily political, is genuinely social. I have experienced this in many contexts, including teenage improvisations in Greater London, which expressed the social injustice participants saw in learning inequalities and offered solutions; improvisations with young adults in the Midlands of England, which vented frustration and anger about schooling, unemployment, and the lack of a future; role plays in Fiji, which demonstrated the racial tensions between native Fijians and East Indians and ways these could be overcome; the improvised dance of North American Indians, which expressed desperation at the denigration of their culture and their hatred of all-powerful white society. What makes dramatic action so significant in such contexts is that it not only provides a social critique but can, unless the situation is desperate, be productive. It is highly effective in educating both the oppressed and the empowered; it teaches players practical problem-solving and activates them to find solutions; and it ensures that what is learned is well learned.

CONCLUSION

Key to these issues is the nature of learning. This is defined in so many ways that here we have avoided a full-scale definition. But it is quite clear from the examples that our concern is with deep-felt and permanent learning – those significant moments of "Aha" learning.

Take reading, for example. The "Aha!" moment when we learn to read is an enormous leap. (So why is it that most research studies address not this moment but issues of remedial reading?) Evidence confirms that children learn to read best when they sit on a parent's (or surrogate's) knee following their finger from word to word; they mouth the words the parent speaks; when well-loved stories are read again and again, the child joining in; and, finally, when the parent slowly withdraws from reading, allowing the child to take over. In this routine the child identifies with and later impersonates the parent. Inner dramatization results in a dramatic act that teaches the child to read.

It is a major assumption of this book that behind much learning lie tacit dramatic acts. Impersonation (standing in someone else's shoes) is the prime activator of most learning. The perspectives from our actual and dramatic worlds, when compared, transform our knowledge and beliefs so that we learn. These cognitive changes increase our potential for intelligence.

CHAPTER ELEVEN

Drama and Dialogue

Dialogue relates to drama practically and theoretically. Practical dialogue is the words players say to each other in a performance – or *dialogue as mutual talk*. Theoretically, dialogue is how people function with others – or *dialogue as mutuality*. This chapter addresses the latter.

We have already seen that dialogue activates two initial structures, the vaunt and the proposition; that drama/speech is the closest expressive media can come to Being; and that dialogue is inherent in any form of dramatic relationship. These factors raise three major issues: (1) dialogue versus dialectic; (2) interpretation (the experiences of the member of an audience, the reader, and the viewer of a work of art); and (3) dialogue as an exemplar (dialogue and its interactions as a model for the dramatic event).

DIALOGUE AND DIALECTIC

Duality, dialectic, and dialogue refer to different cognitive models for understanding existence. Dualism or binarism, based on opposites, was born of ancient Greek and Jewish thought. It began to collapse before the Enlightenment: The duality of either/or was too crude for Kierkegaard and not understood by Blake, for whom "contraries mutually exist." By the nineteenth century, it was replaced by dialectic. The dialectic form of thesis, which led to its opposite, antithesis, with the result being synthesis (described variously by Hegel and Marx), was in the late nineteenth century a major intellectual model for understanding thought as well as action and social processes; it tried to account for the personal and social character of the time – steam power, industrialization, state capitalism, the masses, and poverty.

Dialectic as "triangularity" was at least progressive and ongoing. But in essence it merely patched up duality, positing a triangular model to meet current determinist needs. Dialectic was the underpinning of Hegel's philosophy, perhaps the most significant system of thought since that of Plato. But both Plato and Hegel were philosophic Idealists: In the final analysis both believed that all causes could be attributed to the ultimate, or God. That is, there was something out there (the objective) to which all humans were responsible and by which, to a large extent, history was determined.

Determinism became the fundamental commonplace of the nineteenth century. The intellectual link between dialectics and determinism was made by the major thinkers of the period: Human life was determined by evolution for Darwin, by economic history for Marx, by the unconscious for Freud. For Nietzsche, the opposition of Dionysian and Apollonian forces resulted in a cognitive synthesis in any given society at any given moment of historic time, and there was a determinist cast to this. The influence of dialectics and determinism was not restricted to nineteenth-century thinkers. It is seen in the twentieth-century work of many older structuralists like Lévi-Strauss, who goes looking for binary codes (oppositions) that lead to cognitive synthesis. John Dewey wrote his dissertation on Hegel, which may account for the Idealist and dialectical cast to his pragmatism (as compared, say, to that of William James) and his intellectual acceptance of the behavioural "scientific method" (a logical extension of the dialectic) as first outlined by George H. Mead.

But dialectics and determinism are crude tools. Today determinism hardly marries with our cognitive understanding of the universe, while the triangular dialectic was an attempt to patch up ancient dualism to meet the needs of particular historic period. Einstein better prefigured contemporary ways of thinking. The basis of his thought was "toying with concepts," and he used visual metaphors to represent his theories, which recalls Wittgenstein's notion that modern logic (the cognitive use of specific criteria in particular contexts) had to do with "picturing." Heisenberg's theory of indeterminacy in physics illustrates that modern "truth" is different from the truth of dualism or dialectics: It is arrived at by comparing the perspectives of individual observers, but it does not provide as much certainty as older forms of truth ostensibly did. The terminology used earlier in this book understands truth to be much like that of the first people who heard the parable of the Good Samaritan: We "come to believe" it when it fits our experience.

Many modern thinkers have moved away from dualism and triangularity. The most startling occurrence of this is Jung's break from Freud. Jung discovered that the quaternity structure (wholes) was the major cognitive model in the ancient world and among alchemists and that it was still fundamental to tribal peoples and the East. Jung began a Western movement towards oriental thinking that many American scholars continued in the 1960s. Some contemporary post-structuralists (for example, Derrida) and semioticians (Greimas) have broken out of the dialectical mould by steadily moving away from it. Derrida dislocates classic logic, denies opposition, and looks for what lies "in between." Greimas, doubling binaries, returns to the ancient quaternity. But the four has not replaced the two of duality or the three of dialectics. Rather, *the issue has become the nature of wholes.* Like the founders of Rome (see p. 116), contemporary thinkers have solved the ancient riddle of squaring the circle. The four positions of the quaternity are merely "temporary absolutes" (in Louis Arnaud Reid's famous phrase),[1] which can expand to more than four (including the circle) and contract to less than four, and do so in a gestalt dynamic where figure and ground are in constant oscillation – like the "speech" of two players. This has important implications for cognition and thus for our understanding of intelligence. One significant implication concerns interpretation.

INTERPRETATION

One way of picturing dialogue is as a gestalt. The figure (the first "speech") is the lens through which we see the ground (the second "speech"), and vice versa. In its simplest form the gestalt operates between two players: Two vaunts and two propositions begin a dialogue where truth is revealed in the interaction brought about by the fiduciary contract. A second way of picturing dialogue is through "the voice" of the observer (or reader): The observer-as-player "speaks" a perspective and the observed-as-player is understood to respond by "speaking" a second perspective. This kind of picturing applies to observers, readers, and witnesses in relation to a text. A third way of picturing is psychological: In the manner of metaphor with its two images, one interacts with the other to produce a further meaning. Persons and doubling are at the centre of dialogue, which provides homologies as metaperspectives. Our cognition is not a form of dualism or dialectic but rather a nesting. It represents the continually changing comparison of voices. From this view we can approach interpretation.

Significantly, three major figures of the twentieth century who address the issue of dialogue, Martin Buber, Mikhail Bakhtin, and Kenneth Burke,[2] all use a dramatic perspective. Most of the works of Bakhtin and Burke are in the field of criticism, while many of those of Buber are framed in terms of the person in an audience or on a stage. The focus of all three is the dialogic relation – between I and Thou for Buber, between creator and reader for Bakhtin, and between action and roles for Burke.

Bakhtin sees the contact between reader/audience and work of art as intelligent, that is, dialogic and based on cognitive interaction. In a novel we hear voices even when reading silently; with any text we always arrive, finally, at the human voice (Being). Even if author and reader are separated by history or great distances, they are both located in a fictional world that is oral and aural. "'The fictional world' creates 'the text,'" says Bakhtin. The author, the players (if they exist), and the readers (listeners/audience) who re-create it, all participate equally to create the represented world in the text. Even in the most naturalistic work, the text is never actual, even though it refers to the actual. When the readers or audiences experience the text, they assume that the fictional world exists and that it is in dialogic relation to the actual world. The author-creator also has a dialogic relation to the phenomena of the actual world: S/he is both outside and inside the text, whether using his or her own voice, that of a narrator (in a novel), or that of different personages (in theatre): "He can represent the temporal-spatial world and its events only 'as if' he had seen and observed them himself, only 'as if' he was an omnipresent witness to them ... [I]f I relate (or write about) an event that has just happened to me, then I as the teller or writer of this event am always outside the time and space in which the event occurred. It is just as impossible for me to forge an identity between myself, my own 'I,' and that 'I' that is the subject of my stories as it is to lift myself up by my own hair."[3] This is a dramatic perspective; the author and reader function "as if," just like the dramatist, player, and audience.

Most contemporary critics and semioticians are not directly concerned with cognition and intelligence, dramatic or otherwise. They usually address some aspect of language and critical interpreatation, for example, how we learn to read novels or appreciate theatre. But they express a particular tacit perspective about dramatic thinking and learning. Semioticians are inclined to regard all works of art as texts, whether literary or not, largely because, as linguists, they view art through the lens of language. In their view, texts designate "a certain body of repeatable or recoverable acts of communication."[4] Where art forms are predominantly spatial (art, architecture, etc.) the communication is repeatable. But where the predominant mode is temporal (theatre, dance, music, etc.) the communication is not repeatable but rather recoverable (for example, in film). Performances (texts) carry communicable meanings, cognitive but tacit, as signifiers of what is signified. According to this view, dramatic learning like all textual learning is the learning of a philosophy, whether human beings realize it or not – that is, a set of expectations about the nature of possible contexts. Humans seek errors in order to learn, but they also seek order.[5] These two aspects of learning allow our intellectual abilities to generate sets of alternatives. "All acquired knowledge, all learning, consists in the modification (possibly the rejection) of some form of knowledge, or disposition, which was there previously, and in the last instance of inborn dispositions."[6] This is a particular view of the cognitive that entails learning in modes of thinking and of action.[7]

From texts as dramatic signs, we increasingly learn to discriminate between the actual and the fictional. This is significant because it opens the way to other aesthetic alternatives, which depend on the contrasting qualities of the contexts invoked by a particular message. (In terms of logical types, LEARNING II is the basis for LEARNING III.) Within the aesthetic and dramatic modes, Robert Scholes tells us, we learn six types of fictional conventions:

1 Fiction of sender	*Roleplaying, acting*
2 Fiction of receiver	*Eavesdropping, voyeurism*
3 Fiction of messenger	*Opacity, ambiguity*
4 Fiction of context	*Allusion, fiction proper*
5 Fiction of contact	*Translation, fiction proper*
6 Fiction of code	*Involved in all the above*[8]

Theatre, story, and poem are dominated by such fictions overtly, other art forms, covertly. We learn two things about creating fictions: that we create them around the message that is the focus of our thoughts, and that we do so against a background of actual contexts. Thus we create two gestalt worlds, the aesthetic world, or the play world, where creativity is self-generating; and the art world of specific, self-generating forms (theatre, music, etc.). These two fictional worlds can be pictured as dialogic, as Chinese boxes, as figure and ground, or as a continuum running from spontaneous drama to ritual and theatre.

Aesthetic learning is generated by the intention of the organism (it creates aesthetic worlds out of the environment), whereas artistic learning is generated by the creation of artistic fiction. The maturational sequence that attends our experience of aesthetic worlds involves the growth of empathy and identification, the mediate object, the mirror stage, "the primal act" and impersonation, and play. This same sequence informs dramatic and artistic learning, which are closely linked. Much artistic competence depends on our ability to connect play fiction with artistic fiction. But most of our knowledge remains tacit and unconscious, homologies of childhood models (heroes and heroines, journeys and adventures) condensed into mental structures and dynamics that we replay in a contemporary context, actual, aesthetic, or artistic.

Artistic performance makes available a particular way of learning. In theatre, the signification is shared by actors, directors, and dramatists, while spectators learn by submerging their individuality within the collective personality of the audience. In theatre and all literature, we learn through the art form's reference to its own form. Plays, poems, and novels all comment on the generic traditions of which they are part; and each allow the reader/viewer to learn communication in general – the semantic meaning of both aesthetics as a whole and particular arts. We learn to value the arts through function and form, to see signification as a way of structuring that enables the creator to communicate certain kinds of meaning. The aesthetic sign is both a formal homology and a function of human experience.[9]

The reader learns to create a book, the audience learns to create a performance, and the viewer learns to create an art work (a text) out of a work. An artist creates a painting, but when a viewer comes into a gallery he or she creates it anew. Readers, audiences, and listeners must learn to make texts by understanding a specific cultural code. Artistic learning is gaining knowledge of cultural traditions and acquiring specific skills in interpretation. Traditions are always fluctuating.[10] How do we learn traditions and skills? Semioticians differ in their approaches. For Yuri Lotman,[11] we must learn to re-code our cultural framework through the particulars of a text. In the terms of this book, re-play is the adjustment of present learning to the Being and knowing acquired in the past; we re-learn the sensations of life, the feeling of things, through each unique text. The artist learns to select and order significations to create a work of art; the percipient learns the cultural codes and skills necessary to interpret those significations; and we all learn to discriminate between our imaginative and feeling responses.

All interpretation must accept that aesthetic and artistic learnings have their historic origins in dialogue and dramatic narrative. Tribal cultures had no art as such. Their form of representation was ritual-myth, the enactment (ritual) of origin stories (myths). In this sense, *all contemporary arts grew out of the performance of narrative.* This is most obvious in the mimetic arts of theatre, dance and mime, storytelling, the novel and other written narratives, film, and television drama. The fact that it is less obvious in other arts (music, the visual arts, architecture) does not mean that their suppressed premises do not lie in narrative. Today, narrative learning hinges on learners distinguishing between their own actual situation and a fictional, narrated situation – a skill acquired through play. In terms of logical types, LEARNING II leads to LEARNING III.

Play, dialogue, and narrative teach us that (1) two frames of reference coexist but differ in space-time; (2) events can be doubles present both as fictions and actuality, or present only as fictions *(for us)*; (3) fictional worlds symbolically signify meanings that can affect us in our daily lives, even if we are not able to put those meanings into words; (4) there are tacit meanings signified in art that we learn over time increasingly to interpret; and (5) there are three levels of artistic form:

A *The form as presented:* the immediately available artistic elements (acting, speech, gesture, etc.) in theatrical form.
B *The form as re-presented:* the levels of meaning within the art work (the conscious/unconscious meanings of the dramatist, the performer, and the character, etc.).
C *One form as different from other forms:* one artistic theme can be treated by various forms. For example, *Hamlet* is a play, a ballet, a film, a story, illustrations, etc., all signifying some common meanings, but each form also provides unique tacit meanings.

Each of these levels of artistic form, in the sense used here, derives from acquired discrimination between levels of drama, dialogue, and narration.

Dramatic and theatrical forms share common elements: the player living through fictional experience in the "here and now," metaphoric and symbolic meaning, colour and rhythm, light/dark, noise/silence, and so forth. *In theatre, the art work as aesthetic object oscillates between the subjectivities of its creators.* But child play, creative drama, role play, improvisation, and the drama of life each have their own formal properties. *Spontaneous drama exists processually, medially and liminally: It exists in time, as an aesthetic object characterized by mutuality and dialogue.*

DIALOGUE AND ITS EXTENSIONS

Dramatic actions have a dialogic orientation. That is, the structures and dynamics of human dialogue are a model for the way the player relates with other players and performs with them in dramatic events and contexts. A dramatic act never exists on its own, just as no word or gesture exists in isolation. The act, the word, and the gesture are essentially interactive and social. They only have meaning in relation to *the object they refer to, the player who makes them, and the player who receives them.*

If this applies to the protagonist, it applies with equal force to the second protagonist. The act, word, and gesture of the first player exists in a dynamic environment that includes the acts, words, and gestures of the second. As players, our intellectual potential is constantly tested by *the degree of elasticity* with which we function in a human context.

In our self-presentation in life or as a personage in fiction, we must ask this key question: How well did we function in this dynamic process? The process is dialogic; to deal with it successfully we must act, speak, and gesture in a dialogic manner. The environment a player works in consists of persons and objects. It is not neutral. What we do relates to an object that is already charged with meaning, or to a person who is in the process of valuing, choosing and judging. His or her response is never quite what we expect. The process is ever fluctuating. It is this with which we must deal.

"Speaking is life," Derrida said.[12] Voice is creative. I identify with my breath, like Thoth I breathe life into things and create the "world-for-me." My exhalation of sounds and words makes me a protagonist. But I exist in a mutual relation with another protagonist who has his own exhalation. Together we create the "world-for-us," a world where our voices (speech) substitute for our Being, but a world nonetheless as near to Being as we can get together. Our voice takes shape, and takes its shape, from the thing it substitutes for.

Being and voice appear to be one entity in our "felt world." But voice is distinguishable from Being; it is similar to yet different from itself. Voice is the double of Being, the mask of Being. Our voice is the fiction of our Being. In imitating Being, our voice becomes its sign.

Speech is also *the medium of our Being*. Being requires voice in order to be projected into the environment. Voice is the signifier of Being. It obeys it, conforms to it, yet replaces it and becomes the playing and the plaything of it. Voice is the mimic and the player. Simultaneously, it is felt to be our Being and it acts as the creative impulse in our interactions. It is many things in one.

Living speech and all dramatic acts are active parts of dialogue. They conceptualize the environment in highly complex ways. In the environment they meet with persons and objects that are already imbued with past and present words, acts, and meanings. Yet the utterance and the act must also "make their mark"; they must create their own values and meanings by intervening in the living process. The concepts that result strike a particular balance between the forces in their interplay; these vary from moment to moment, from player to player, and from context to context. Speech, like any act, is purposive. It directly reflects human intention. Its aim is to be assimilated into the ongoing conceptual system and then feed back to Being what is understood.

To this end, dramatic acts and speech generate two related dynamics: *responding* and *understanding*. Responding is a feeling dynamic in me, a cognitive reaction ("disturbance") generating sensation, awareness, and concentration. In responding to an external stimulus (for example, another's utterance or act), the protagonist meets with the subjective belief system of the listener, projected into the mutual action or dialogue. The listener's attention focuses on the protagonist, and some sort of accommodation between their two belief systems is called for. An internal stimulus (for example, an imagining) triggers feeling entirely within the protagonist. These two kinds of responding, to external and internal stimuli, are what Robert W. Witkin calls object response and subject response. Although both *exist* in the present tense, they can also be *about* the past and future.[13]

Understanding arises from response. It cannot exist without response. The protagonist assimilates an utterance or act and his response into a new conceptual system – one of "coming to believe" – just as Jesus's listeners did after hearing the parable of the Good Samaritan. By striving to understand, the protagonist creates a series of complex interrelationships with the utterance or act of the second protagonist.

Thus the purpose of dialogue is cognitive. The protagonist tacitly intends to improve his intelligence. His attitude towards the second protagonist is a projection into a specific conceptual framework, into another cognitive world, which introduces totally new elements into the world of the first protagonist. This is a dialogic interaction that is paradigmatic for dramatic interaction; it is the way we discover different perspectives and points of view. As Bakhtin tells us, "The speaker tries to get a reading on his own word, and his own conceptual system that determines the word, within the alien conceptual system of the understanding receiver; he enters into dialogic relationships with certain aspects of this system. The speaker breaks through the alien conceptual horizon of the listener, constructs his own utterance on alien territory, against his, the listener's, apperceptive background."[14]

CONCLUSION

Dialogue is a model for dramatic action that results from human intention. Tacitly we try to understand the other person dramatically/dialogically. As players who live through the text, we assume that the fictional world exists, that it has a dramatic/dialogic relation to the actual. The author-creator has a dramatic/dialogic relation to the phenomenon of the actual world both outside and inside the text. The player uses the Being/voice of the self, or of a narrator (in a novel), or of various personages (in dramatic acts), to create performances (texts) that carry communicable meanings. Players then are media – signifiers of mostly tacit signifieds. Theatrical signification is shared between actors, directors, and dramatists, and spectators learn meanings by participating in the communal reaction of the rest of the audience. Thus dramatic learning like all textual learning is the learning of a philosophy (whether the audience realizes it or not), that is, a set of expectations about the nature of possible contexts. The relation of the reader or spectator to an art work is always intelligent because it consists of dramatic/dialogic learning.

Dialogue, speech, and dramatic actions only have meaning in relation to the object they refer to, the player who makes them, and the player who receives them. These interrelationships are highly complex because they apply with equal force to both protagonists. Understanding comes from response. We assimilate the total utterance of dramatic event, and project a response into a new conceptual system. Then we have improved the potential of our intelligence.

CHAPTER TWELVE

In Conclusion

I have used a cognitive theory to show that the actor on a stage, the person in an audience, the child at play, the improviser, the man or woman on the street – all are in the continual process of improving their cognitive abilities and therefore they are trying to fulfil their intellectual potential. I am aware that, as given here, the theory is incomplete. A gardener can only grow flowers and vegetables in their proper season; I have primarily addressed the intelligence of dramatic action because that is the main concern in the field today.

If I were a critic, this incompleteness might occupy me. But the critic should note that my purpose has been not to rake over my ideas and display them as a unity (although this may be another matter for another time) but rather to use a theory to explicate a very practical matter. In our post-structural climate of today, readers should be able to "fill in" the holes themselves. Still it must be acknowledged that the way the book has turned over the ground has meant that there are a number of unsightly holes and lumps left around. The most important of these I will now briefly discuss: probability and aspects of playing, learning, theatre art, and study.

When we say that dramatic intelligence helps us to fulfil our potential, we mean in an Aristotelian sense that dramatic action helps the acorn become an oak. This idea is simple and might well fit with the theory of creative evolution expressed by Shaw and Bergson. But the causal nature of the idea fits neither our dramatic experience nor the new atomic theory (quantum mechanics) that has enriched physics with the theory of probability. For dramatic purposes, the probability that an event will take place is affected by the context in which the event occurs. In Karl Popper's famous example, if we are tossing a penny that is not biased, its probability of falling heads up is equal to 50 percent. But if we toss a penny over a table with cracks and slots designed to catch a coin upright, then its propensity to fall heads up will be less than 50 percent.[1] This contextual dependence applies to our own experiences in life or drama. If, for example, we are designing costumes for *The Three Musketeers,* it is probable that our final designs will be affected by the production's location: New York offers all possible fabrics, colours, and textures, while central Siberia restricts the amount and type of usable material. A second example: When one member of an improvisational group imagines something new and expresses it to the others, it changes the possibilities open to the group. Newly emergent ideas introduce new potentials or possibilities or propensities into a situation; a new field of ideas and actions is created, which is exactly what makes creative drama creative. If the idea comes from within the group there is a greater chance that it will be accepted than if it comes from outside the group.

Probability also affects our ideas about learning. The question Is human learning genetically founded, or is it an acquired ability? is unsatisfactory. The ability to use language and dramatic action appears to have a genetic basis; yet specific language and dramas, different from group to group, are made by human beings. The question does not deal adequately with three factors: the specific situation in which learning happens; the achievement of an individual; and subjective experience.

All normal children acquire skills in particular languages and dramas through hard work and intellectual achievement. The degree of effort and the level of success both affect the child's personality as well as his or her interactions with other people and the environment. According to probability, children are partly products of their achievement. The newly found ability to speak and act with the effect intended, particularly using speech and gestures indicating personal pronouns, which usually occurs after the primal act, rapidly increases the child's mastery and consciousness of environment, self, and others (and thus personality). The implications of this view are considerable. For example, it is unlikely that perception, imaging, imagining, and action are "given" to us, but it is probable that we help others create them while we ourselves learn to use and to interpret them.

We are all born into an environment of the languages and dramas of others. Like costume designers in Siberia and New York, each of us acts within a context that shapes probability. A child cannot develop appropriate cognitive skills without an adequate milieu. But this is not to say that we are determined by our environment. Experimental surgery on the brain performed by Wilder Penfield and repeatedly replicated shows that,[2] when certain areas of the cortex are stimulated in a fully conscious patient, vivid visual and auditory experiences are re-played in the patient's mind. This clearly indicates the existence of subjective states of consciousness. We are as dependent these as we are on the situations in which we live.

Longitudinal studies of spontaneous drama in schools show[3] that children are not *determined* by genetics, the environment, intellectual achievement, or subjective states of consciousness but rather are *dependent* on these things. Groups in the same culture exhibit similar dependencies. Between cultures, however, groups vary in how dependent they are on specific factors. Additionally, in each culture children demonstrate that they can break dependencies in any number of ways; the only common factors among those who do so are increased experience in dramatic playing and improved trust in the other players.

The issues of play and playing are complex because of the variables involved. We have seen that the essence of dramatic action is doubling: identifying and empathizing with others, impersonating them, thinking from their point of view, and transforming our metaphoric imaginings into external symbols that create multiple meanings. Simultaneously, others are working likewise on our behalf. But there are aspects of human playing that need further discussion. It has not been said clearly enough, for example, that teachers should ensure their learners are active – intellectually, physically, and dramatically active, as Rabelais would have it. If the teacher wishes the learning task to become deeply embedded in the self, then in the vast majority of cases they should be on their feet. Embodied learning is as permanent as learning can be. At the same time the fiction of drama should be engaged. For example, history improvisations will provide learning that is both embodied and embedded. Teachers may find such strategies more difficult in mathematics or grammar, but those working at the level of LEARNING III will find tasks that are tacitly dramatic in such subjects.

In this sense, scientific and dramatic methods are parallel: The hypothesis must come before the observation. This is the case in the logic of the human organism, both its nervous system and its psychology. Dramatic acts are practical hypothesizing: We try out in the not-really-real what we need to know in the real. This is the antithesis of the lecture method, and it is appropriate not only for children in schools but also for teaching the experimental method in science. Good university mathematics teachers give flesh and blood to abstract ideas. One, for example, taught me the nine dimensions with two (imagined) billiard balls, a cloth, and a small table. To cite another example, in teaching an undergraduate course in theatre history I set each student the task of solving in practice a major staging problem of the Elizabethan-Jacobean theatre; one student who tackled the arbour scene in Kyd's *The Spanish Tragedy* did so through practical hypothesis (i.e., he actually performed it) and he learned more efficiently than he would have through the lecture method or by merely reading the relevant sources.[4] And in a graduate course in comparative literature where we were dealing with discourse in late nineteenth-century novels (Tolstoy, Dostoevsky, Zola, Hardy, etc.), students prepared and enacted various novelists' dialogue on a theme (for example, the trial) prior to discussing it. Compared with other sessions where the dramatic method was not used, these sessions showed that graduate students markedly improved both their understanding of the texts and their ability to express ideas.

Some players perform on stages in plays. But a play like *Hamlet* or *A Winter's Tale* has an odd kind of existence. At one time it existed in Shakespeare's mind, but it probably never existed there as a totality; at the beginning it was a series of attempts; later, in his memory, he probably never retained it as a complete whole. When written down it became a script, but this, like a musician's score, is not identical with a play as a work of art; it consists merely of the words, not even of the speech, while such stage directions as "Exit pursued by a bear" are mere hints of possible actions. A script is a written form of encoding that is conventionally and arbitrarily related to dramatic ideas; this encoding tries to give the words and language more permanent form. It attempts to capture in space what exists in time. Thus we may say that *Hamlet* is *not:*

1 The script.
2 The sum total of the imagined experiences that Shakespeare had while writing it.
3 An ideal performance.
4 Any of the performances.
5 All the performances together.
6 The class of all possible performances.

While there may be superb performances of the script, there is no one ideal performance. Rather, a script is a series of ideas in writing that can be interpreted in performance; it offers the possibility of performative interpretation. Total depth and meaning is captured not in any one performance but rather in a series of performances giving different interpretations. In other words, it exists by virtue of the potential interpretation of others.

This might lead us to assume, falsely, that a play is a real (but ideal) object that exists in and of itself but that can be reinterpreted by others. If so, then *Hamlet* in script form has the potential of being recaptured again, if only partly, by human minds. This is the position of Popper,[5] who regards it as part of a world that comes into existence through the development of language. What Popper imagines is a type of Platonic world of ideas that exists nowhere but has a kind of existence through interaction with human minds. However, Popper sees these ideas as active processes (including intuition) that we make, or re-play, and that require us in storytelling or dramatic fiction "to distinguish between truth and falsity." Thus Popper, in a way similar to Ryle and Russell, ends up with the false proposition of truth versus fiction; he fails to consider that truth can equal fiction.

My idea of *Hamlet* is not a replica of yours. Dramatist, director, actors, and audience *create* the play. *Hamlet,* thus, exists mediately, between the subjectivities of those who create it;[6] it is a "mediate object," like Linus' security blanket (see p. 45). As it proceeds in time, its energy oscillates between its creators who, by comparing it with life, discover its degree of truth. While other forms of dramatic activity (everyday self-presentation, children's play, improvisation, etc.) are not usually works of art, they too exist aesthetically in a similar way.

While it is tempting, in the mode of Howard Gardner,[7] to claim that there is something called dramatic intelligence, we must take great care here. If as Gardner says there is a musical intelligence that underpins musical activities, it is distinct from, say, linguistic intelligence. Should we, in a similar manner, claim that there is a dramatic intelligence? What would it underpin? Dramatic activities, presumably. But these cover far more territory than Gardner's other intelligences. As we have seen in this book, dramatic acts are part of the dramatic world, the fictional world, and social worlds. The kind of intelligence we are hypothesizing, in fact, would underpin the most significant activities we live through. To put it another way, if there is a dramatic intelligence it differs from Gardner's other intelligences because it can be viewed in two different ways: as being behind the specific dramatic/theatrical activities within the theatre art form (limited sense); and as part of general intelligence (general sense). This does not appear to support or deny Gardner's theory of multiple intelligences.

When we turn from the nature of dramatic activity to the study of it, as in Developmental Drama,[8] our discussion goes far beyond intelligence per se, even beyond the so-called psychological domains, to an examination of life processes. In academic terms, Developmental Drama resembles a science. Science, in the strictest sense, investigates the natural universe, but its principles have been used in the social sciences to examine cultural life. But can science properly investigate the universe as a whole, natural as well as cultural? Can the view that the objective and the subjective are mutually exclusive be broken? If so, can the discipline of drama bridge C.P. Snow's duality of science and the humanities?

Developmental Drama focuses on dramatic acts embodying a practical, indeed a technological, method of inquiry. It is much like normal science in being *experimental,* but it is unlike science in being simultaneously *experiential.* Dramatic activity affirms the integrity of the subjective experience while using objective methods in a subjective context. Thus while Developmental Drama is aggressively committed to the active defence of consciousness, it assumes that both subjective and objective ways of knowing are valid. Developmental Drama, with Heisenberg, acknowledges indeterminacy (perspectives and comparisons) in the examination of data, but it denies the Faustian quest for absolute knowledge. Developmental Drama is not, then, a science in the mechanical mould. It is not solidly objective or concerned only with number-crunching. But it is certainly scientific in its mode of operation and may indicate future ways in which science can cease bifurcating knowledge and once more address the totality of human experience and the universe.

What does this mean for programs at the school and university levels? When personal, sociocultural, aesthetic, and artistic (theatrical) considerations form the foundation of drama curricula in schools and universities, drama as an educational medium becomes highly significant. Where it is used today, it infuses all other aspects of a school curriculum or of a university drama/theatre program. It is steadily increasing as a way of training teachers, particularly drama teachers. Although the increased use of spontaneous drama in Western schools is one of the best-kept secrets of the twentieth century, educational drama goes beyond schooling. Dramatic transformation is inherent in parenting, social learning, learning to learn, increased differentiation, maturation, and re-creation. Developmental Drama is the study of dramatic transformation as a total educative process, and it is holistic in its effect. Unifying imaginative thought and dramatic action, drama produces positive changes that transform the way we think, the way we learn, and our moral and ethical attitudes. Thus it can result in a change of consciousness.

Finally we should note that this book suggests ideas for a plan of future research. It is genuinely what McLuhan called a probe – a way of exploring the issues in order to lead us onward. Its ideas are meant not as ends in themselves but as means to continue exploration. What could be more appropriate in a book that addresses dramatic action?

Notes

INTRODUCTION: DRAMA AND INTELLIGENCE

1 For an excellent discussion of this issue, see Philip E. Vernon, *Intelligence and Cultural Environment* (London: Methuen 1969, 1972).
2 This theory of Howard Gardner's received hostile press, particularly by those who believe in a single intelligence, behaviourists, and preordinate thinkers. It has, however, many attractions for arts educators. The discussion here is briefly continued in the chapter 12. See *Frames of Mind: The Theory of Multiple Intelligences* (New York: Basic Books 1983).
3 Michael Polanyi, *Personal Knowledge: Towards a Post-Critical Philosophy* (New York: Harper and Row 1964).

CHAPTER ONE: DRAMA AND FICTION

1 Richard Courtney, "Drama and Aesthetics," *British Journal of Aesthetics,* 8, no. 4 (Winter 1968): 378–86.
2 Richard Courtney, "Theatre and Spontaneity," *Journal of Aesthetics and Art Criticism* 32, no. 1 (Fall 1973): 79–88.
3 Richard Courtney, *The Quest: Research and Inquiry in Arts Education* (Lanham, Maryland: University Press of America 1985); *Practical Research* (Sharon, Ontario: Bison Books 1988).
4 E.J. Burton, *Reality and "Realization": An approach to a Philosophy* (London: St. Alban Press 1966). See also H.J. Blackham, James Britton, and E.J. Burton, "A Theory of General Education," *The Plain View* 13, no. 4 (1961).
5 Thomas G. Pavel, *Fictional Worlds* (Cambridge, Massachusetts: Harvard University Press 1986). An important work on the theory of fiction, I have followed this in many respects here.

6 Carl Jung, ed., *Man and His Symbols* (New York: Dell 1968).
7 Claude Lévi-Strauss, "L'Analyse morphologique des contes russes," *International Journal of Slavic Linguistics and Poetics 3* (1960): 122–49; *Structural Anthropology*, 2 vols. (New York: Basic Books 1966, 1973).
8 Roland Barthes, "Introduction to the Structural Analysis of Narratives," in *Image, Music, Text* (New York: Hill and Wang 1977), 123–4.
9 Vladimir Propp, *Mortphology of the Folktale* (Austin, Texas: University of Texas Press 1968).
10 C.K. Ogden and I.A. Richards, *The Meaning of Meaning* (London: Routledge and Kegan Paul 1923; 8th ed. 1946). See also I.A. Richards, *Principles of Literary Criticism* (New York: Harcourt, Brace 1925).
11 P.F. Strawson, "On Referring," *Mind* 59 (1950); "Identifying Reference and Truth Value," *Theoria* 30 (1964): 96–118. See also Bertrand Russell, "Mr. Strawson on Referring," *Mind* 66 (1957): 385–9.
12 Richard Courtney, "Imagination and the Dramatic Act: Some Comments on Sartre, Ryle and Furlong," *Journal of Aesthetics and Art Criticism* 30, no 2 (Winter 1971): 163–70.
13 Gilbert Ryle, "Imaginary Objects," *Aristotelian Society: Supplementary Volume* 12 (1933): 35.
14 Pavel, *Fictional Worlds*, 17.
15 Ibid., 10.
16 Richard Ohmann, "Speech Acts and the Definition of Literature," *Philosophy and Rhetoric* 4 (1971): 14.
17 Barbara Herrnstein Smith, *On the Margins of Discourse* (Chicago: University of Chicago Press 1987), 14–40.
18 John Searle, "Indirect Speech Acts," in P. Cole and J.L. Morgan, eds., *Speech Acts (Syntax and Semantics 3)* (New York: Academic Press 1975).
19 H.H. Price, "Some Considerations about Belief," in A. Phillips Griffiths, ed., *Knowledge and Belief* (London: Oxford University Press 1967).
20 Peter Slade, *Child Drama* (London: University of London Press 1954).
21 John Seely, *In Context* (London: Oxford University Press 1976), 22–3.
22 Pavel, *Fictional Worlds*, 22.
23 John Searle, "The Logical Status of Fictional Discourse," *New Literary History* 6 (1975): 331–2.
24 Willard V. Quine, *Ontological Relativity and Other Issues* (New York: Columbia University Press 1969), 48.
25 Pavel, *Fictional Worlds*, 25.
26 Ibid., 26.
27 Searle, "Logical Status," 325.
28 Terence Parsons, *Nonexistent Objects* (New Haven: Yale University Press 1980).
29 Saul Kripke, "Naming and Necessity," in D. Davidson and G. Harman, eds, *Semantics of Natural Language* (Dordrecht: Reidel 1972).

30 Aristotle, *Poetics* 9. 1.

31 Robert Howell, "Fictional Objects: How They Are and How They Aren't," *Poetics* 8 (1979): 137–40.

32 David Lewis, "Anselm and Activity," *Nous* 4 (1970): 175–88; *Counterfactuals* (Cambridge, Massachusetts: Harvard University Press 1973).

33 Pavel, *Fictional Worlds*, 50.

34 For ontological metaphors, see Ellen Winner, *Invented Worlds: The Psychology of the Arts* (Cambridge: Harvard University Press 1982); and Gerald Prince, *Narratology* (The Hague: Mouton 1982). For aesthetic theory, see Nicholas Wolterstorff, "Worlds of Works of Art," *Journal of Aesthetics and Art Criticism* 35 (1976): 121–32. For phenomenology, see Roman Ingarden, *The Literary Work of Art* (Evanston, Illinois: Northwestern University Press 1965). For categorization, see Felix Martinez-Bonati, *Fictive Discourse and the Structure of Literature* (Ithaca: Cornell University Press 1981).

35 Kenneth Burke, *Language as Symbolic Action: Essays on Life, Literature and Method* (Los Angeles: University of California Press 1966); Hugh Dalziel Duncan, *Symbols in Society* (New York: Oxford University Press 1968); Erving Goffman, *The Presentation of Self in Everyday Life* (New York: Doubleday, 1959); Stanford M. Lyman and Marvin B. Scott, *The Drama of Social Reality* (New York: Oxford University Press 1975); Victor W. Turner, "Social Dramas and Stories about Them," in W.J.T. Mitchell, ed., *On Narrative* (Chicago: Chicago University Press 1980); *From Ritual To Theatre: The Human Seriousness of Play* (New York: Performing Arts Journal Publications 1982); Peter L. McLaren, *Schooling as a Ritual Performance* (London: Routledge and Kegan Paul 1986).

36 Alvin Plantinga, *The Nature of Necessity* (Oxford: Clarendon Press 1974).

CHAPTER TWO: DRAMA AND COGNITIVE PROCESSES

1 Algirdas Julien Greimas, *On Meaning: Selected Writings in Semiotic Theory,* translated by P. Perron and F.H. Collins (Minneapolis: University of Minnesota Press 1987), chapter 10. This is the best introduction to Greimas' work currently available in English; a number of ideas it contains underpin this chapter.

2 This famous phase by McLuhan, by which he meant that the most significant meanings of messages are provided by the media that carry them, is used slightly differently here.

3 The use of this parable as exemplary has been previously employed by others, including Greimas and Daniel Patte.

4 The particular concern of Greimas, the semiotic square is an analytic tool

that can be used for both binary/categorical and alternative logics (Richard Courtney, *Aesthetic Learning* [Ottawa: Social Sciences and Humanities Research Council of Canada 1985], chapter 5).

5 Richard Courtney, *Re-Play: Studies of Human Drama in Education* (Toronto: Ontario Institute for Studies in Education Press 1982).

6 *Overload* is a term used by improvisers for the director's intervention under certain conditions (Keith Johnstone, *Impro: Improvisation in the Theatre* [London: Methuen 1979]; Viola Spolin, *Improvisation for the Theatre* [Evanston, Illinois: Northwestern University Press 1963]).

7 The fiduciary contract is a term particular to Greimas and semioticians who follow him.

CHAPTER THREE: COGNITIVE WORLDS

1 For the variety of improvisation, see Courtney, "Spontaneity."

2 Thomas G. Pavel, *Fictional Worlds,* (Cambridge, Massachusetts: Harvard University Press 1968) 51.

3 John Searle, *Speech Acts* (London: Cambridge University Press 1969), 19–21.

4 Pavel, *Fictional Worlds,* 53.

5 Ibid., 54.

6 Kendall Walton, "Do We Need Fictional Entities? Notes towards a Theory," in *Aesthetics: Proceedings of the Eighth International Wittgenstein Symposium* (Vienna: Holder, Pichler, Temsky 1984), 179.

7 Pavel, *Fictional Worlds,* 55.

8 Walton, "Do We Need Fictional Entities?"

9 Gareth Evans, *The Varieties of Reference* (New York: Oxford University Press 1982).

10 For the isomorphism of drama, see Bernard Beckerman, *The Dynamics of Drama* (New York: Knopf 1970), chapter 1.

11 Richard Courtney, *Play, Drama and Thought* (Toronto: Simon and Pierre 1968; 4th ed. 1989), chapter 8; Courtney, *Re-Play; Studies of Human Drama in Education* (Toronto: OISE Press 1982), chapter 1. See also the works of Mircea Eliade and Joseph Campbell.

12 Arthur Danto, "The Artsworld," in Joseph Margolis, ed., *Philosophy Looks at the Arts* (Philadelphia: Temple University Press 1978), 137, 139.

13 F.E. Sparshott, "Truth in Fiction," *Journal of Aesthetics and Art Criticism* 26 (1967): 3–7.

14 Richard Courtney, "Indigenous Theatre: Indian and Eskimo Ritual Drama," in Anton Wagner, ed., *Contemporary Canadian Theatre: New*

World Visions (Toronto: Simon and Pierre 1985), 206–15. See also entries in *Oxford Companion to Canadian Theatre* (Toronto: Oxford University Press 1989).

15 Marie-Laure Ryan, "Fiction, Non-Factuals and the Principle of Minimum Departure," *Poetics* 8 (1980); "Fictions as a logical, Ontological and Illocutory Issue," *Style* 18 (1984): 121–39.

16 Jacques Derrida, *Speech and Phenomena* (Evanston, Illinois: Northwestern University Press 1973); *Mimesis/des articulations* (Paris 1975); *On Grammatology* (Baltimore: Johns Hopkins University Press 1976); "Signature, Event, Context," *Glyph* 1 (1977): 172–97; "Limited Inc abc.," *Glyph* 2 (1977): 162–254; *Dissemination* (Chicago: University of Chicago Press 1981); Jacques Lacan, *Ecrits: A Selection* (London: Tavistock 1977); Julia Kristeva, *La révolution du langage poétique* (Paris 1974); Paul De Man, *Blindness and Insight: Essays in the Rhetoric of Contemporary Criticism* (New York: Oxford University Press 1971); *Allegories of Reading: Figural Language in Rousseau, Nietzsche, Rilke and Proust* (New Haven: Yale University Press 1979).

17 D.W. Winnicott, *Playing and Reality* (Harmondsworth: Penguin 1974). See also the works of Melanie Klein.

18 Richard Courtney, "A Dramatic Theory of Imagination," *New Literary History* 2, no. 3 (Spring 1971): 445–60, reprinted in David Booth and Alistair Martin-Smith, eds, *Re-Cognizing Richard Courtney: Selected Writings on Drama and Education* (Markham, Ontario: Pembroke Publishers 1988) 98–109; Richard Courtney, *The Dramatic Curriculum* (London, Ontario: Althouse Press, University of Western Ontario 1980), chapter 5.

19 Richard Courtney, "Drama and Metaphor," in Judith Kase-Polisini, ed., *Creative Drama in a Developmental Context* (Lanham, Maryland: University Press of America 1985), 39–64.

20 Philippe Lacoue-Labarthe, "Typographie," in, Jacques Derrida, *Mimesis/des articulations* (Paris, 1975).

21 Pavel, *Fictional Worlds,* 89.

22 To those of us who once performed Victorian melodrama in British repertory theatres ("twice nightly, three times on Saturdays"), this is no surprise. Even Mrs Henry Wood's *East Lynne,* where the heroine, on hearing of the death of her son Little Willie, cries: "Dead! Dead! And never called me mother!" demands to be played "straight." The prompter said during each interval, "There's not a dry eye in the house tonight." Today as we watch Keith Johnstone's improvisational group, The Loose Moose Company, performing his "theatresports" to an amused audience, we are amazed that such incongruous creations should be based on the ordinary.

And those of us who have had the good fortune to use spontaneous improvisation in schools can only watch in wonder as students take mundane situations and instantly create the most imaginative worlds.

23 See chapter 5. See also A.J. Greimas, *Structural Semantics: An attempt at a Method* (Lincoln, Nebraska: University of Nebraska Press 1983); Floyd Merrell, *Semiotic Foundations: Steps towards an Epistemology of Written Texts* (Bloomington, Indiana: Indiana University Press, 1982). The latter is not only a good introduction in English to Greimas' ideas but also contains many ideas relevant to this book.

24 For example, the appearance of spontaneous drama in schools at the beginning of this century (see H. Caldwell Cook, *The Play Way* [London: Heinemann 1919]).

CHAPTER FOUR: THE DRAMATIC WORLD

1 See pp. 54–6.

2 Jean Piaget, *Play, Dreams and Imitation in Childhood* (New York: Norton 1972), and other works.

3 Richard Courtney, "A Dramatic Theory of Imagination," *New Literary History* 2, no. 3 (Spring 1971), reprinted in David Booth and Alistair Martin-Smith, eds., *Re-Cognizing Richard Courtney: Selected Writings on Drama and Education* (Markham, Ontario: Pembroke Publishers 1988).

4 It is interesting to note that Being/body/voice have been the three major categories in actor training for many years (see Yori Lane, *The Psychology of the Actor* [New York: John Day Company 1960]).

5 E.H. Gombrich, *Meditations on a Hobby-Horse and Other Essays,* 3rd ed. (London: Phaidon 1978).

6 Courtney, "A Dramatic Theory."

7 See p. 46.

8 Richard Courtney, *Re-Play: Studies of Human Drama in Education* (Toronto: Ontario Institute for Studies in Education Press 1982), 108–25.

9 Richard Courtney, "Theatre and Spontaneity," *Journal of Aesthetics and Art Criticism* 32, no. 1 (Fall 1973): 79–88.

10 Richard Courtney, *The Quest: Research and Inquiry in Arts Education* (Lanham, Maryland: University Press of America 1985).

11 Richard Courtney, "Indigenous Theatre: Indian and Eskimo Ritual Drama" in Anton Wagner, ed., *Contemporary Canadian Theatre: New World Visions* (Toronto: Simon and Pierre 1985), 206–15.

12 Edward Gordon Craig, *On the Art of the Theatre,* rev. ed. (London: Heinemann 1905), 1–53.

13 G. Wilson Knight, *The Wheel of Fire* (London: Methuen 1930). Gordon

Craig and Wilson Knight represent a British tradition of highly imaginative actor-director-scholars whose poetic works have had a great influence on dramatic theory and practice. Their diverse symbolic views of *Macbeth* indicate the style of interpretation that still influences dramatic practice in the English-speaking world.

CHAPTER FIVE: THE DRAMATIC METAPHOR

1 Aristotle *Poetics* 1457 b. 1–1458 a. 17.
2 Ibid., 1457 b. 6–9
3 When Aristotle turns to metaphor proper he uses two examples:

A "Then he drew off his life with the bronze sword," and "Then with the bronze cup he cut the water [that is, the flow of blood, or life]." Both are examples of two ideas, *X* and *Z*, that overlap at *Y*. In other words, *Y* is the genus of which *X* and *Z* are the species. This form of metaphor implies two underlying processes:
a Identification: *Y* is identified with parts of *X* and *Z*;
b Absorption: *Y* absorbs parts of *X* and *Z*.

B Aristotle uses the forms *A*/*B* = *C*/*D*. That is, where old age/life = sunset/day, then "old age" = "the sunset of life" and "evening" = "day's old age." This form of metaphor has a sort of propositional function where noncoincident traits can be dropped while those in common are reinforced. They are culture-bound, as is the poetic tradition (Umberto Eco, *Semiotics and the Philosophy of Language* [Bloomington, Indiana: Indiana University Press 1984].

4 Aristotle *Rhetoric* 1401 b. 14–25.
5 Ibid., 1412 a. 11–12.
6 Paul Ricoeur, *The Rule of Metaphor: Multi-disciplinary Studies of the Creation of Meaning in Language* (Toronto: University of Toronto Press 1977).
7 George Lakoff and Mark Johnson, *Metaphors We Live By* (Chicago: Chicago University Press 1980).
8 Experimental psychology has indicated that the use of mental or visual imagery in metaphor is a key element in verbal effectiveness. The significance of the double in metaphor has been shown to improve language production, comprehension, and memory; on the other hand, it has also been suggested that root metaphors of a culture can best be identified in ritual contexts (Allan Paivio, *Imagery and Verbal Processes* [Hillsdale, New Jersey: Lawrence Ehrlbaum 1979]).
9 Ricoeur, *The Rule of Metaphor*, 6.

10 Max Black, *Models and Metaphors* (Ithaca: Cornell University Press 1962); Nelson Goodman, *The Languages of Art* (Indianapolis: Hackett 1972).

11 Ricoeur, *The Rule of Metaphor*, 7.

12 O.B. Hardison, Jr, *Christian Rite and Christian Drama in the Middle Ages: Essays in the Origin and Early History of the Drama* (Baltimore: The Johns Hopkins University Press 1965, reprinted 1969), 39–40.

13 Roger S. Jones, *Physics as Metaphor* (Minneapolis: University of Minnesota Press 1982), 4.

14 William Shakespeare, *The Tempest*, IV. i. 156–8.

15 For aesthetics and art criticism, see Elliott W. Eisner, "Educational Connoisseurship and Educational Criticism" (paper privately circulated, n.d.); "The Perceptive Eye: Towards the Reformation of Educational Evaluation" (paper presented at A.E.R.A., 1975); *The Educational Imagination: On the Design and Evaluation of School Programs* (New York: Macmillan 1979). For literary criticism, see E.F. Kelly, "Curriculum Evaluation and Literary Criticism," *Curriculum Inquiry* 5 (1975): 87–106; D. Jenkins and B. O'Toole, "Curriculum Evaluation, Literary Criticism, and the Paracurriculum," in G.M. Willis, ed., *Qualitative Evaluation: Concepts and Cases in Curriculum Criticism* (Berkeley, California: McCutchan 1978). For journalism, see T. Barone, "Education as Aesthetic Experience: 'Art in Germ,'" *Educational Leadership* 40, no. 4 (1983): 21–6; B. MacDonald, "The Portrayal of Persons" (paper privately circulated, 1976). For music, see Elliott W. Eisner, "The Art and Craft of Teaching," *Educational Leadership* 40, no. 4 (1983): 4–13. For theatre, see M.R. Grumet, "Curriculum as Theatre," *Curriculum Inquiry* 8, no. 1 (Spring 1978): 37–64; R. Oram, "In Defence of Curriculum Criticism," *Cambridge Journal of Education* 13, no. 1 (1983): 7–13. For drama, see Richard Courtney, *The Dramatic Curriculum* (London, Ontario: Althouse Press 1981). See also Geoffrey Milburn, "Derivation and Application of a Dramatic Metaphor for the Assessment of Teaching" (Ed. D. dissertation, University of Toronto 1983); "On Discipline-Stripping: Difficulties in the Application of Humanistic Metaphors to Educational Phenomena" (paper presented to the Canadian Society for the Study of Education, 1983).

16 K.A. Leithwood, ed., *Planned Educational Change: A Manual of Curriculum Review, Development, and Implementation (CRDI) Concepts and Procedures* (Toronto: OISE Press 1986); ed., *Studies in Curriculum Decision Making* (OISE Press 1982); et al., *Making a difference through Performance Appraisal* (OISE Press, 1988).

17 F. Michael Connelly and Jean Clandinin, "Personal Practical Knowledge at Bay Street School" (paper privately circulated, n.d.); *Teachers as Curriculum Planners* (Toronto: OISE Press 1988).

18 Peter L. McLaren, *Schooling as a Ritual Performance* (London: Routledge and Kegan Paul 1986).

19 Richard Courtney, *Aesthetic Learning,* (Ottawa: SSHRC 1985); Richard Courtney and Paul Park, *Learning through the Arts,* research report, 4 vols. (Toronto: Ministry of Education, Ontario, 1980); Richard Courtney, David Booth, John Emerson, and Natalie Kuzmich, *Teacher Education in the Arts* (Sharon, Ontario: Bison Books 1985); *No One Way of Being: The Practical Knowledge of Elementary Arts Teachers,* research report (Toronto: Ministry of Education, Ontario, 1988).

20 Various bibliographies exist. For Canada, see Richard Courtney, *Drama Education Canada* (Sharon, Ontario: Bison Books 1987).

21 Lynne McGregor, Maggie Tate, and Ken Robinson, *Learning through Drama* (London: Heinemann 1977), 59.

22 Floyd Merrell, "Of Metaphor and Metonymy, *Semiotica* 31, no 3/4 (1980): 289–307; *Semiotic Foundations. Steps towards an Epistemology of written texts* (Bloomington, Indiana: Indiana University Press 1982).

23 Gary Schwartz and Don Merten, "Social Identity and Expressive Symbols: The Meaning of an Initiation Ritual," *American Anthropologist* 70: (19??): 1117-31.

24 Edmund Leach, *Culture and Communication: The Logic by Which Symbols Are Connected* (Cambridge: Cambridge University Press 1976); 5.

25 Merrell, *Semiotic Foundations.*

26 Leach, *Culture and Communication,* 5.

27 Ibid., 22.

28 Anthony Wilden, *System and Structure* (London: Tavistock 1972).

29 John McLeod, "Metaphor and Metonymy in the Arts" (Melbourne, Australia: Drama Resource Centre 1982).

30 Helen B. Schwartzman, *Transformation: The Anthopology of Children's Play* (New York: Plenum Press 1978).

31 A.J. Greimas, *Structural Semantics: An Attempt at a Method* (Lincoln, Nebraska: University of Nebraska Press 1983).

32 These are the concepts of Thomas S. Kuhn, Stephen C. Pepper, Lucien Goldmann, and Ludwig Wittgenstein.

33 McLeod, "Metaphor and Metonymy."

34 Robert W. Witkin, *The Intelligence of Feeling* (London: Heineman 1974).

CHAPTER SIX: DRAMA AND LOGIC

1 For Edward Sapir, "language is a guide to 'social reality.'" It not only refers to experience but actually defines experience for us. Benjamin Lee Whorf extended this to the idea that language acts as a mould for thought.

(*Collected Papers on Metalinguistics* [Washington, D.C.: Department of State/Foreign Service Institute 1952]; *Language, Thought and Reality* [Cambridge, Massachusetts: MIT Press 1956]).

2 Umberto Eco, *A Theory of Semiotics* (Bloomington, Indiana: Indiana University Press 1976); also *Semiotics and the Philosophy of Language* (Bloomington, Indiana: Indiana University Press 1984), hereafter cited as SPL.

3 H. Marshall McLuhan, *Understanding Media: The Extensions of Man* (London: Routledge and Kegan Paul 1964).

4 P. Rosenthiehl, "Labyrinthologie Mathematique," in *Mathématiques et Sciences Humaines 9* (Paris: Centre Culturel Pompidou 1971); "Les Mots du labyrinthe," in *Cartes et Figures de la Terre* (Paris: Centre Culturel Pompidou 1980).

5 Karl Popper, *Conjectures and Refutations* (New York: Harper and Row 1963); *Objective Knowledge* (London: Oxford University Press 1972); *The Philosophy of Karl Popper,* 2 vols. (LaSalle, Illinois: Open Court Publications 1974); *Popper Selections,* edited by D. Miller (Princeton, New Jersey: Princeton University Press 1985).

6 Peter Slade, *Child Drama* (London: University of London Press 1954).

7 Ludwig Wittgenstein, *Tractacus Logico-Philosophicus,* translated by D.F. Pears and B.F. McGuinness (New York: The Humanities Press 1922, 1929).

8 Werner Heisenberg, *Philosophic Problems of Nuclear Science* (London: Faber and Faber 1952).

9 Alfred Korzybski, *Science and Sanity* (Lakefield, Connecticut: International Society for General Semantics 1958).

10 David Best, *Expression in Movement and the Arts* (London: Lepus 1974).

11 Ibid., 92–3.

12 E.R. Emmett, *Learning to Philosophize,* (Harmondsworth: Penguin 1968).

13 Best, *Expression.*

14 Popper, *Objective Knowledge,* 420–2.

15 Best, *Expression.*

16 Ludwig Wittgenstein, *Philosophical Investigations,* edited by G.E.M. Anscombe (New York: Macmillan 1953).

17 Best, *Expression.*

18 Here we are referring not only to scholarly research but also to the remarkable experiments carried out by contemporary storytellers (see Bob Barton, *Tell Me Another* [Markham, Ontario: Pembroke Publishers 1987]).

19 Keith Johnstone, *Impro: Improvisation in the Theatre* (London: Methuen 1979).

20 M.A. Bonfantini and G. Proni, "To Guess or Not to Guess," in Umberto Eco and T.A. Sebeok, eds, *The Sign of Three: Dupin, Holmes, Peirce*

(Bloomington, Indiana: Indiana University Press 1983). See also Eco, *A Theory of Semiotics*, 2.14; *SPL*, 41–3.

21 A.J. Greimas, *Semantique structurale* (Paris: Larousse 1966), 188.

22 A.J. Greimas, *Structural Semantics: An Attempt at a Method* (Lincoln, Nebraska: University of Nebraska Press 1983), IV.3.d, VI.2.a.

23 Gregory Bateson, *Steps to an Ecology of Mind* (New York: Chandler 1972); Nelson Goodman, *The Languages of Art.* (Indianapolis: Hackett 1972) Floyd Merrell, *Semiotic Foundations: Steps towards an Epistemology of Written Texts* (Bloomington, Indiana: Indiana University Press 1982); John von Neumann, *The Computer and the Brain* (New Haven: Yale University Press 1958); Thomas A. Sebeok, *Style in Language* (Cambridge, Massachusetts: MIT Press 1972); Anthony Wilden, *System and Structure* (London: Tavistock 1972).

CHAPTER SEVEN: DRAMA AND INTUITION

1 Nell Noddings and Paul J. Shore, *Awakening the Inner Eye: Intuition in Education* (New York: Teachers' College Press, Columbia University 1984), 2–3.

2 Eric Berne, *Intuition and Ego States: The Origins of Transactional Analysis* (San Francisco: TA Press, 1977), 25–6.

3 Jean Piaget, *Play, Dreams and Imitation in Childhood* (New York: Norton 1972).

4 Jerome S. Bruner, *The Process of Education* (Cambridge, Massachusetts: Harvard University Press 1977).

5 Jerome S. Bruner, *Towards a Theory of Instruction* (Cambridge: Harvard University Press 1966), 102.

6 Gabriele Lusser Rico and Mary Frances Claggert, *Balancing the Hemispheres: Brain Research and the Teaching of Writing* (1980).

7 Brewster Ghiselin, ed., *The Creative Process* (Berkeley, California: University of California Press 1952).

8 Douglas R. Hofstadter, *Gödel, Escher, Bach: An Eternal Golden Braid* (New York: Basic Books 1979), 371, 375.

9 Ibid., 385.

10 Ibid., 201, figure 43.

11 E.T. Hall, *The Hidden Dimension* (New York: Doubleday 1966); Ray L. Birdwhistell, *Kinesics and Context: Essays on Body Motion Communication* (Philadelphia: University of Pennsylvania Press 1970).

12 Robert W. Witkin, *The Intelligence of Feeling* (London: Heinemann 1974).

13 I am grateful to my colleague, Dr. Chester Carlow, for this point.

14 Jacob L. Moreno, *Psychodrama*, vol. 1 (New York: Beacon House 1946).

CHAPTER EIGHT: DRAMA AND SYMBOL

1 Raymond Firth, *Symbols, Private and Public* (London: Allen and Unwin 1973), 66–7.
2 Umberto Eco, *Semiotics and the Philosophy of Language* (Bloomington, Indiana: Indiana University Press 1984), hereafter cited as *SPL.*
3 Ernst Cassirer, *Substance and Function,* translated by W. Curtis and M. Swabey (Chicago: Open Court Publishers 1923); Claude Levi-Strauss, "Introduction à l'oeuvre de Marcel Mauss," in M. Mauss, *Sociologie et Anthropologie* (Paris: PUF 1950); Tzvetan Todorov, *Les Genres du Discours* (Paris: Seuil 1978).
4 Eco, *SPL.*
5 Sigmund Freud, *The Interpretation of Dreams* (London: Allen and Unwin 1899, reprinted 1954).
6 Mircea Eliade, *The Sacred and the Profane* (New York: Harcourt Brace 1959).
7 Alexander Marshack, *The Roots of Civilization* (New York: McGraw-Hill 1972).
8 Frank Waters, *Book of the Hopi* (New York: Viking Press 1963).
9 Juan Eduardo Cirlot, *A Dictionary of Symbols,* translated by J. Sage (New York: Philosophical Library 1962), xx.
10 Eco, *SPL.*
11 Dante *Divine Comedy,* epistula XIII.
12 Eco, *SPL.*
13 Cirlot, *Dictionary*, xxiii.
14 Wilhelm Goethe, *Werke,* 1809–32 (Leipzig: Bibliographisches Institut 1926), n. 111–13.
15 Eco, *SPL.*
16 Georg Friedrich Creuzer, *Symbolik und Mythologie der Alten Volker* (Leipzig-Darmstadt: Leske 1810-12), 1: 35.
17 G.W.F. Hegel, *Philosophy of Right,* translated by T.M. Knox (Oxford: Clarendon Press 1817, reprinted 1942), 2: 83.
18 Ibid., 8.
19 Freud, *Dreams.*
20 Paul Ricoeur, *The Rule of Metaphor: Multi-disciplinary Studies of the Creation of Meaning in Language* (Toronto: University of Toronto Press 1977).
21 Eco, *SPL.* 162–3.
22 Carl Gustav Jung, ed. *Man and his Symbols* (New York: Dell 1968).
23 Carl Gustav Jung, "Über die Archtypen des Kollektiven Unbewussten," in *Von den Wurzein des Bewusstseins Studien über des Archetypus* (Zurich: Rascher 1934).

24 Carl Gustav Jung, *Basic Writings* (New York: The Modern Library 1959), 19.
25 Ibid.
26 Jerome S. Bruner, *On Knowing: Essays for the Left Hand* (Cambridge, Massachusetts: Harvard University Press 1962).
27 Jung, *Basic Writings,* 195.
28 Carl Gustav Jung, *Alchemical Studies,* translated by R.F.C. Hull (London: Routledge and Kegan Paul 1967), 150.
29 Marie-Louise Von Franz, "The Process of Individuation," in Jung, *Man and His Symbols*, 246.
30 Ricoeur, *The Rule of Metaphor.*
31 Aniela Jaffe, "Symbolism in the Visual Arts," in Jung, *Man and His Symbols*, 267.
32 *Ibid.*, 268–9.
33 *Ibid.*, 269–73.
34 Eco, *SPL.*
35 C.S. Peirce, *Collected Papers* (Cambridge, Massachusetts: Harvard University Press 1958), 2: 228.
36 For symbol communication (versus language), see Louis Hjelmslev, *Prolegema to a Theory of Language,* translated by F.J. Whitfield (Madison, Wisconsin: Wisconsin University Press 1961). Or as identified with the subject of the sign, see Julia Kristeva, *Semiotike* (Paris: Seuil 1969), 69.
37 For symbol as only linguistic, see B. Malmberg, *Signes et Symboles* (Paris: Picard 1977), 22. As performed speech act, see E. Buyssens, *Le langage et le discours* (Brussels: Office de publicité 1943). As only in a text, see Roland Barthes, "The Structuralist Activity," *Partisan Review* 34 (Winter 1967): 82–8; Derrida, "Limited Inc abc.," *Glyph* 2 (1977): 162–254.
38 Eco, *SPL*. 46.
39 Charles E. Shannon, "The Mathematical Theory of Communication," *Bell System Technical Journal* (July–October 1948): 379–423, 623–56. See also Roman Jakobsen, *The Framework of Language* (Detroit: Michigan Studies in the Humanities, 1980).
40 Lévi-Strauss sees all myths, culture, and language as rule-governed, and seeks a universal code (see *Structural Anthropology,* 2 vols. [New York: Basic Books 1966]).
41 Eco, *SPL.*
42 Shannon, "Mathematical Theory."
43 Jeremy Campbell, *Grammatical Man: Information, Entropy, Language and Life* (New York: Simon and Schuster 1982). Eco defines this as an "s-code" that has the possibility of a correlational use of its elements *(SPL).*
44 Petr Bogatyrev, "Semiotics in the Folk Theatre" (1938), in Ladislaw

Matejka and Irwin R. Titinuk, eds., *Semiotics of Art: Prague School Contributions* (Cambridge, Massachusetts: MIT Press 1976), 35–6.

45 Jiri Veltruvsky, "Man and Object in the Theater" (1940), in Paul L. Garvin, ed., *A Prague School Reader on Esthetics, Literary Structure and Style* (Washington: Georgetown University Press 1964), 84.

46 Eco, *SPL*.

47 M.M. Bakhtin, *The Dialogic Imagination: Four Essays,* translated by C. Emerson and M. Holquist (Austin, University of Texas Press 1981), 210–18.

48 A.J. Greimas, *On Meaning: Selected Writings in Semiotic Theory,* Translated by P. Perron and F.H. Collins (Minneapolis: University of Minnesota Press 1987).

49 Nancy Munn, "Symbolism in a Ritual Context: Aspects of Symbolic Action," in John J. Honigmann, ed., *Handbook of Social and Cultural Anthropology* (Chicago: Rand McNally 1973), 582.

50 Ibid., 580.

51 Stanford M. Lyman and Marvin B. Scott, *The Drama of Social Reality* (New York: Oxford University Press 1975).

52 Munn, "Symbolism."

53 Roy A. Rappaport, "Adaptation and the Structure of Ritual," in N.B. Jones and V. Reynolds, eds, *Human Behavior and Adaptation: Symposia: Society for the Study of Human Biology* 18 (1978): 77–102; *Ecology, Meaning and Religion* (Richmond, California: Atlantic Books 1979); "Concluding Remarks on Ritual and Reflexivity," *Semiotica* 1/2, no. 30 (1980): 181–93.

54 Victor W. Turner, *Process, Performance and Pilgrimage: A Study in Comparative Symbology* (New Delhi: Concept Publishing 1979).

55 Abner Cohen, *Two-Dimensional Man: An Essay on the Anthropology of Power and Symbolism in Complex Society* (London: Routledge and Kegan Paul 1974); *Symbolic Action and the Structure of the Self* (London: Academic Press 1977).

CHAPTER NINE: DRAMA AND PERFORMANCE

1 Robert W. Witkin, *The Intelligence of Feeling* (London: Heinemann 1974).

2 Jacques Derrida, "Signature, Event, Context, *Glyph* 1 (1977): 172–97; *Dissemination* (Chicago: University of Chicago Press 1981).

3 Keir Elam, *The Semiotics of Drama and Theatre* (London: Methuen 1980).

4 Aristotle, *Poetics* 22.

5 D.W. Winnicott, *Playing and Reality* (Harmondsworth: Penguin 1974).

6 Jean Piaget, *Play, Dreams and Imitation in Childhood* (New York: Norton 1972).

7 C.S. Peirce, *Collected Papers* (Cambridge, Massachusetts: Harvard University Press 1958), 7.337.

8 Floyd Merrell, *Semiotic Foundations: Steps towards an Epistemology of Written Texts* (Bloomington, Indiana: Indiana University Press 1982), 138.

9 Gregory Bateson, *Steps Towards an Ecology of Mind* (New York: Chandler 1972), 317–18.

10 Merrell, *Semiotic Foundations.*

11 David Bohm, *Causality and Chance in Modern Physics* (Philadelphia: University of Pennsylvania Press 1957); Marjorie Grene, *The Understanding of Nature: Essays in the Philosophy of Biology* (Dordrecht, Holland: D. Reidel 1974); Merrell, *Semiotic Foundations*, 146; Karl Popper, *The Philosophy of Karl Popper,* 2 vols. (LaSalle, Illinois: Open Court Publications 1974).

12 B.F. Skinner, *Science and Human Behavior* (New York: Macmillan 1953); *The Technology of Teaching* (New York: Appleton-Century-Crofts 1968); Abraham H. Maslow, *Motivation and Personality* (New York: Harper and Row 1954); *The Farther Reaches of Human Nature* (Harmondsworth: Penguin 1972).

13 Konstantin Stanislavsky, *Creating a Role,* translated by E.R. Hapgood (New York: Theatre Arts Books 1961); Bertolt Brecht, *The Messingkauf Dialogues,* translated by J. Willett (London: Methuen 1965).

14 Brian Way, *Development through Drama* (London: Longman 1967); Gavin Bolton, *Towards a Theory of Drama in Education* (London: Longman 1979); *Drama as Education* (London: Longman 1984).

15 J.A. Hadfield, *Dreams and Nightmares* (Harmondsworth: Penguin 1954).

CHAPTER TEN: DRAMA AND HUMAN LEARNING

1 Richard Courtney, "On Culture and Creative Drama," "Creative Drama in English-speaking and Hunting Societies," "Creative Drama in Agricultural Societies," and "Culture and the Creative Drama Teacher," in *Youth Theatre Journal* 3, no. 1 (Summer 1988): 3–9; 3, no. 2 (Fall 1988): 6–10; 3, no. 3 (Winter 1988): 14–20; 3, no. 4 (Spring 1989): 18–23.

2 Richard Courtney and P. Park, *Learning through The Arts* (Toronto: Ontario Ministry of Education 1980).

3 Joseph Lee, *Play in Education* (New York: Macmillan 1917).

4 Richard Courtney and Gertrud Schattner, eds, *Drama in Therapy,* vol. 1: *Children*, and vol. 2: *Adults* (New York: Drama Book Specialists 1982).

5 Peter Slade, *Child Drama* (London: University of London Press 1954).

6 Alfred N. Whitehead and Bertrand Russell, *Principia Mathematica* (Cambridge: Cambridge University Press 1910–13). The most important

commentaries are Gregory Bateson, *Steps to an Ecology of Mind,* (New York: Chandler 1972) and Floyd Merrell, *Semiotic Foundations: Steps towards an Epistemology of Written Texts* (Bloomington, Indiana: Indiana University Press 1982).

7 Bateson, *Steps to an Ecology,* 251–2.

8 Benjamin Lee Whorf, *Language, Thought and Reality* (Cambridge, Massachusetts: MIT Press 1956).

9 Rudolf Carnap, *The Logical Syntax of Language* (New York: Harcourt, Brace 1937).

10 Bateson, *Steps to an Ecology,* 254.

11 Ibid., 262–3.

12 Ibid., 264.

13 C.S. Peirce, *Collected Papers,* (Cambridge, Massachusetts: Harvard University Press 1958), 5.388–410.

14 Nicholas Rescher, *Conceptual Idealism* (Oxford: Blackwell 1973).

15 Peter L. Berger and Thomas Luckman, *The Social Construction of Reality* (New York: Doubleday 1966); Thomas S. Kuhn, *The Structure of Scientific Revolutions* (Chicago: University of Chicago Press 1962); Ervin Lazlo, *Introduction to Systems Philosophy* (New York: Harper and Row 1972).

16 Paul Feyerabend, *Against Method* (London: New Left Books 1975); N.R. Hanson, *Patterns of Discovery: An Inquiry into the Conceptual Foundations of Science* (Cambridge: Cambridge University Press 1958); Kuhn, *Scientific Revolutions;* Michael Polanyi, *Personal Knowledge: Towards a Post-Critical Philosophy* (New York: Harper and Row 1964).

17 Bateson, *Towards an Ecology,* 266–72.

18 Lawrence Kohlberg, *Recent Research in Moral Education* (New York: Holt, Rinehart and Winston 1978).

19 Bateson, *Towards an Ecology,* 274–5.

20 H. Marshall McLuhan, *Understanding Media: The Extensions of Man* (London: Routledge and Kegan Paul 1964).

21 Bateson, *Towards an Ecology,* 101–25.

22 Viola Spolin, *Improvisation for the Theater* (Evanston, Illinois: Northwestern University Press 1963).

23 Bateson, *Towards an Ecology,* 115.

24 H. Howard Russell, *Generic Skills/Economic Development: First Interim Report* (Toronto: Ontario Institute for Studies in Education 31 March 1986); and subsequent reports; Richard Courtney, "Drama as a Generic Skill," *Youth Theatre Journal* 1, no. 1 (Summer 1986): 5–27.

25 Author's private research papers.

CHAPTER ELEVEN: DRAMA AND DIALOGUE

1 Louis Arnaud Reid, "Feeling and Understanding," in Ralph A. Smith, ed., *Aesthetic Concepts and Education* (Urbana, Illinois: University of Illinois Press 1970).
2 Martin Buber, *I and Thou,* translated by W. Kaufmann (New York: Scribner's 1970); M.M. Bakhtin, *The Dialogic Imagination: Four Essays,* translated by C. Emerson and M. Holguist (Austin, Texas: University of Texas Press 1981); Kenneth Burke, *Language as Symbolic Action: Essays on Life, Literature, and Method* (Los Angeles: University of California Press 1966).
3 Banktin, *The Dialogic Imagination,* 256.
4 Robert Scholes, *Semiotics and Interpretation* (New Haven: Yale University Press 1982), 18.
5 Karl Popper, *Objective Knowledge,* (London: Oxford University Press 1972), 23–4, 70.
6 Ibid., 71.
7 Floyd Merrell, *Semiotic Foundations: Steps towards an Epistemology of Writter Texts* (Bloomington, Indiana: Indiana University Press 1982), 103.
8 Scholes, *Semiotics and Interpretation,* 31.
9 Ibid., 33–5.
10 Paul Ricoeur, *The Rule of Metaphor: Multi-disciplinary Studies of the Creation of Meaning in Language* (Toronto: University of Toronto Press 1977), 74.
11 Yuri M. Lotman, *Semiotics of the Cinema* (Ann Arbor: Michigan Slavic Publications 1976); *Analysis of the Poetic Text* (Ann Arbor: Michigan Slavic Texts 1976).
12 Jacques Derrida, *Dissemination* (Chicago: University of Chicago Press 1981).
13 Robert W. Witkin, *The Intelligence of Feeling,* (London: Heinemann 1974), 4–5.
14 Bakhtin, *The Dialogic Imagination,* 282.

CHAPTER TWELVE: IN CONCLUSION

1 Karl R. Popper and John C. Eccles, *The Self and Its Brain: An Argument for Interactionism* (London: Routledge and Kegan Paul 1977, 2nd ed. 1983), 27.

2 Wilder Penfield, "The Permanent Record of the Stream of Consciousness," *Acta Psychologica* 11 (19??): 47–69.
3 See footnote 1, chapter ten.
4 M.D. Faber and Collin Skinner, "*The Spanish Tragedy:* Act IV," *Philological Quarterly* 49, no. 4 (October 1970): 444–59.
5 Popper and Eccles, *The Self and Its Brain,* 43–50.
6 Richard Courtney, "Drama and Aesthetics," *British Journal of Aesthetics* 8, no., 4 (Winter 1968): 378–86.
7 Howard Gardner, *Frames of Mind: The Theory of Multiple Intelligences* (New York: Basic Books 1983). See also Robert W. Colby, "On the Nature of Dramatic Intelligence: A Study of Developmental Differences in the Process of Characterization by Adolescents," Ed. D. dissertation (Harvard University 1988).
8 Richard Courtney, *Dictionary of Developmental Drama* (Springfield, Illinois: Charles E. Thomas 1987).

Index

Also by Richard Courtney

EDUCATIONAL DRAMA

College Drama Space (editor)
Drama for Youth
Teaching Drama
The School Play
The Drama Studio
Play, Drama and Thought
The Rarest Dream: "Play, Drama and Thought" Re-Visited
The Dramatic Curriculum
Re-Play: Studies of Human Drama in Education
Drama Education Canada
Dictionary of Developmental Drama
Re-Cognizing Richard Courtney: Selected Papers in Drama and Education (D. Booth and A. Martin-Smith, editors)

DRAMA THERAPY

Drama in Therapy, 2 vols. (edited with G. Schattner)

ARTS EDUCATION

The Arts in Society (editor)
Teaching and the Arts
The Face of the Future (editor)
The Quest: Research and Inquiry in Arts Education
Practical Research
Aesthetic Learning
Learning through the Arts (with P. Park)
Teacher Education in the Arts (with D. Booth, J. Emerson, and N. Kuzmich)
Basic Books in Arts Education (with D. Booth, J. Emerson, and N. Kuzmich)
No One Way of Being: Practical Knowledge of Elementary Arts Teachers (with D. Booth, J. Emerson, and N. Kuzmich)

HISTORY

Outline History of British Drama

CRITICISM

Shakespeare's World of War

Shakespeare's World of Love

Shakespeare's Comic World

Shakespeare's Tragic World

POETRY

Wild Eyed Girl

Beasts and Other People

Tales of a Travelling Man

The Turning of the World

PLAY

Lord of the Sky